The NOTE THROUGH the WIRE

The NOTE THROUGH *the* WIRE

THE INCREDIBLE TRUE STORY
OF A PRISONER OF WAR
AND A
RESISTANCE HEROINE

DOUG GOLD

wm

WILLIAM MORROW

An Imprint of HarperCollins*Publishers*

This book is a fictionalized account of Bruce and Josefine's story.
In some cases, names of people, places, dates, sequences,
and the detail of events have been changed where the
fundamental facts are known but corroborating details are
uncertain. The author has stated to the publishers that, except
in such respects, the contents of this book are true.

Maps by Area Design

Photographs on page v from the author's family collection

HarperCollins books may be purchased for educational, business,
or sales promotional use. For information, please email the
Special Markets Department at SPsales@harpercollins.com.

Originally published as *The Note Through the Wire* in
Australia and New Zealand in 2019 by Allen & Unwin

FIRST U.S. EDITION

Library of Congress Cataloging-in-Publication
Data has been applied for.

ISBN 978-0-06-301229-5
ISBN 978-0-06-307254-1 (international edition)

21 22 23 24 25   LSC   10 9 8 7 6 5 4 3 2 1

In memory of Bruce Murray and Josefine Lobnik,
who found love in the midst of a bloody conflict

Contents

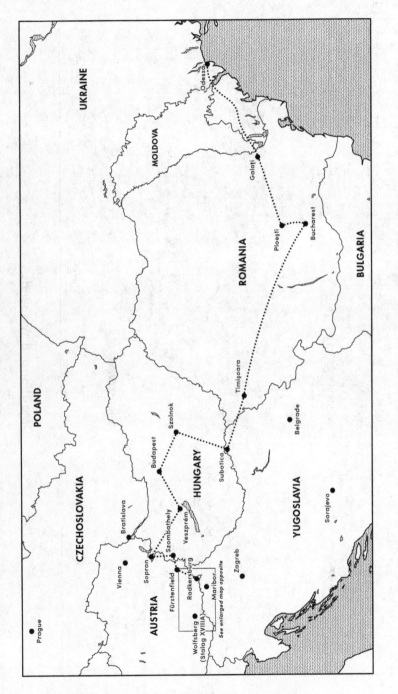

Bruce's route from Radkersburg to Odessa in 1945

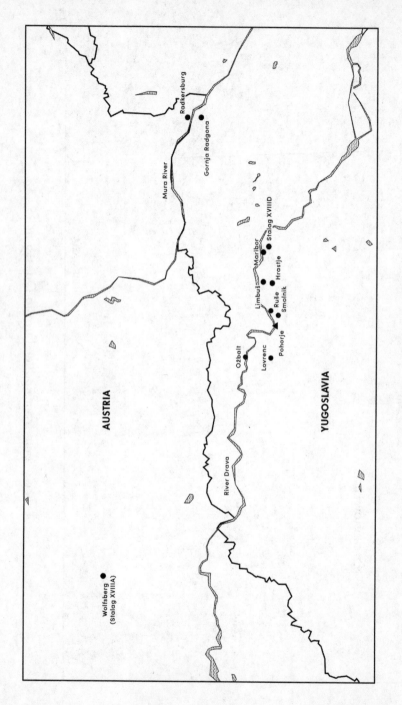

Maribor and surrounds

Chapter One

—

Bruce, Stalag XVIIID, February 15, 1942

He was nursing a sledgehammer hangover. It took Bruce Murray several minutes to reorientate himself. The hut gradually came into focus—the rough timber of the walls, the muddy floorboards, the grimy window in the door.

It was Sunday. That was a good thing. That was a bloody good thing, considering the state he was in. He imagined what it would be like if the German guards came hammering at the door, as they did on most other days, ordering him to fall in for a compulsory work detail at some Slovene factory or, worse, at one of the railway sites near the Maribor POW camp.

He shuddered. Disconnected pieces of the previous evening came back to him. Shouts of laughter. The fug of smoke, of course. The eye-watering burn of the homebrewed hooch—some infernal potion the boys had concocted in secret from filched potatoes and hoarded sugar, or so he understood.

Lofty. That's right. It was Lofty Collier's twenty-first birthday, and this had seemed like enough of an occasion to break out the booze. Bruce had had hangovers before, more than he cared to remember, but this one was a real doozy. It felt as though a pneumatic drill was boring through his temple and there was a coating of cement on his tongue that fixed it to the roof of his mouth. Now his guts were churning.

He groaned.

The mood had swung wildly over the course of the evening. First there was hilarity—jokes and laughter and good fellowship. Then it had developed a hard edge, when the latest outrage committed by some guard or another riled the men. Inevitably, it had grown maudlin, as stories and reminiscences of home were shared. Toward midnight, they had rallied, and the singing had begun. Some time and several tin cups of grog later, the joy had leached from it all again as many hoarse throats joined a chorus of "Auld Lang Syne"—it sounded more like "Old Lands Shine" in their rendition. There were tears. Bruce might have shed a few himself.

After that, he didn't remember much.

The hut reeked. His shirt reeked. He reeked. He had to get out.

Bruce heaved himself into a sitting position and swung his legs over the edge of the bunk, his coarse gray blanket slithering to the floor. The hut spun, and Bruce belched ominously. Steeling himself, he lurched to his feet, averted his eyes from the hazy scrap of mirror, pulled on his boots, shrugged into his greatcoat, and staggered to the door. A gust of freezing air greeted him as he opened it, and he screwed up his eyes against the glare from the snow. Perhaps, he thought, sitting out in the bitter wind would purify him, purge him of the toxic aftermath of the night before. He sat heavily on the upturned Red Cross crate where he sometimes sat in warmer weather, drew his coat about him, and wondered whether a cigarette would make him feel better or worse.

That's where Frank Butler found him.

"Get up, ya ugly sod," Frank said.

"Piss off, Frank," Bruce replied.

"Come on, Brucie. Get off yer arse. Let's take a turn, blow out the cobwebs."

Frank grabbed Bruce's arm and heaved him to his feet. It was their routine on Sundays to take a stroll around the perimeter of Stalag XVIIID: partly for the exercise, partly because it gave them another opportunity to taunt the goons with jibes as barbed as the wire surrounding them, mostly to relieve the unrelenting boredom.

"Cor, you look a right bloody mess," Frank said, eyeing him sideways. Insults were the stock-in-trade of their conversation, but Frank meant it. By this hour of the morning, Bruce was usually freshly scrubbed, his hair combed and slicked down, and he would have done what he could with his clothes. Not today.

It was all Bruce could do to grunt in reply.

They walked in companionable silence, an inch of fresh snow squeaking beneath the soles of their boots. The gloom overhead thinned a little and the light brightened. It was agony on Bruce's bleary eyes. He closed them tightly and gritted his teeth.

"Hello," Frank breathed softly beside him. "What have we here?"

Bruce opened his eyes.

They were thirty yards from a point on the southern perimeter fence that was out of the direct eyeline of the guards in the watchtowers. There was a figure standing motionless on the other side of the wire—a brave or desperate thing to do since, needless to say, the guards didn't exactly encourage interaction between the locals and the camp inmates. It was an old woman, to judge from her attire—she wore a shapeless woolen dress and a black-fringed knitted shawl.

Her presence there was something out of the ordinary, something that stood out from the monotony of camp life.

"Come on," Bruce said. "Let's see what she wants."

Frank looked all around them carefully. There weren't any guards in sight, but that meant little. A goon might appear at any moment.

"Best not," he said. "They'll shoot you if they see you."

"Nah," said Bruce. "She'll be right."

The hangover had relented a little. He had regained his will to live.

Frank stayed where he was. Bruce walked briskly to the wire. Unlike most prisoner-of-war camps, which had two wire perimeter fences, one inside the other with ten yards of dead ground between them, Stalag XVIIID had been a Slovene Army barracks and was surrounded by only a single high wire fence. Despite the dangers, the locals occasionally traded items—eggs, bread, woolen mittens—for rare luxuries such as the tinned meat or chocolate bars that came in Red Cross parcels.

The woman watched him approach. Bent and shapeless as she was, she reminded Bruce of old Sis Moore who used to terrorize the kids of his neighborhood when he was growing up. It was rumored she would beat—and even eat—kids who strayed onto her property.

"Hello," he said, as he neared the wire, and smiled. She stepped forward, and held out her hand toward him. His smile faltered as he met her eyes—green and unmistakably youthful beneath the fringe of the shawl.

"*Bitte*," she said. "*Bitte hilf mir.*"

She said more—a few sentences in a low, urgent voice, the voice of a young woman—but Bruce didn't speak German. He understood the appeal for help, but he didn't understand the rest. He shook his head.

"I'm sorry—" he said, but stopped. Her gaze had shifted past his shoulder, and her eyes—beautiful eyes, he registered—widened slightly.

"*Bitte*," she repeated, and thrust her hand at the wire again. Bruce reached out and felt her fingers press a scrap of paper into his. Then she was gone. Another observer might have imagined they were witnessing a miracle, as the old crone straightened, hitched up the skirts of her dress, and set off like a gazelle down the gentle slope toward the trees a hundred yards away.

"Halt!"

Bruce turned and saw one of the guards stalk past Frank, working the bolt of his rifle. The guard waved at Bruce to get out of the way, but he stood his ground. The guard stepped to his left to try to clear his line of fire. Bruce stepped to his right to block it.

"Halt!" the guard yelled again, his voice cracking with fury.

"Run!" yelled Bruce, still facing the guard. "Faster!"

The dogs began barking, a wild, savage sound. The guard made to step past Bruce, but Bruce lowered his shoulder and shoved him. Instead of firing at the fleeing girl, the guard rounded on Bruce. His face was white with rage, and he spluttered something in German. Bruce grinned at him. The guard leveled his rifle, but when Bruce didn't flinch he lowered it, changed his grip, and jabbed at him with the butt. Bruce twisted and took the blow in the small of the back.

"Bastard!" he said.

He was feeling fully alive now, his hangover quite gone. He and the guard faced each other, their breath steaming in the air between them. After a few moments, the guard swore, spat on the ground, and marched off, hell-bent, Bruce had no doubt, on making trouble for him.

He rejoined Frank.

"Did she make it?" he asked.

"Dunno. She was running very fast. She fell just before she got to the trees. Must have hurt herself. She crawled the rest of the way in. She's a goner if they let those dogs go."

The dogs were still barking. But as Frank and Bruce resumed their stroll in a show of nonchalance, the growling began to subside. Someone shouted at the animals in German. A minute or two later, the camp was quiet again.

"Well, was it worth getting your arse kicked?" Frank said. "What did she give you?"

Bruce surreptitiously opened his palm to show Frank the paper.

"You was robbed," Frank said.

Bruce didn't say so, but he was still thrilled with the encounter. If nothing else, it was something out of the ordinary. And his hangover was cured.

Chapter Two

———

Josefine, Maribor, February 12 to 15, 1942

On the day that everything changed—February 12, 1942— Josefine Lobnik was walking through the streets of the old part of Maribor toward Vetrinjska ulica, affecting innocence. She was dressed in typical Slovene fashion: a black high-waisted, ankle-length skirt, a white embroidered blouse, and a red silk-lined jacket. A lace-trimmed headscarf concealed the lovely fall of her jet-black hair, and concealed in the lining of her jacket was a package of documents she was carrying from one partisan group to another.

As she neared Glavni trg—like most Slovenes, she refused to call the town square Adolf-Hitler-Platz as the Nazi occupiers had decreed—there were suddenly German soldiers everywhere. Her breath caught in her throat. The documents she was carrying would not only sign her death warrant if they were found, but likely lead to the unmasking of dozens of other Slovene patriots besides.

The soldiers used their rifles to herd everyone into the central courtyard. At first Josefine thought she was about to be arrested and searched, but as soon as she entered the square she realized what was going on.

Twenty people were standing in a tight group at the far end of the plaza. The snow sifting from the eaves of the Rotovž, the graceful Renaissance-style town hall, settled on the shoulders of their jackets. Snow fell from the leaden skies and softened the outlines of the Ludwigshof house and the other steep-roofed buildings flanking the square; it ought to have been a beautiful scene. But German soldiers in their gray uniforms stood guard at every exit, and several more were cradling submachine guns a few paces away from the twenty captives.

A ripple of horror ran through the melee as, like Josefine, the people realized what they were about to witness. The soldiers were forcing the men and women into a rough line, and cries of anguish were rising from the crowd as the onlookers recognized faces. Josefine saw four she knew. Everyone knew the short, barrel-shaped Miljenko. No one knew his surname, but everyone knew his bloated, florid face with its bulbous, blue-veined nose. He was always somewhere around the center of Maribor, either sleeping in a doorway or reeling along the streets, and invariably surrounded by the waft of cheap wine.

Josefine also recognized Franc Gudek, a friend of her father. Franc was in his seventies, a bookkeeper by trade but retired now, a slight, mild-mannered man with soulful, sagging eyes, narrow, drooping shoulders, a mirthless, thin-lipped smile and sparse, snow-white hair. He had a permanently quivering lip and an uncontrollable twitch in his left eye, the combined effect of which made him look perpetually on the brink of tears.

And, with a jolt, Josefine recognized two of the Milavec brothers: Albin and Marjan. Albin was eighteen, the same age as Josefine; Marjan a year younger. They were both tall but slightly built, Marjan with brown, brushed-back hair and Albin with bushy jet-black curls parted in the center. Josefine had taken some of the same classes as Albin at school. She didn't know him well, but he was studious and always polite to her—certainly not the type who got into schoolyard fights. As far as Josefine was aware, he had harmed no one.

"Albin," she gasped. "Why you?"

A man close by glanced at her. "No reason," he said. "It could have been anyone. It could have been you or me. It's because of what happened up there."

He jerked his thumb toward Pohorje, the mountains rising to the west of the town. Josefine knew better than most that, a few days before, the partisans had ambushed a Nazi patrol on the wooded slopes. The poorly equipped partisans should have been no match for this disciplined enemy and their modern weapons, but knowledge of the rugged terrain gave them a decisive advantage, particularly in winter when the deep, deceptive snowdrifts made the conditions even more difficult. In the ensuing short and sharp fray, four Germans had been killed. The partisan casualty count was two—both wounded, neither seriously—and they were quietly triumphant as they made their way into the mountain recesses and the security of their own well-hidden base. The mood of celebration in certain clandestine circles in Maribor had been tempered with a sense of foreboding, because all knew that the commander of the occupying forces had issued a directive that fifty Slovene lives should be taken for every German life. For expediency rather than mercy, it was a smaller assembly of twenty lined up in Glavni trg. The victims had been mostly chosen at random; they were merely the first twenty Slovenes the Nazi death squad had happened upon as they swept toward the square. The day had started out for them like any other—buying bread, tending to chores, walking dogs, and, in Miljenko's case, drinking wine—but now it was about to end in death. Half an hour earlier and Josefine may have been caught in the executioner's net.

"But they're not even partisans," Josefine said, then she threw the man a frightened look, realizing what might be read into what she had said.

He nodded. "That's the point," he said grimly.

Four of the victims, including Franc and Albin, faced their executioners with nothing but contempt and defiance in their eyes. If anything, Franc's features had firmed; Josefine couldn't help thinking she had underestimated his courage. She could hardly bear to look at poor Albin.

A German officer was trying to speak, but his voice was drowned out by the wails from the crowd. He was growing frustrated. There was a gasp as two of the twenty collapsed, and those standing next to them hauled them to their feet again, keeping them upright with arms around their waists.

Someone called for a priest to be summoned to administer last rites, and the cry was taken up by the crowd. The appeals were ignored. Then, suddenly, one of the victims lifted his voice. It was full of fear, but also defiance.

"*Naš Oče, ki je v Nebesih* . . . Our Father, who art in Heaven . . ."

The twenty reached for one another's hands. The crowd stilled momentarily, then joined in as the victims recited the Lord's Prayer. Even Miljenko, who was permanently drunk and reckoned to be a bit simple besides, seemed to know what was about to happen. He squared his shoulders and mumbled along.

Before the prayer ended, one of the women standing in the line collapsed, slumping to the ground in spite of the efforts of those alongside to hold her up. There was a sharp clatter of gunfire. Josefine never even heard the order to fire. A moan rose from the crowd. Hundreds of pigeons erupted from the nooks and crannies of the old stone buildings framing the square and took flight, like so many startled souls. A crimson stain crept through the slushy snow beneath the untidy pile of bodies.

With deliberate, unhurried movements, the Nazi commander unholstered his Walther P38 pistol and walked up to the woman who had fainted; she now lay whimpering on the ground. He aimed carefully and fired two shots into her head. The screams from the crowd were underpinned by a dark mutter. Perhaps, Josefine reflected grimly, Adolf-Hitler-Platz was the more appropriate name.

"Mongrels," she whispered.

"Yes," said the man standing next to her. "They think this will make us too afraid to support the partisans." He spat on the ground. "They'd better think again."

Apart from a handful of people who tried to move toward the bodies—they were kept back at gunpoint—the crowd began to drift away. Josefine allowed herself to be carried along. Her initial numb shock had been replaced by wild, reckless rage. A frightened-looking German soldier stood at an exit from the square, and was being jostled by those shuffling by; Josefine spat on him as she passed.

"I hope you burn in hell!" she yelled, but the curse was lost among the louder curses being heaped upon him by others.

Any thought she had of completing her mission was gone. The documents were still safe in the secret pocket in her jacket, but while she had set out that afternoon feeling she was doing her bit to defy the occupation, it all now seemed far too little. She vowed that she would do everything in her power—sacrifice her life if necessary—to rid her country of the Nazi vermin.

As she walked across the bridge to her home in the small village of Limbuš, she felt a sudden, violent chill. It was hitting home; it was all hitting home for the first time. When her brother Polde had been arrested ten days before, she had felt certain that he was safe. In captivity, but safe. She had heard the rumors of summary executions—young men and women dragged off into the woods surrounding the town and shot—but she had either doubted them or, if she were honest with herself, refused to confront the truth. Like the other horrors of war, it felt too remote. Now, after what she had witnessed in Glavni trg, anything, even the worst, was suddenly and terribly possible.

As she neared her home, she began to run, slowly at first, then faster, as though the horror were at her heels. As she burst through the door of her house, she could no longer contain her sobs.

Her older sister, Anica, appeared in the kitchen doorway.

"What is it, Pepi?" she asked, referring to Josefine by her family nickname. "What's happened?"

Josefine shook her head, unable to speak. Anica gathered her in her arms and stroked her hair.

"What is it?" she repeated after a minute or two, during which Josefine sobbed. Anica's voice had the flat, expressionless tone that it had acquired since she had reappeared after her own unexplained absence a few weeks previously. It was the voice of someone who had been face-to-face with terror, and expected to meet it again.

"Anica," Josefine whispered. "They killed Franc. Franc Gudek. They shot him, and the others. Albin, Marjan . . ."

She couldn't go on.

"Albin? The Milavec boy?" Anica asked.

Josefine nodded. "And his brother, Marjan."

"That's tragic. They were so young. And Father will be devastated," Anica went on. "Franc was such a good friend. A good man. Tell me what happened."

"They shot twenty people in Glavni trg," Josefine gasped. "Twenty. They just . . . shot them."

She shook her head to rid it of the afterimage: the black mounds of the bodies with the seeping stain beneath them. The crack of the pistol: once, twice. The spasmodic movement of the woman's leg. Josefine had seen dead bodies before—the custom among Catholic Slovenes was to mount a vigil over the dead in open coffins—but she had never seen anyone die, let alone such a violent death.

Anica was silent, her arms about Josefine, one hand mechanically stroking her hair.

"Polde," Josefine managed to say. "What about our dear brother?"

"We must hope for the best." Anica was reciting the family mantra, but there was no comfort in her voice. She was silent for a moment. Then she said, almost as though to herself, "They'll stop at nothing, these animals. They'd murder every last one of us without a second thought. To these pigs, a Slovene life is worthless."

Josefine had heard others say the same thing, but for the first time she felt the truth of the words for herself.

———

The morning after Glavni trg, Josefine crossed the bridge into Maribor again. This time, she made her rendezvous with her contact and handed over the documents. Then she started the search for her brother. Someone, she had decided during the long, sleepless night, must know something.

She talked to Polde's old friends in case they had any information. She sought out people who frequented his regular haunts. She pestered her contacts within the partisan movement, and she even spoke to people who she knew had been arrested by the Nazis and released. Several people were aware that Polde had been captured— that kind of news spread fast—but no one knew much about the circumstances, and no one had the faintest idea what had happened to him. Josefine's best friend, Jelena Kunstek—Jelka—worked as a night cleaner at the *Kommandantur*, the German administrative office, and often had access to information that she passed on to the resistance, but not even she could find anything that shed light on Polde's fate.

Swallowing her disgust, Josefine even approached a prewar

acquaintance who she suspected was a collaborator, but the woman had heard nothing, either.

The best anyone could offer was theories. Perhaps Polde had been sent north into Austria or east into Germany, where there were rumored to be camps for "resettled" dissidents? Perhaps he was languishing in one of the local prisons, such as the one beneath Maribor Castle? That would likely mean he was being tortured; Josefine couldn't bear to believe this was true. None of those she spoke to voiced the other possibility that she dared not contemplate: that Polde's body was lying in a shallow grave somewhere in the forest. But it hung there, unspoken, nonetheless.

The only glimmer of actual hope came from a man with partisan connections who had friends who were often called to do repairs at Stalag XVIIID, the prisoner-of-war camp on the outskirts of Maribor. Josefine knew Slovenes were being held in the Eastern compound and she asked whether it would be possible to make inquiries there, but the man shook his head.

"My friends never go in there. And you couldn't speak to the prisoners from outside, either. The Slavic compound is too heavily guarded. You'd never get close to it."

Seeing Josefine's face, he went on. "Your best chance of finding out if your brother is there would be to get someone to ask one of the English prisoners. They might be able to find out from the Slavs."

"How would I talk to the English?" Josefine asked eagerly.

"People occasionally go up there to trade," he replied. "There's a place on the fence that the guards don't patrol very often." He paused. "You said 'I.' You're not thinking of trying to do it yourself, are you? It's far too dangerous."

"Of course not," Josefine lied. "It was a figure of speech."

———

Josefine had learned that the English prisoners, who were usually sent out on work details, were confined to the camp on Sundays. And, because it was a day of rest, it was regarded by those who dared take contraband to Stalag XVIIID as the safest day, since the guards themselves also seemed to be taking it easy.

So, on Sunday, Josefine stood shivering in the eaves of the pine forest at the bottom of the slope that led up to the wire fence surrounding the camp. She was dressed as an old woman—her habitual disguise when she was on errands for the resistance in Maribor—but her coarse woolen garments were no match for the thin breeze, which cut straight through them.

Her stomach was churning. She knew that the Germans shot on sight anyone acting suspiciously near the wire—or, almost as bad, they set the dogs on them. She had taken many risks on her missions in Maribor, but the danger had always seemed abstract. Now, with the memory of the day of terror in Glavni trg fresh in her mind and the occasional glimpse of guards with rifles on their shoulders patrolling the camp, it was all very real.

Twice she had just about plucked up the courage to break cover and set off for the wire when a guard had appeared and she'd been forced to duck back into the trees, heart thumping. It occurred to her that she should perhaps give up her quest, but the note in her pocket made her stay. Finally, after a guard had made his leisurely way along the fence and disappeared around the corner of a building, she took a deep breath and forced herself forward.

It was the longest hundred yards she had ever walked. When she reached the wire, there was no one there. It was as though the camp were asleep. She hadn't bargained on this. She had assumed there would be someone she could pass the note to at once and then get away. Instead, she was forced to stand there, feeling as conspicuous as though she were naked.

Eventually, two men came into sight, both in an unfamiliar

uniform. She guessed they were English. One of them saw her and stopped. The other glanced up.

After a moment, the second man walked toward her.

"Please," she said in German, holding out the note. "Please help me. The Nazis have taken my brother and we think he might be a prisoner here. He has been missing for two weeks."

She looked directly into his face. He was unshaven and bleary-eyed, and there were dubious-looking stains on his shirt. She saw him react to the glimpse he got of her face: his hand went instinctively to his hair—a strange gesture, given how greasy and unkempt it was.

Men, she thought. The only thing they can think about is what impression they have on women.

"Please help my family find out what has happened to him," she said.

The man began to speak in English, but a movement beyond him caught Josefine's eye—a flash of gray. A German soldier.

She thrust the note through the wire, and the man took it. The soldier shouted, and she turned and ran, expecting a shot at any moment. Her breath came in short, panicky rasps that hurt her throat. The trees didn't seem to be getting any closer.

There came another shout, and then another. Still there was no shot. She was twenty yards from the trees. The dogs were barking now, and she was seized with an ancient, primal fear. Just then, her foot caught on something—a stone, a tree root, a hole in the ground—and her lower leg twisted painfully. She screamed and pitched forward. Her knee was ablaze. She tried to clamber back to her feet but her knee wouldn't bear her weight. She crawled frantically toward the trees.

Please, she was thinking. Please. Not the dogs.

Chapter Three

Bruce, Stalag XVIIID, February 15, 1942

Back in their hut, Bruce and Frank studied the note, written in a cramped longhand that slanted to the left.

"What language is that?" Frank asked.

"Kraut for sure," Bruce replied, peering at the note shortsightedly.

"Ah. Taffy speaks Kraut. You could ask him."

"Why German?" Bruce mused. "They speak Slovene here. Is it some sort of trap?"

They went and found Taffy, a genial Welshman who had been brought in a few months before.

"It's in Kraut," Bruce explained. "But I'm wondering why it's not in Slovene."

"Not surprising," Taffy replied. "I was talking to one of them over yon." He waved in the direction of the segregated part of the camp in which the Slovene prisoners were kept, along with Russians, Poles, and other non-British or Commonwealth nationalities. "Turns out this part of the world has been Austrian before. The Austrian border is only a few miles off. They all speak German, too. I suppose she thought you wouldn't be able to make heads or tails of a note in Slovene."

"She was right there," Bruce said. "So what does it say?"

"*Please help me,*" Taffy read. "*I'm looking for my brother Leopold Lobnik, also known as 'Polde,' from Limbuš, who has been missing for two weeks. Can you please find out if he is a prisoner in the camp? I'll come back to the fence at the same time next Sunday.*"

"That's all?"

"That's all," said Taffy.

"You was robbed," said Frank again.

———

The Eastern compound was a dire place. Bruce pitied Polde if he were held there. The guards hated the Eastern European POWs and treated them with naked contempt. Their food—what little there was of it—wasn't fit to be served to a pig, and their tattered clothes hung loosely off their emaciated frames like torn and grimy sheets flapping around on scarecrows. The English-speaking prisoners lived a life of luxury by comparison. Any attempt to fraternize or communicate with the Slavs was swiftly dealt with, usually with a rifle butt, a swat from a baton, or a dangerously close warning shot. The punishment was even worse for the Slavs.

Nevertheless, when he was sure he was unobserved, Bruce walked up to the Eastern compound wire, caught the eye of a gaunt prisoner on the other side, and delivered a carefully rehearsed phrase in Russian.

"*Ty govorish po-angliyski?*"

It was the best anyone could do when he asked if anyone knew the Slovene phrase for "Do you speak English?" The camp linguists assured him that the Slavic languages were all pretty closely related, and the Slovenes would get the drift of the Russian.

The first prisoner dropped his eyes and shuffled away from the wire, as did one or two others. No one seemed to want to meet his eye. He repeated the phrase, once, twice, three times. The most he got from the mob on the other side was a blank, bovine stare or two, and a single shake of the head.

He was about to give up when a skeletal figure pushed past the others. He had a ragged, badly stitched wound stretching from his forehead to his jaw on one side of his face, and an unnaturally twisted nose.

"I spik Englis some," he said, approaching the wire.

Bruce opened his mouth to speak, but there was a shout from behind him. He wheeled, shoved his hands in his pockets, and started to walk away from the wire, but a hand grabbed his shoulder and spun him half around. He was about to retaliate when a wooden object—a pick handle, Bruce thought—fetched him across the bridge of the nose. He fell to his knees, but scrambled up again as fast as he could, stumbling backward with his hands in front of his face to ward off any further blows. None came, but a torrent of angry German followed him as he hurried away. Other shouts came from the direction of the Eastern compound. Bruce shuddered to think what might happen to the man he'd spoken to. He clamped his hands over his nose to try to staunch the blood and, for the thousandth time since he'd arrived in the camp, he cursed the Germans.

———

Over the next two days, Bruce took any opportunity he could find to hover close to the wire of the Eastern compound. On the third day, he saw the scarred man again. When each was sure that there were no guards about, they approached the wire.

"Bruce," said Bruce, placing his palm against the wire.

"Brush," the other repeated, placing his palm on the wire opposite Bruce's. "Kristian," he said, pointing to his chest, although his voice was so low and his accent so thick that Bruce thought it might have been "Kristof."

"Do you know if Leopold or Polde Lobnik is with you guys?" he asked slowly.

"What you want, Brush?" the Slovene replied, plainly failing to understand the question.

"Polde Lobnik," Bruce repeated, articulating his words carefully to ensure he pronounced them correctly.

"Pula Lobec?"

"No. Polde Lobnik," Bruce reiterated, emphasising the "d" and the "n."

"Ah, Lobnik," the Slovene responded. "I look," he said, and was gone.

Three days later, on Saturday, the day before the girl had promised to return, Bruce saw the Slovene near the wire and sidled up. It was difficult to understand exactly what Kristian (or Kristof) was saying, but he gathered that a few of the Slovenes interned at the camp knew of Polde Lobnik. But no one knew where he was or what had happened to him.

"*Spasibo,*" he said. The Slovene nodded curtly, and he and Bruce melted back into their respective crowds.

———

Sunday found Bruce pacing slowly along the perimeter fence, pretending to be deep in thought but actually scanning the field beyond the wire. He was clean-shaven, his hair was carefully combed, and his frayed and well-worn dress uniform was as neat as he could make it.

He was barely recognizable as the wretch he'd been when the Lobnik girl had last clapped eyes on him.

He'd arrived at the meeting place early, so as not to risk missing her. He'd resisted the urge to loiter, which might have attracted attention, and instead tried to keep as closely as possible to his Sunday-morning ritual without letting the spot on the fence and the field beyond it out of his sight. The promised hour came and went. Still Bruce paced, reluctant to give up hope. As luck would have it, when someone did emerge from the trees in the distance—a young woman, as timid as a deer—he was well away from the perimeter.

Bruce paused in his walk, lit a cigarette, then resumed walking in the other direction, toward the fence. The girl—she was too far off for him to decide whether it was the same girl or not—had taken a few hesitant steps out into the field. She stood there, as though undecided as to whether to approach. It was all Bruce could do to keep from waving at her or rushing to the wire. He concentrated on swinging each foot loosely forward, taking unhurried steps, and appearing to look anywhere but at the girl.

Something spooked her. She turned and half walked, half ran into the trees. Just like that, she was gone.

From the corner of his eye, Bruce saw a guard mooching along in the yard. He didn't appear to have seen the girl. But, even when the guard was out of sight and Bruce passed the meeting place again, the girl didn't reappear.

Bruce was disappointed. It seemed too much of a coincidence for it to have been a different young woman approaching the wire at the appointed day and time. But some instinct told him it wasn't her. This girl seemed to lack the courage that had brought Polde Lobnik's sister right up to the wire. Perhaps she had sent someone else in her place?

Over the next couple of days, he wondered whether the young

woman had seen him and known that he had tried to keep the rendez-vous. He thought she probably couldn't see him from where she had been standing. Even if it were the same girl, she wouldn't have seen him clearly enough to be certain it was him—especially since he'd taken the trouble to scrub up. He wondered if she would dare try again. He resolved to wait and see if she reappeared at the same time the following Sunday.

In the meantime, mostly as a way to occupy the time that weighed so heavily on his hands, he thought about how it might be possible to get a message to her. He could bribe a guard; plenty of them would do anything for a bar of chocolate or a packet of cigarettes. But he decided it was way too risky. If the communication were intercepted, or the guard decided to renege on the deal, Bruce imagined it would put not only him but also the girl and anyone with her surname in danger from the German authorities. And, even if a guard faithfully delivered the message to the Lobnik family's home without reading it, the unexplained appearance of a German soldier at their door would bring them under suspicion from the locals. Bruce had heard rumors of the ferocity with which collaborators were treated by the local partisans.

Either way, he decided, he couldn't ask a Kraut to carry the message.

The only real option left was one of the tradesmen who regularly visited the camp to perform maintenance. Electricians, builders, plumbers—even the dunny men who carted the shit out each night in the appropriately named "Smelly Nellie"—were all regulars at Stalag XVIIID. One of them might know the Lobniks. Or at least know how to get a message to them. But there was no real way of knowing where their loyalties lay. Bruce supposed they must all naturally resent the German occupation, but who knew for sure? They were plainly trusted by the prison administration, and might turn out to be Nazi sympathizers after all.

The next Sunday came and went, and Bruce scanned the field beyond the wire in vain. There was no sign of the girl. He began studying the tradesmen, and settled upon a plumber for no better reason than that he had a friendly face.

When he spied an opportunity to get close to the plumber, Bruce stood there, half turned away, and uttered his Russian phrase through the corner of his mouth.

"*Ty govorish po-angliyski?*"

"*Ne govorim angleško.*" The man shrugged.

"*Deutsche?*" Bruce queried.

There was a pause.

"*Ja,*" came the guarded response.

Bruce made a "wait there" motion with his hand and rushed off to find Taffy before the plumber finished what he was doing and left for the day.

Through Taffy, Bruce could communicate with the Slovene. Yes, he said, he did indeed know the Lobnik family from Limbuš. Why was Bruce interested?

Even across the language barrier, Bruce could sense the man's wariness. The open, friendly expression that had drawn Bruce to him in the first place was gone, replaced by a mask of mistrust.

"Tell him Polde Lobnik's sister passed me a note asking me to find out if Polde was here. I have an answer for her. I'd like him to take a note to her."

Taffy translated. The man paused in his work, and fixed Bruce with a suspicious stare. Bruce could almost see him calculating the odds that this prisoner might be a German stooge, trying to shake loose information that could be traded for valuable privileges from the camp authorities.

The plumber turned back to his work, and finally gave a slight nod. Bruce surreptitiously slipped the note he had written into the pocket of the plumber's coat where it lay on the ground nearby. He and Taffy strolled away. Soon afterward, the man packed up his tools, wiped his hands, and put on his coat. He left.

For the first couple of days, Bruce was half waiting for the sound of jackboots approaching his door as the goons came to drag him away to where some arch-goon would smile cruelly and wave the captured note at him. But the fear subsided and, as it did, his expectations mounted.

He rushed to the wire again on Sunday at nine thirty in the morning. For fully two hours, he paced to and fro, watching the forest carefully for any sign of movement. There was none. Even as he decided he'd waited long enough and started to walk away, he couldn't prevent himself shooting glances over his shoulder. But there was no one there.

Face facts, he told himself. You won't see her again.

Chapter Four

———

Bruce & Josefine,
Wellington and Maribor

Bruce Gordon Murray was born on March 3, 1916, and lived in Wellington, the capital city of New Zealand. In 1939, the year that war was declared, Bruce—"Boy" to his family—was twenty-three years old. He had four siblings: Alan, Betty, Jo, and Norm. Five foot seven and a handsome devil (or so the girls told him), he was slightly built with a prominent nose, high forehead, and a cheeky smile. He took great pride in his appearance. He wore his dark, wavy hair cut in short-back-and-sides with not a hair out of place, and he habitually sported trousers with knife-edge creases and shoes polished to a mirror shine.

Bruce's parents weren't wealthy—they might have been, had his father not gambled the family's vast Northland farm in a card game and lost—but they were comfortably off. By the end of the 1930s, the hard years of the Depression were a fading memory, and New Zealand enjoyed one of the highest standards of living in the developed

world. Bruce himself was on a good wicket. He held down a senior
position as production manager at the famous Prestige Hosiery factory, makers of fine silk stockings, lingerie, and nightwear. He could
therefore afford to live as a Kiwi man-about-town. Saturday night
was the big one. Bruce and his mates might go to a rugby game in
the afternoon, and follow it up with a few jugs at the Midland Hotel.
Then it might be a bring-a-flagon party in one of the suburbs, a dance
at the town hall, or a back-row seat at the De Luxe Theater to watch
the "talkies"—especially if a Mae West movie was showing. Bruce
was secretly in love with Mae West, as was most of the male population of New Zealand. Movies with sound were still something of a
novelty, after the silent cinema of a few years previously with a lone
pianist providing the accompaniment.

Like most New Zealanders of his age, Bruce kept a weather eye
on the political situation in Europe. New Zealand newspapers were
dominated by foreign news, and the rise of Adolf Hitler—being of
vital importance to British interests—was exhaustively reported in
Great Britain's far-flung dominion. Bruce had joined the crowds in
joyously toasting the coronation of King George VI on May 12, 1937,
but that event wasn't the most significant of that year so far as Bruce
was concerned. Nor, if he was being honest, was his marriage to
Doreen. Everything paled into insignificance beside the All Blacks'
sole win over the touring Springboks at Wellington's Athletic Park
on August 14. Bruce was on the Western Bank for the match:
tickets were cheaper on the bank and there was always plenty of
good-natured banter. A typical Wellington gale was blowing that
day and Bruce's fedora hat was a definite flight risk. Bruce and his
best mates, "Blackie" White and "Logie" Logan, kept warm by taking turns swigging from Bruce's hip flask of Macallan's whisky, and
cheered as the All Blacks went on to win 13–7. After the game, they
headed straight to the Midland Hotel to celebrate the historic win,

piling up the jugs to beat the six-o'clock closing time and filling a few flagons for later.

At first glance, the three mates seemed an unlikely trio. Joe "Blackie" White was everything Bruce wasn't. He was six-foot-something tall, had a shock of unruly black hair—seldom combed— a misshapen nose from one too many bar brawls, and striking black-rimmed eyes. Blackie had a vulgar tongue, which was responsible for many of the contours of his nose, but despite appearances he was a gentle soul and surprisingly timid—until he was riled. He owned one pair of rugged twill trousers, frayed around the cuffs, for everyday wear and one pair of crumpled, beer-stained "good strides" for special occasions. His shirttail was always hanging out from the back of his trousers. A hand-rolled cigarette was almost permanently glued to the corner of his mouth, so firmly fixed to his bottom lip that he could engage in animated debate without any danger of it falling out. Sometimes, but not always, he would remove the fag to eat.

If he wasn't such a good friend, Bruce might have called him slovenly. But they were best mates and Bruce would never say anything to offend his close pal. Blackie had looked out for Bruce ever since they'd first met, and his imposing figure had intimidated many would-be bar-room assailants.

Cecil "Logie" Logan, on the other hand, was slender, about half a head taller than Bruce, with square shoulders and a ramrod-straight back. He was a softly spoken chap with blond, curly hair, an aesthete's full, pouting lips, and rather extraordinarily large ears accentuated by his customary pudding-basin haircut. His oversized, perfectly round glasses made his hazel eyes seem larger than they were. Summer and winter, he wore the same permanently creased herringbone jacket with brown suede elbow patches and knotted leather buttons. He looked like a distracted professor.

By 1939, Bruce's marriage was the sole blot on an otherwise

pleasant landscape. His mates—especially Blackie and Logie, who knew him best—had advised against the match. They couldn't see much to like in Doreen, whom they thought shallow and a bit of a shrew. He scoffed at their concerns, but only a few months into the marriage he admitted to himself (if not to them) that they had been right. Doreen had never liked Bruce's two best friends; he supposed she was jealous of the strong bond they shared. Nevertheless, he resolutely focused on Doreen's good points and hoped for the best on the others; he supposed he wasn't the easiest person to live with, either. He was stuck with it, and determined to make it work.

Not even rumors of war troubled him unduly. The prospect was occasionally mentioned in the newspapers, but it seemed unlikely—particularly after the four-power Munich Agreement was announced by the pacifist British Prime Minister Neville Chamberlain on September 29, 1938. "Peace in our time," Chamberlain proclaimed, and the newspapers took up the call.

Consequently, in 1939, it wasn't war but the £500,000 Centennial Exhibition that preoccupied Wellingtonians. Bruce was one of the three million visitors who were amazed by the exhibits—futuristic buildings, wide boulevards, ornamental pools, fountains, and a majestic equestrian statue with a naked female rider—and who rode the roller coaster and marveled at Mexican Rose, "The 54 Stone Fat Girl." Sideshows and curiosities aside, the Exhibition offered a vision of a glittering future, a brave new world—a world and a future that would, as it turned out, have to wait.

———

It was harder to ignore the shadow of war on the other side of the world, in the Maribor district of Slovenia where Josefine lived. Josefine Lobnik—"Pepica" or "Pepi" to her family—was born on June 15 or 16, 1923 (no one knows for sure as she had two different birth certificates). She lived in the village of Limbuš, just across the River Drava from Maribor. She too had four siblings: Anica (sometimes known as Ani), Leopold (Polde for short), Roman, and the much younger Mitzica. Josefine's mother died when she was thirteen. Her father, Jožef Lobnik, provided for his family as best he could but there was hardly enough for food and essentials, let alone luxuries. Once, when Josefine was just a small child, Jožef had given her a one-dinar note to go toward the purchase of a doll that she had set her heart upon. It was all he could spare. The doll cost ten dinar, but Josefine was resourceful: she cut the note into ten pieces.

Slovenia was part of the Kingdom of Yugoslavia in the 1930s. At the 1936 Berlin Olympics, while Bruce had been toasting Reefton-born Jack Lovelock's gold medal in the 1500 meters, Josefine was cheering the Slovene gymnast Leon Štukelj, who won a silver— Yugoslavia's only medal. What made his victory even sweeter for Slovenes is that it was one in the eye for Adolf Hitler, who everyone knew was using the Games to showcase Germany's glory. The threat from Germany was growing daily.

Times were hard in Slovenia, as they were in wider Yugoslavia: unemployment was rampant, the economy was failing, and living standards were dropping. These were troubled times and, inevitably, there was civil unrest. Yugoslav society was a complicated morass of political and ethnic divisions. The clandestine Communist Party, outlawed since 1921, was attacking the royalists, the Catholic activists, and its other adversaries; the anti-communist groups were, in turn, intent on destroying the communists; Slovene nationalists were opposed to the union with the Serbs and Croats; the leftist radicals were up against the rightist radicals. And, as the 1930s wore on, there were skirmishes between the pro-Nazis and the anti-Nazis. In June '39, just before her sixteenth birthday, Josefine had witnessed for herself an attack on the house of Dr. Karl Kieser, head of the Nazi movement in Maribor, who had openly incited violence and racial hatred. Meanwhile, the Yugoslav Army had begun mounting large-scale military exercises to prepare against the eventuality of a German invasion.

Despite the poverty, hardship, and civil unrest, Josefine led a relatively carefree existence, and was as full of life as every teenager has the right to be. An accomplished skier, she headed to the slopes as often as she could in winter; in summer, it was swimming, walks in the countryside, Sunday picnics, and—an unusual hobby—making elaborate costumes from chestnut leaves. Josefine loved to paint and might have been an artist of some note had Hitler not seized her paintbrush.

In 1939, on the eve of the war, Josefine was still at secondary school. She wanted to pass all her exams with merit. She wasn't the best student in the class, but she was well above average and she excelled in both Russian and German—little knowing how useful her talent for languages would soon become. She spent her evenings at home, cooking for her father, mending clothes, and helping mind Roman and Mitzica. On the weekends, when her chores were finished, she liked nothing better than to socialize with her friends—usually in the local village, sometimes in Maribor itself. Once a month, they might take in a badly dubbed foreign film at the Kino Udarnik or share a strudel and *Prekmurska gibanica*, a layered pastry covered in cream and stuffed with a variety of tasty fillings, at the Kavarna Astoria. On the even rarer occasions when she could afford it, she might go to the Slovene National Theatre in Maribor to watch a play, ballet, or opera.

Needless to say, wearing fancy clothes was out of the question. The best Josefine could do was rummage through Anica's castoffs to find something presentable when she took her trips across the bridge to town to meet her friends. Her best friend in the world—they called each other sisters—was Jelena Kunstek. Jelka was one of the very few people outside Josefine's real family who called her by her pet name, Pepi. They even looked like sisters—at sixteen, both dark-haired and vivacious. They had lately discovered boys. Josefine wasn't as successful in the romantic stakes as Jelka, but she had had a couple of boy-friends. Her family had encouraged her to cultivate Aljoša Kovačič, a nice young lad from the neighboring village, but Josefine wasn't interested. He was a pleasant enough boy, not overly bright, with a reasonable farm job, but he was just not Josefine's type. She had gone out for a while instead with Goran Krajnc, but her interest had fizzled out after a few dates. He was dirty, she told Jelka, and he smelled bad.

Chapter Five

Bruce, Cairo,
February 1940 to March 1941

Do your duty!" the posters screamed. "Don't Sit Doing Nothing!"
read an advertisement in Wellington's *Dominion* newspaper. And
it wasn't just the recruitment ads: articles and editorials spoke loftily
of the need to play one's part, to pull one's weight in the imperial war
effort. "Enlist today," they enjoined, "and help your pals overcome the
forces of evil. The Spirit of ANZAC calls you."

It was a powerful plea to young men thirsty for adventure, whose
imaginations had filled the void their fathers left when they answered
with silence questions about what it had been like to fight in the Great
War. For most, it was probably the lure of travel to faraway desti-
nations. Blackie and Logie were no different. The pubs were full of
young men just like them, egging one another on with fantasies of
foreign fields and exotic women.

"Right," said Blackie one evening, as their elbows stuck to the top of the bar in the smoke-filled Midland. "Don't know about you jokers, but I'm going down there first thing tomorrow to join up."

"If you're in," said Logie slowly, "then I'm bloody in."

Bruce finished his last half-glass.

"I suppose I'd better come too, then," he said. "Can't leave all those foreign sheilas to a pair of shifty sods like you."

"Hear that?" Blackie yelled over the roar of the six-o'clock swill. "We're off to fight for King and Country!"

There was a rowdy cheer, their backs were slapped, and their glasses filled and filled again. There was no going back after that.

The next morning, they took their place in the queue, which mostly comprised young blokes nursing hangovers and doing their best to pretend they weren't prisoners of their own bravado. After a few cursory questions from the recruiting officer—a stern-looking fellow their fathers' age in a crisp, neatly pressed uniform with a highly polished medal or two pinned on the breast—they were passed to the doctors for a medical. Bruce, Blackie, and Logie were all pronounced A1 and fit for service. Bruce was allocated Service Number 32673, and he and his two mates were officially enlisted in 25 Battalion of the 2nd NZEF and given a day and time to report to the military training camp at Trentham. The only thing left to do then was to tell their loved ones. It was as he contemplated telling Doreen what he had done that Bruce felt the first stirrings of unease.

———

At Trentham, they were issued with a smart new uniform—and told not to wear it. Instead, they were given parade-ground denims. Bruce winced when he saw himself in a mirror wearing these shapeless garments. The only consolation was that no one looked any better. Basic training occupied fifteen weeks, in which time they were taught to polish their boots, keep their kit tidy, march in step, and fire a .22 version of the Lee-Enfield SMLE, the same rifle their dads had used at Gallipoli and in France. Once the Army felt it had knocked them into some sort of shape, they were given their final leave. The last ten free days on New Zealand soil didn't go so well for Bruce. Doreen was less than impressed that he had decided to do his patriotic duty. As the days ticked down to his embarkation, she pointedly went out with friends and came in late, and after she'd come to bed she would lie with her back to Bruce. If he went to stroke her shoulder, she would make an irritated noise and shrink away from his touch. Part of Bruce wished he'd never enlisted. Most of him was fiercely glad he had.

———

After their leave expired, they were told to report back to Trentham, where their status was changed to "On Active Duty" and they spent a few days in frantic preparation. On August 17, 1940, they were allowed to put on their flash new uniforms and they were paraded along the streets of Wellington. Ten days later they marched to the Overseas Terminal, where two troop ships—luxury cruise liners only months before, now painted in drab naval gray—were moored. Bruce's unit was to embark on the former Cunard liner *Mauretania*.

"Blimey," said one young bloke in the same rank. "Looks like we're traveling in style, then."

Bruce didn't leave New Zealand or Doreen on exactly the best of terms. Bruce had looked in vain for his wife as he marched, but he saw her, front and center, as he was walking up the gangplank. He could hear her shouting at him above the hubbub of endearments, promises, and tearful farewells.

"Go on, then!" she yelled. "Piss off and leave me here! I'm not going to let the grass grow under my feet, you know. I'm an attractive woman, and here you go leaving me at home alone."

Bruce's cheeks flamed. There was laughter from those around him, but a few grimaced in sympathy.

"Don't worry, mate. There'll be plenty to keep you busy where we're going."

That was how Bruce decided he would quiet his misgivings: he would focus on the adventure that lay ahead.

Outside the harbor, they wallowed in Cook Strait for an hour or so, awaiting another ghostly gray liner coming up from the south. Once *Orcades* had joined them, the long, lethal silhouette of a battle cruiser appeared, slicing the water with menace and purpose. It was *Achilles* of the New Zealand Squadron, hero of the battle of the River Plate. The soldiers cheered her until their throats were hoarse as she passed to the head of their little convoy.

Achilles quietly left them in the charge of an Australian warship off the Aussie coast. A long, rolling sea took hold, and Bruce wasn't alone in feeling queasy, lying in a hammock slung in the cavernous bowels of the ship, from which every shred of luxury had been removed for present purposes.

After that, all was monotony, relieved only by training, training, and more training. They weren't allowed to march around the decks because the hobnails in their boots marked the woodwork, so they spent long periods of time with nothing to do but watch for enemy submarines. That, and speculate on what lay ahead. They knew they were bound for Cairo, but beyond vague images of the pyramids and other antiquities half remembered from schoolbooks and newspapers, they had no real idea what to expect. A couple of days out, Bruce, Logie, and Blackie were part of a group that buttonholed an NCO who was a veteran of the last war.

"What's Cairo like, Corp?" someone asked.

A fond, unfocused smile crossed the old boy's face.

"Cairo," he sighed. "Well, now. There's only one Cairo."

"Hear that?" Bruce nudged Logie. "There's only one Cairo!"

It was five weary weeks before they docked at Port Tewfik and got to find out for themselves the truth of what became one of Bruce's favorite sayings. There the ship was boarded by a frenzied horde of Arab baggage handlers. Crates and luggage were thrown everywhere amid shouting and screaming, but somehow, out of the chaos, every solider seemed to end up matched with the right bag.

Once ashore, they were marched a short distance from the port to the railway station. For Bruce, who was accustomed to high standards of personal and public hygiene, the train was an affront. It was hot and squalid, and the carriages stank of unwashed bodies before the sweating contingent of Kiwis even embarked. And this was just the prelude. After a long wait and then a short ride, they paused at a station in the outskirts of Cairo, where a full-scale assault on the senses began.

It was the pandemonium that first hit Bruce: people rushing in all directions but seeming to get nowhere; oxen pulling rickety carts loaded as high as tower blocks; the hostile stare of Arabs loitering in the shade of filthy side streets; shopkeepers touting their wares. Every time the train stopped—and it stopped often—dozens of hawkers clambered up the sides of the carriages and thrust their skinny arms through the windows, offering God knows what for sale for who knows how much. Nothing had prepared these raw recruits for the hubbub, filth, poverty, hustle, commotion—and magnificence—of Cairo.

"Looks like there *is* only one bloody Cairo," Bruce said to the goggle-eyed, grinning Blackie, who nodded.

His first impressions of Cairo both excited and repelled Bruce. It was a city of confusing contradictions: the majesty of the pyramids and the Sphinx towering above the ancient run-down alleys—lined with dingy mud huts and traders' stalls—where donkeys, goats, and the occasional dilapidated bicycle offered the only affordable means of transport. And Bruce had the advantage of hailing from a city. Some of his comrades-in-arms were dairy farmers who milked cows in

Taranaki, or back-country sheep farmers from Mangaweka, who were still reeling from the culture shock of Lambton Quay. None of them were prepared for the bedlam that was Cairo. It was a far cry from the parade grounds at Trentham and the (as it now appeared) small-town tranquility of Wellington.

Their destination wasn't Cairo itself, but the New Zealand Expeditionary Force camp at Maadi, on the outskirts of the city. Although it comprised only a handful of semipermanent buildings and a sprawl of canvas bell tents, it seemed like an oasis of order and calm after what they had just glimpsed. As he unpacked his kit bag and followed a quartermaster's directions to the tent that he would temporarily call his own, Bruce felt homesick for the first time since leaving New Zealand. He was also apprehensive, with their arrival at Maadi bringing them one step closer to active duty. He wondered whether he had what it took, when all around him he saw nothing but cheerful bravado. The prospect of panicking in front of his mates—of letting them down—didn't bear thinking about.

He confessed his misgivings to Logie when they caught up later that evening.

"You're a bit scared?" Logie cried. "I'm shitting myself! Look around you. Everyone is. Anyone who says he's not is either lying or drunk."

Bruce nodded. The reality was that none of them knew what to expect, apart from the handful of older World War I veterans. None of the rest knew how they would handle themselves on the battlefield. Bruce decided that all he could do was his best.

———

Life wasn't easy at Maadi. From the bugle call at 6 a.m. sounding the reveille to Last Post at night, life was one long chore. Morning parade from nine to noon was a bitch and the afternoon parade was even worse, so much so that the intensive training they received, which was hard slog, was a welcome relief. They were put through close-order drill, weapon skills, route marches, map reading, desert navigation, and other maneuvers, again and again and yet again.

After a couple of weeks, they were declared fit to take part in desert training.

"What's the desert like?" someone asked.

"Miles and miles of fuck all," an old hand replied. So it proved. The most prominent feature of the desert was the pounding heat. It should have been a profound relief after the monotony of the parade ground and kit inspections, but humping up to 100 pounds of pack and weaponry wasn't Bruce's idea of fun. Occasionally, live rounds were fired over their heads to give them a feel for real battle conditions. If they were lucky, they got to practice bayonet charges, or learn unarmed combat techniques, or—Bruce's favorite—lob grenades and fire Bren guns. But mostly, life at Maadi was dull.

———

Like everyone else, Bruce couldn't wait for his first leave, when he, Logie, and Blackie had agreed to pool their resources and go and see the sights of Cairo. When the day came, they caught a ride in a donkey cart into the city. Bruce had heard that the Empire Services Club ran organized tours of the city. He couldn't understand Blackie's reluctance. Logie seemed torn.

"Bugger the pyramids," Blackie muttered. "I'll be happy if I don't see nothing but the ceiling of a cathouse all day."

Logie's casting vote saw them present themselves to the Services Club. Eight piastres each got them a half-day tour of the pyramids, the Sphinx, the zoo, and other attractions, after which they enjoyed a cold beer among the palm trees in the Services Club bar. The next day, they signed up for a full-day tour to the Delta Barrage. Blackie grumbled about the price—fifteen piastres—but Bruce pointed out it included lunch. For his part, Bruce loved playing tourist. But the next day, when he proposed they join one of the tours visiting Memphis and Sakkara, or the River Nile, or Old Cairo and the dozens of museums, mosques, and bazaars scattered all over the city, Blackie rebelled. He asked the driver of their donkey cart to drop him at the entrance to a dubious-looking alley into which a stream of men wearing the uniforms of the New Zealand Army were disappearing.

"See you back at camp." He waved, and vanished into the gloom of the alley.

———

The following day, Blackie announced that this time around, he was going to be their tour guide. Logie looked pleased, and agreed at once. Bruce reluctantly nodded, and wondered what he was getting himself in for.

At Blackie's direction, they were dropped off in the same general vicinity that he had visited the day before.

"This way," he said, and led them into a narrow side street. Although it was winter, the day was stinking hot, literally. Bruce had never quite adjusted to what he called the "Cairo Fragrance": the putrid stench of rotting garbage piled high in side alleys mingling with the sweetish scent of strong Egyptian tobacco and hashish being smoked in hookah or shisha pipes in the cafés and bars; the reek of open sewers and the stale odor of millions of unwashed bodies competing with the aroma of a thousand spices; the pong of the still-steaming oxen shit that strewed the roads strangely harmonizing with the smell of burning incense drifting from windows.

The other aspect of Cairo that took some adjusting to—if you ever managed to adjust to it—was the ceaseless appetite of the city's population for whatever you might have to give, willingly or not. Everywhere they went, Bruce, Blackie, and Logie were harangued and beseeched, wheedled and cajoled, hectored and harried by men, women, and children selling anything and everything, from shoeshines and souvenirs and artifacts and antiquities to their bodies. Sleight-of-hand dice games, smoke-and-mirrors trickery, bait-and-switch scams, slick-as-snake-oil sales pitches, and quick-as-lightning pickpocketing—all were in the repertoire of ruses the locals used to take money from the naïve soldiers.

As they pushed through the crowds, an ancient-looking stone object on a hawker's table caught Logie's eye. He stopped and picked it up speculatively.

"You have good eye, Kiwi," said the jelly-bellied, profusely sweating man behind the table. "This is *ushabti*. Ancient and very sacred. It is three thousand years old and from the tomb of King Tut himself."

"Piss off," said Logie, sounding impressed despite himself. He studied the object carefully.

"I do not lie," the man protested, sounding injured. "Ask anyone. I am Abdul. Ask anyone if Abdul lies. They will tell you. Abdul sells only genuine articles. He is famous for it."

"How much?" Logie asked.

Abdul named a price. Logie put the object down and made to walk away. Abdul called him back. With a show of barely controlled anguish, much muttering about his poor wife and many children, he offered a sharper price.

Logie accepted at once, looking smug.

They pressed on through the throng toward the railway station. There was a crowd gathered around a table. Craning over the heads of the locals and the soldiers, Bruce, Blackie, and Logie saw that the focus of all the attention was a wizened old man whose gnarled fingers were deftly moving three upturned cups around the surface of a table. When he stopped, his client—another diminutive Egyptian man—tapped one of the cups. The host uttered a cry of anguish and turned over the chosen cup to reveal a pea. He passed over a handful of piastre notes and shook his head grimly. There was a happy buzz from the crowd.

"That's me!" said Logie, and shoved his way forward.

The pea-and-shell gamer welcomed him with a solemn handshake, took Logie's money, and placed it almost delicately in his lap. He held up the pea to Logie, set it on the table, covered it with a cup, and began whirling the three cups around. Logie watched intently, a confident smile twisting the corners of his lips. Sure enough, when the cup he tapped was raised, there was the pea.

So it went for the first two or three rounds.

"He's done his dough," grinned Blackie on the fourth. "Bet you."

The cups came to a rest. Without hesitation, Logie tapped one. There was a pause, and the pea-and-shell man slowly lifted it to reveal . . . nothing.

"What?" yelled Logie, and the crowd roared with laughter.

For the next round, he focused every bit of his attention on the shells. He lost again, much to the delight of the crowd, and again, and again, and again.

A furious-looking Logie rejoined Blackie and Bruce.

"Thief!" he said. "There's some trick. There's a hole in the table or something."

"Cheer up," Blackie began, but Logie had stopped, a stricken look on his face.

"What is it?" asked Bruce.

Logie took his hand from his pocket. Sand trickled through his fingers, and in his palm lay a few fragments of what looked like stone. Abdul's "genuine' *ushabti* had turned out to be plaster, painted with tea to make it look old.

"Pack of thieves!" shouted Logie. "The whole lot of them. Pack of thieves!"

Bruce and Blackie were doubled over with laughter.

———

On their second leave, they caught a train to Bab-el-Louk, the main station in the Sharia Wagh el Birket district, universally known to Kiwi soldiers as The Birka. The moment they stepped out onto the platform, they were besieged: boot polishers, cab drivers, souvenir sellers, street vendors, horse-drawn gharry drivers, pimps, and pickpockets all converged on the khaki uniforms; a raucous rabble of rogues and shysters tugging sharply on uniforms and persistently peddling their wares. It was almost enough to send them scrambling for the next train back.

"Let's get the fuck outta here, Bruce," Blackie's loud, uncultured voice boomed, as he swatted at the hands groping and grabbing at every inch of his body. "Jesus Christ! I can't stand it! All these foreign buggers pokin' and proddin' me like I'm a friggin' pin cushion!"

Bruce feared there might be a brawl before they got as far as the station entrance. But if the locals took offense, they didn't show it. He and Logie managed to steer Blackie through the crowd to the relative safety of the street outside, where they were surrounded by distractions of a different order.

The Birka was famous for its brothels, all sporting alluring names such as Tiger Lil's, Fleur's, and Maxine's House of Pleasure. Beautiful, provocatively dressed girls stood outside, enticing the customers indoors, but the bordellos seldom delivered the exotic experiences their lurid signs promised. The real hookers, whose best days were firmly behind them, kept to the dimly lit interiors, which were kinder on their faded charms and where off-duty soldiers—desperate, dateless, and almost always drunk—pursued them as though they were beauty queens.

Blackie led them under a sign reading "Fifi's Fantasy Palace." They climbed a shabby stairwell and entered a tiny, dimly lit, smoke-stained reception room with paint peeling from the fading walls.

"My treat, Bruce!" Blackie yelled, and waved at the wall beside the entrance. A "Menu of Services" hung lopsidedly by the door, offering a smorgasbord of sexual services in pidgin English. Bruce thought he knew what some of them were. Others he could only guess at.

Bruce ordered a beer—at least Fifi's had real beer instead of Stella, the local brew that was plausibly rumored to involve onions—and settled down to wait for Blackie and Logie who had chosen to partake. He was as randy as any other red-blooded twenty-four-year-old—perhaps more than most, given how unsatisfactory his marital bed had been in the months before his departure. It wasn't lack of libido, or even pangs of conscience on Doreen's account. It was fear, pure and simple. In Bruce's case, the lectures delivered back at camp by the grim-faced nurses before they were presented with their quota of Army-issue condoms had fallen on fertile ground. He couldn't imagine how he'd live with the humiliation if he caught an STD and had to line up for treatment in the Droopy Dick parade back at Maadi, or had to tell Doreen, or his parents . . .

He hadn't even finished his beer when first Blackie, then Logie emerged, looking pleased with themselves.

"Aren't you afraid of catching something?" Bruce asked.

Blackie shrugged. "I'd rather die," he said casually. "But I take precautions. And for all we know, this might be the last bit of slap and tickle we get for a while. Might be the last bit ever."

———

This was the routine of their time in Cairo: the hard slog and monotony of camp lightened by their time off. Drinking was a favorite pastime. When they got into town, their preferred watering hole was Mannering's Bar, which advertised itself as a "friend to every New Zealander." They also favored the New Zealand Forces Club on Sharia Malika Farida, and when they were off-duty in camp the courtyard of The Lowry Hut was a shady refuge from the unrelenting desert sun.

Of course, they made their own fun, too. One day, Bruce saw Logie deep in conversation with one of the newspaper boys who plied their trade in camp, hawking the *Egyptian Mail*. Logie seemed to be giving the lad a language lesson, as he would speak very slowly and clearly and get the boy to repeat what he'd said. Finally, he nodded approvingly, sent the boy on his way with a clap on the back, and wandered over to Bruce.

"What's up?" Bruce asked, sensing mischief.

"Wait for it," Logie said.

"Very good news," yelled the newspaper boy. Although they spoke no English, the boys were all very good mimics. "Very good news," he repeated. "General Freyberg Caught Shagging a Camel." Off he went, announcing the headline around the camp to the cheers and laughter of the Kiwi troops.

Needless to say, the camp brass would have dearly loved to have found out who was responsible for this stunt. Logie would have spent a few weeks in the cooler if anyone had let on, but no one did.

Most nights, an Aussie entrepreneur by the name of Thomas Shafto—Shifty Shafto to the Kiwis—ran a poxy old fleapit cinema playing reruns of B- and C-grade movies. The "theater" comprised flimsy wooden walls and a crude roof that Shifty had stitched together from surplus canvas and any other scraps of sacking or fabric he could lay his hands on. Inside this ramshackle big top, three piastres would get you a perch on an arse-achingly hard wooden bench. For five piastres, you could upgrade to a ragged wicker chair, which would prick you with loose strands of rattan. The bugs didn't discriminate: they bit everyone in the cheap seats and the posh chairs regardless. Like most privates earning five shillings a day, Bruce, Blackie, and Logie opted for the benches.

Once, when the projector broke down—which it did with monotonous regularity—some drunken British Army lout pushed Blackie off his perch. Blackie resumed his seat, choosing to ignore the deliberate provocation.

"Move over, you cockless Kiwi git," the Pom said, giving him another shove. "Ain't room 'ere for us both."

Blackie feigned interest in the blank screen.

"What's the matter. Are you dumb as well as ugly?" asked the Pom, giving Blackie yet another shove.

Everyone was studying Blackie with interest. He wasn't known to turn his back on the opportunity for a fight. Sure enough, after a moment's pause, he swung his fist foursquare into the Brit's nose and stood up.

"Anyone else for some of that?" he asked the other tanked-up British soldiers, as he rolled up his sleeves. It was all on. Half the theater joined in the brawl, while the other half cheered and yelled encouragement.

"Best movie ever," Bruce told Blackie afterward, as Blackie nursed his bleeding knuckles.

———

In early March 1941, the Cairo winter was giving over into spring. The days were getting longer and warmer, hovering around twenty-two degrees. The nights were pleasantly mild, even as the rumor mill at Maadi ran red-hot. Everyone at the camp—and it seemed half of Cairo as well—was talking about 25 Battalion's imminent deployment. The prospect of facing the Hun provoked a mix of excitement and fear among the men. After all the arduous training and long, sweat-soaked hours lugging rifles and rucksacks in the heat and dust, they were now well prepared, militarily if not mentally.

No one on high was letting on about where they were likely to be sent, and that made the matter the subject of speculation and more than a few wagers. Some thought it might be Libya. Most plumped for Greece. Others professed to not give a damn—they just wanted to get on with it. The Egyptian traders, the dhobi wallahs, the bus drivers, the newspaper boys—even the Cairene tarts—seemed better informed than the young men whose lives were shortly to be on the line. "You're on your way to Greece" they would say with an air of authority. Or, "You're leaving for Athens on Tuesday," accompanied by a nod and a wink.

Bruce supposed he felt ready. The rifles had been issued, their bayonets were gut-piercingly sharp, and the rest of their gear was polished, oiled, cleaned, checked, checked again, and then treble-checked. Whatever needed to be done had been done. It was now or never.

Finally, on March 17, 25 Battalion boarded a train for Alexandria, where they embarked on the HMS *Orion*. Still, there was no official word of their final destination. Some desk wallah at HQ had plainly decided that the soldiers, some of whom had drawn a one-way ticket in life's lottery, should be kept in the dark "in the interests of secrecy." Bruce couldn't see the point of it. Every man jack of them knew they were heading for Greece. He'd have been very surprised if the Hun didn't know, too.

In the end, he reflected, it hardly mattered. It was time to do what they were there to do.

Chapter Six

———

Josefine, Maribor, April 1941 to January 1942

The Wehrmacht had marched into Maribor on the night of April 8, 1941. Almost three weeks later, on April 26, Polde, Josefine, Jelka, and a group of others had gone to hear Adolf Hitler himself speak. It was raining that late spring day, but that didn't stop the hordes from turning out. The town square was packed to capacity, proud parents hoisting young children to their shoulders to get a better view and the sycophantic crowd waving frantically and shouting encouragement to their German heroes. They listened to Hitler roar from the balcony of the Rotovž—the town hall—that their land would be "made German again."

"The man's not much taller than us," Josefine shouted to Jelka above the clamor of the crowd. "How can someone so short have so much power?"

A man with a child perched on his shoulders and a swastika armband rounded on her.

"Shut up, bitch!" he snarled at her in German. "Have some re-spect!"

She was taken aback by the fury that twisted his face. She rec-ognized him. He was a baker whose shop she visited occasionally, and he was Volksdeutsche—a member of the well-represented ethnic German minority. Maribor, part of the Lower Styria region of Slovenia, had been a predominantly German-speaking territory as recently as 1919. Tensions ran high between the Volksdeutsche and the local Slovenes.

She could understand the Volksdeutsche's support for the German invasion, and almost forgive it. But many of those cheering that day were Slovenes. That filled her with disgust. Polde led their little group in a chant—"Slovenia for the Slovenes!"—but it was largely ignored by the crowd, who applauded Hitler's message and fluttered little swastika flags like so many red-and-black butterflies.

The Nazi presence became more obtrusive and oppressive as days passed. Even before Hitler's visit, the *Kommandantur*, a kind of administrative office, had been established in Maribor, with 2,500 *Sturmabteilung*—the feared Nazi storm troopers, known as the Brown-shirts for the uniform they wore—attached as enforcers. Gauleiter Uiberreither, the Nazi administrator, was ordered to impose a pol-icy of "re-Germanization." Slovene street names were taken down and replaced with German ones. The town square, Glavni trg, was renamed Adolf-Hitler-Platz, and Slovene-language shop signs—even those over stores owned by Slovenes—were switched for their Deutsche equivalents. Maribor was renamed Marburg an der Drau. Limbuš became Lembach bei Marburg. Teachers were deported and replaced by Nazi Austrians who taught only in German. Anything reflecting the Slovene culture or character was destroyed. Even the use of the Slovene language in public was forbidden.

Josefine was a common enough name in both Slovenia and Ger-many so she was saved the indignity of a Nazi-dictated name change, and as Lobnik had no German equivalent her family preserved some self-respect.

Every Sunday for as long as she could remember, Josefine had rung the bell of the Catholic church in Limbuš, summoning the congregation. It was all she could do now to keep her expression neutral when she looked around and saw men in the hated gray uniform of the occupier piously making the sign of the cross alongside her Slovene compatriots. After praying for the safety of her family, she asked that God would cast down the Nazis and return Slovenia to the Slovenes.

———

Josefine met Jelka one summery afternoon, as she often did, for a coffee and chat, but Jelka was preoccupied. When she was certain they were alone in a narrow street, she stopped Josefine with a hand on her arm.

"Pepica, listen. It's Polde," she said. "I saw his name on a list. They're going to arrest him."

Josefine frowned at her friend. "What list? What are you talking about?"

"I was working," Jelka replied. "On one of the officer's desks, I saw a list of people the Švabi have given the mark 'E.' That's code for 'prominently anti-German.' Polde's name was on it, and it said he was to be arrested and resettled. You have to warn him."

Josefine stared at her. Jelka was a night cleaner in the *Kommandantur*, where the *Reichssicherheitshauptamt*, the State Security Office, was also housed. She often gathered useful pieces of information, which she passed on to those who had connections to the partisans.

Slowly, Josefine nodded, feeling sick at heart. The fact that her brother's name was being spoken by the Švabi—the derogatory term Slovenes used for the Nazis—made the war suddenly very personal to her.

"Thank you, Jelka," she said. "Thank you."

She embraced her friend, and they parted.

———

"Where's Polde?" she asked as soon as she arrived home.

Roman, her younger brother, looked up from the book he was reading and shrugged.

"Fetch Papa," Josefine said. "It's important."

Josefine's father, Jožef, entered the room, his habitually bleak expression bleaker than usual. These were times when, more than ever, no news was good news.

"What is it, Pepi?" he asked.

Josefine repeated what Jelka had told her.

"What has that foolish boy done now?" Jožef sighed, sinking into a chair. "Where is he?"

"I don't know, Papa," said Roman, looking from his father to Josefine anxiously. "Should I go and find him?"

"Yes, see if you can," Jožef said.

An anxious wait ensued. It was half an hour before Polde breezed into the room with Roman at his heels. In that time, Josefine had imagined him already arrested, beaten, or worse. She was weak with relief at the sight of him.

"What's up?" he asked.

"Tell him," Jožef said.

Josefine told her brother that he was marked for arrest and "resettlement." None of them had any illusions about this Nazi euphemism. But if Polde was worried he didn't show it. He merely shrugged.

"How did this happen?" Jožef said. "Why can't you be more careful about who's listening when you bad-mouth the Nazis?"

Polde snorted. Caution wasn't a concept he grasped.

"Like everyone my age, I was invited to volunteer for the *Steirischer*

Heimatbund, Papa," he said, placing a heavy emphasis on the word "invited." "Of course, I refused."

The blandly named Styrian Youth Corps had recently been established to assist with the "re-Germanization" policy. Its members were encouraged to intimidate anyone heard speaking Slovene, or using Slovene names, or speaking ill of the Nazis or their Führer. All who received an invitation such as Polde had received knew full well that there was no option to refuse. He refused nonetheless, and this had evidently brought him to the attention of the *Reichssicherheitshauptamt.*

"You must go to my brother," Jožef said. "You can work for his family. He will keep you safe."

Polde shook his head. "Too dangerous," he said. "If they find me there, they'll take him and his family, too. No, I'll go north and try to get work somewhere in Austria, keep my head down."

He turned his dazzling smile on Josefine, who was fighting back tears. "Don't worry, Pepi," he said. "I'll be fine. The Švabi won't catch me!"

———

Polde wouldn't allow any of his family to accompany him to the station, where he caught the first available train for Graz, across the border in Austria.

"We don't want to make a fuss," he said. "Besides, it's not like I'm going away forever. I'll be back as soon as they've forgotten about me. I promise."

He kissed Josefine and gave her a brief squeeze. He stuck out his hand to shake Roman's, but then dragged him into a bear hug, tousling the boy's sandy curls.

And now he was gone. It was several days before a letter arrived from him, telling the family that he had got a job as a laborer just outside Krieglach, north of Graz. The people, the place, and the pay were all satisfactory, he reported. He promised to visit as soon as he thought the danger had passed.

The family argued about Polde. Jožef was angry at him for ignoring advice to keep quiet and thereby putting his own life—and the lives of his family—in danger. They also argued about how to respond to the Nazi occupation.

"So what are we supposed to do, Papa?" asked Anica one night over dinner. "Get on with our lives and watch the Švabi take over everything?" She shook her head.

"Yes," said Jožef. "That's exactly what we have to do. We have to keep our views to ourselves and toe the line. That's how we'll get through." He ran a calloused hand over the salt-and-pepper stubble on his cheek and passed it across his eyes. "It wasn't that long ago when almost everyone here spoke German, and it was Slovenes who were in the minority. That was before you were born, Anica. We were part of Austria then. The soldiers will soon be replaced by bureaucrats and life will go on as normal, you'll see. We have to wait it out this time, just like we waited before."

"No," Anica said. "I can't."

She paused, as if considering whether to go on.

"And I'm not. Papa, I've joined the partisans."

Jožef looked up from his plate of thin soup, an expression of horror on his face. Josefine and Anica knew he supported the partisans in his own quiet way—he sent food when he could spare it, and he had agreed to let a man who was suspected of being a partisan fighter lie low in an outbuilding on the Lobniks' small property.

"Fighting isn't work for a woman," he said. He would have said more, but Anica cut him off.

"Papa, I was walking home the other night and I saw something that will haunt me forever." Her face contorted. "I saw a girl, the body of a girl, hanging from a tree. There was a sign around her neck saying she was a partisan and she had killed a soldier. She can't have been more than sixteen, Papa. Not much older than Roman. She was just a child. And the Švabi murdered her!"

Anica began weeping as Josefine and Roman stared at her.

"That will be you if you try to fight them," Jožef said. "Leave the fighting to the men."

"I would rather die like that," Anica said passionately, "than sit and wait until it's my turn to be raped and murdered. If it's the last thing I do, I'm going to kill a Švabi for what they did to that girl. For what they're doing to our country."

———

Despite her father's threats and entreaties, it seemed Anica was as good as her word. She never spoke to the family about her activities—not even to Josefine, to whom she had always told everything. She would merely announce that she was going away for a while and tell them not to worry about her. Of course, they did worry, and they tried to imagine where she had gone and what she was doing. They knew very little for certain about the partisan movement. Josefine had the vague idea, based upon rumors and hearsay, that there were two wings: one devoted to paramilitary operations and sabotage, and the other to gathering intelligence and facilitating communication. Anica, she supposed, being Anica, had signed up to be a fighter. Occasionally, news would ripple through the patriotic Slovene community of partisan victories—a railway line blown up here, a motor vehicle convoy ambushed there, Švabi soldiers killed—and Josefine would wonder if Anica had been involved. She would glow with pride at the thought that she might have been.

But not all of the news was good. Soon after the occupation had begun, posters had started appearing around Maribor. They were bloodred, and beneath the word "Notice"—"*Bekanntmachung*" in German and "*Razglas*" in Slovene—there was a list of names: the roll of those who had been executed for "crimes against the Third Reich." These grisly notices proliferated like poppies. Every time a new one appeared, Josefine had to read the list, terrified that one day she would find the name "Lobnik' posted there. Whenever she saw the posters—and they were plastered all over town—she felt sick with worry for Anica, and for Polde.

On Sunday, November 30, 1941, Josefine was sitting on a pew next to Anica when she became aware that her sister was silently weeping. She glanced at her inquiringly, but Anica gave a slight shake of her head.

It was as they were walking home from the church that Anica murmured to Josefine, "Ivan Milavec is dead."

"Luka Milavec's son?"

Anica nodded.

"My God. I went to school with his brothers, Albin and Marjan. How did he die?"

"He was killed in a fight with the Švabi two days ago. We . . . he was ambushing a supply train. Someone must have betrayed them."

"You said 'we.'"

Anica was silent. She wouldn't give any further details. And, when Josefine told her that she had made up her mind to join the partisans too, Anica shook her head vehemently.

"No, Pepi. No, you mustn't. You're too young. It's too dangerous."

"You sound like Papa," Josefine said. "Anica, promise me you'll be careful."

"For me, the time to be careful has gone," Anica replied.

———

Nonetheless, Anica was at home over the next two weeks. She hardly went out during the day and slept in her own bed at night. When, on December 17, Josefine found her buttoning up her overcoat and pulling a woolen hat down over her ears, she said that she would be back by dinnertime.

She wasn't.

Josefine went to bed feeling anxious, and couldn't sleep. By morning, when there was still no sign of her sister, she pulled on her boots and picked her way through the snow to the little shed at the bottom of the property.

Srečko Loburg was already up and about, fetching firewood with which to feed the shed's little stove.

"Morning, Pepi," he called cheerfully. "What brings you down here? Do you have news?"

"Srečko, it's Anica," Josefine replied, hearing the tremor in her own voice. "She was supposed to be home last night, but she didn't come back."

Srečko was silent for a moment as he piled a few more sticks onto the armful he was holding. Then he shot her a glance from beneath his dark fringe.

"I have to go into town later today," he said gravely. "I'll see if I can find out anything."

He lowered his voice. "Don't worry," he said. "Sometimes plans change. Sometimes in Anica's line of work your day doesn't turn out the way you expected it to, and it's safer to do something different."

He forced a smile, and Josefine tried to force one in return. Srečko was a good-looking young man, a couple of years older than Josefine, and most of her friends were smitten as soon as they set eyes on him. But to Josefine he was just a good friend she had known since she was a child.

Srečko returned from his visit to town later that morning. Josefine heard him speaking in a low voice to Jožef, and when she went in the house she found her father sitting at the kitchen table with a rosary in his calloused hands.

"Your sister has been arrested," Srečko said. "She was seen passing an envelope to a known partisan sympathizer. It seems she was being watched. They moved in and took her right away."

"She was being watched?" Josefine asked. "How do you know? How did *they* know?"

"There was a battle a little while ago. The Švabi knew the partisans were setting up an ambush, and they were waiting for them. We lost some good fighters."

"Ivan," said Josefine.

Srečko nodded. "They must have been betrayed. Since then, Anica knew she was being followed, which is why she's been so careful lately. But she must have thought the danger had passed. The Švabi were just waiting for an excuse, and she gave them one."

"Foolish girl," exclaimed Jožef, his voice no more than a broken whisper.

"Where have they taken her? What will happen to her?" Josefine asked.

Srečko was silent for a long time, as though considering how much to tell them.

"They'll take her to one of their prisons, probably the castle. They'll try to make her admit she's a partisan, and to betray her comrades."

"Make her? What does that mean?"

Srečko hung his head. "Anica is strong," he said. "She won't talk. If they can't make her talk, they'll let her go. They have no proof that she's done anything wrong."

"What about the envelope?"

"The person she gave it to got away. That's how I know what I know."

"What will they do to her?"

Srečko just looked at her, then shook his head. Not long after he had first come to live in the shed, Josefine had overheard Anica and

Srečko talking. She'd heard him say he had lately been arrested and, while she hadn't caught the rest of his words, she'd heard her sister gasp and mutter, "Nazi scum!" Nor, when Josefine had pressed her afterward, would Anica tell her what he had endured. Josefine could imagine the kinds of torture they had used—or thought she could.

"What can we do?" she asked.

"You must wait," he said. "It's all you can do."

————

With its picturesque whitewashed walls and red-tile roofs surrounded by three busy squares, Maribor Castle had once been a source of immense pride to Josefine. It was hundreds of years old, built in the Baroque style in the fifteenth century, with an elaborate facade and a tall, black-domed tower. Now, with swastika flags hanging from the flagstaffs on either side of the main entranceway and her sister languishing somewhere in the bowels of the building, it was nothing more than a symbol of oppression. Josefine stood in the square staring at the castle until a brownshirted German noticed her and moved toward her.

"*Was ist Ihr Geschäft?*" he asked. "What are you doing here?"

"I was supposed to meet my friend here," she replied lamely.

He leered. "Perhaps I can be your friend," he said.

She couldn't prevent a spasm of disgust crossing her face. She lowered her eyes, shook her head, and walked away, willing him not to follow her. She was in luck.

There was nothing she could do. She went home to Limbuš, to join her father and Roman in prayer for Anica's safe return.

————

Then it seemed their world was falling apart. Two days later, they received word that Roman had also been arrested. Srečko knew about this, too. He tried to reassure the family.

"Roman should come through okay," he offered. "He'll be scared to death and they'll rough him up, that's for sure, but the Gestapo will be mainly interested in pumping him for information on Anica and her partisan comrades. In the end, I'm sure they'll let him go. He's just a kid, after all. Still at school."

Srečko paused. "As for me," he said, "I must go. If I stay, they'll come looking for me, and if they find me here your lives will be in danger. Anica and Roman weren't the only ones arrested. They took others who may not be as strong as Anica, and I could easily be betrayed."

He left Josefine and her father hugging each other, both sobbing. It was the first time she could remember hearing her father cry, his thin frame heaving in her arms.

Just before he left, Srečko looked in on them again. "Write to me at my uncle's house in Villach. You know the address," he said. "Tell me when you have news. Be careful what you say!"

———

It was more than a week before they heard anything. Then, on the morning of December 27, 1941, the front door opened and there was Anica, her face pale and bruised and her normally lustrous hair hanging in greasy hanks. She moved as if every motion cost her a great deal in effort and pain. She recoiled when Josefine flung her arms around her. Josefine drew back.

"My poor Anica," she said. "What have they done to you?"

Anica never told her. But Josefine found out enough from Anica's friends to piece together what had happened. After she was captured, Anica was taken to a cell in the depths of the castle. She protested her innocence—she claimed that the envelope she was carrying contained nothing more than an official decree from the Gauleiter—but this had convinced no one. The Nazis believed it was partisan propaganda or, worse, stolen intelligence. Anica was chained to a metal pole and interrogated for three hours, during which time she wasn't given so much as a sip of water or the chance to relieve herself.

When this proved to be unproductive, her captors had progressed to torture. Still shackled to the pole, Anica was stripped. She feared she was about to be raped, but at the direction of another man who had joined the proceedings—an older man known as "The Marquis" after the infamous de Sade—she was repeatedly immersed in iced water and held down until she thought she would drown. Josefine could scarcely bear the thought of what liberties the Nazi scum might have taken as they manhandled her beautiful sister. When Anica still refused to admit that she had any connections to the partisans, they changed tactics again. This time, she was made to stand with her legs apart and her hands clasped over her head for four hours without moving. If she dropped her hands, she was beaten with a rubber nightstick. Still they couldn't break her, so they burned her breasts with cigarettes.

But Anica had told them nothing, and they had eventually let her go. Josefine was fiercely proud of her. She wondered if she would have been able to find the courage to continue to defy them if she had been in her sister's place.

"What about Roman?" Josefine said.

"Roman? What do you mean?" Anica responded, clearly puzzled by the question.

Then it dawned on her. "Oh my God, no! Not Roman! My God, it's all my fault! The Švabi have taken him because of me. He'll be grilled and beaten until he tells them what they want to know. Poor Roman. He's still only a boy."

Tears dripped from her black and swollen cheeks.

"We can only pray" was all Josefine could say as she pulled her sister closer.

Three days later their prayers were answered. There was a knock at the door and there stood Roman, battered and bloodied, leaning on the toothless old peasant who had found him where he'd been lying in a street on the other side of town. He had survived, barely. Despite his age—he was just fifteen—he had been beaten with a knobbled wooden baton and flogged with a metal-spiked cowhide whip. But he didn't talk.

When violence failed to deliver the desired effect, the Nazis tried another strategy. Roman was being held in the same prison as Anica. Every day he was taken to a cell overlooking the courtyard, where he could see Anica and observe the extent of the injuries she had sustained from the days of torture, but she never saw nor even suspected he was there. Twice, he was taken to the town square to witness the executions of suspected partisans. The message was clear. Sooner or later—probably sooner—Anica would be among them. All he had to do was tell them about his sister's connections and they would let both him and Anica go.

Roman didn't believe them. He didn't say a word.

Finally, he was bundled into the trunk of a Mercedes staff car—the driver took care to put covers down so that his blood didn't stain the floor—and dumped where the peasant found him.

Josefine wrote to Srečko as promised and received his carefully worded reply a few days later.

Dear Pepica! I received your letter today, thank you very much. I am pleased to hear the news about Anica. I am pleased to learn that she has been freed as she has done nothing wrong—this was included for the benefit of the German censors in case his letter was intercepted—*I'm keen to know if Anica will come back to us now that she has been released* . . . He was referring to the likelihood of Anica returning to her partisan unit;

some who had been tortured had subsequently dropped out of the resistance movement or were too traumatized to play any useful role.

Anica had no such concerns. She did return and was immediately promoted to liaison officer.

It was after what had happened to Anica and Roman that Josefine finally made her mind up. Without telling Jožef or Anica, she made contact with the partisans and, like Anica a few months before, she swore an oath "to destroy the Fascist conquerors, and to fight mercilessly against the bloodthirsty enemies . . . without sparing our blood or our lives."

Chapter Seven

———

Bruce, Greece,
March to April 1941

he Greeks welcomed them as heroes.

Crowds lined the streets, ten or more deep, and cheered the Kiwis on as they marched through the thronged avenues of Athens. Bruce was proud to be wearing the khaki uniform of 25 Battalion. Pretty young girls threw bunches of flowers at the troops and the older Athenians waved and shouted encouragement, fervently hoping that these brave young lads would be their saviors.

The soldiers had been granted a few days' leave. The more learned and curious among them—Bruce included—took the opportunity to look around this fabled metropolis of the ancient world, while others did nothing, nervous about what lay ahead, and, as always, there were plenty who wanted to whore it up or drink themselves senseless. At least they'd be bulletproof until they sobered up.

Athens was a far cry from the craziness of Cairo. The Greeks were enthusiastic hosts, generous to a fault despite their own hardships, and quite innocent of the devious commercial practices of the wily old gents in Egypt. Bruce did what every tourist in peacetime did: he trekked up to the Acropolis and marveled at its architectural magnificence; he strolled around the ruins of the ancient Agora marketplace, his feet ringing on the same stone that those of the ancients had trodden thousands of years before; he stared skyward at the massive pillars of the Temple of Olympian Zeus; he visited the museums, bought cheap souvenirs in the Monastiraki area, and dined on moussaka and taramasalata at one of the many restaurants in the Plaka neighborhood. The cafés and tiny bars tucked away in narrow lanes represented a completely different culture from what the Kiwi boys were used to back home, but Bruce embraced this new lifestyle. Although beer was still his poison of choice, ouzo soon became a close second. The coffee, though, was no better than Cairo—it tasted like dirty silt dredged from the bottom of the Ilissos River.

"I can handle this sort of war. Can't you?" Blackie sighed one evening, as a smiling young woman refilled his glass with retsina.

"Doing your patriotic duty, there, Blackie," Logie said. "Making your country proud, I see."

Bruce laughed. As the sun set over the Aegean, it was hard to imagine there was a desperate struggle taking place in the hills just to the north.

A few days later, their leave expired and they were called back to reality. At first, the war news—filtered as it was through the military rumor mill—was good: the attempted invasion of the Greek peninsula by the Italians had been repulsed. But it was widely anticipated that the Germans would have a go instead. On March 25, 25 Battalion received its marching orders. Crowds of cheering Greeks lined the street once again as they made their way to the station, where they boarded a train for Katerini, a town on the Gulf of Salonika two hundred miles or so northwest of Athens. It was a hideous journey, fully twenty-three hours spent huddled on the floor of cattle trucks. They emerged, blinking, into the morning sunshine in a little clutch of stone houses nestled at the foot of a towering, snowcapped mountain.

"What mountain's that?" Bruce wondered aloud.

"That," said his company sergeant, who seemed to have a pretty good grasp of Greek geography, "is Mount Olympus. Heard of Olympus, boys?"

Several of Bruce's comrades shook their heads, squinting up at the cloud-wreathed summit.

"Home of the gods," said Bruce.

"That's right. Home of the Greek gods. Jupiter and them," the sergeant said, enjoying showing off his superior knowledge.

"Zeus," corrected Bruce.

"Him too," the sergeant replied. "Now move your sorry arses."

The battalion marched out of the village that afternoon and bivouacked in a meadow full of wildflowers. It was bitterly cold, with a keen breeze sweeping down from the snowfields. The following day, they moved north through a narrow mountain pass to a position where a unit of the Greek Army was well dug in. The Greeks welcomed them with flashing grins and thumbs-up, as well they might: they were being withdrawn. The next morning, waving to the Kiwis, they formed up and began marching out. Bruce and his mates were ordered to carry on the work of digging rifle pits and filling sandbags to surround machine-gun and mortar nests. All around him, soldiers grumbled and whined but they got on with it anyway. Bruce was sure everyone felt as he did. It was good to have real work to do at last. It took his mind off the butterflies churning in his stomach.

At dawn on April 6, there was a series of dull booms to the north. The grapevine was alight with stories, soon confirmed, that Germany had declared war on Greece and Yugoslavia at midnight. The sound they had heard was the sound of demolition charges being detonated in forward positions to destroy roads and bridges, in order to slow a German advance.

Bruce heard this news with the rest of D Company in the mess tent late that morning.

"This is it, then," someone said. "Looks like we're finally going to meet Fritz."

Work on their defenses redoubled over the next couple of days. On April 8, the heavily overcast sky to the north was splashed red. Salonika was on fire.

———

Two days later, they were ordered to withdraw back through the Olympus Pass. The weather had reverted to winter, and snow lay on the ground. To general disgust, they were told to fall in and march. The reason soon became clear: the road through the pass had been marginal in good weather. Now, in snow, it looked impassable to anything with wheels. Greek civilians—men and women, girls and boys, some as young as ten and many gnarled and wrinkled with age—were working on improving it. Bruce gave one little girl a chocolate bar from his rations, and was rewarded with a dazzling smile from both the girl and what may have been her grandparents.

Every now and again, when there was room for the men to move to the side of the road, they gathered there as a lorry or a Bren carrier ground its way over the treacherous surface. At times it looked as though the vehicles must surely slither off and plunge over the bluff on the outside of a corner. But the drivers kept the trucks on course, and the men cheered.

"Hope they keep them on the road. We don't want to walk everywhere we go," said Bluey, a Hawke's Bay farmer with whom Bruce had become good mates back at Trentham.

"Amen to that," Bruce said, massaging his aching calf.

Late that afternoon, the sound of artillery and even machine-gun fire could be heard to the north and, with a roar, a lone aircraft swept through the pass, heading in that direction.

"One of ours?" Bruce asked.

"Nah," said Bluey. "Bloody Kraut. Must have been saving his ammo for someone else. Lucky for us."

"Amen to that, too," said Bruce.

———

By April 16, they were beginning to dig in on the high ground overlooking one of two roads that ran south toward the town of Elasson. Bruce was no military strategist, but even he could see the defensive advantages of the location. The road was flanked on one side by steep hills and on the other by a deep swamp. A tank wanting to pass through would have to stick to the road, where it would be an easy target for their anti-tank guns. Churchill had said—Bruce had seen it in the papers—that the Allies would not surrender Greece. This was where they would make their stand, and it looked like a good plan.

Just then, it began to rain, and not just rain, but bucket down.

"Oh, shit. This is all we need," groaned Bruce.

"Be grateful," the sergeant said. "It keeps the Boche planes on the ground."

The rain persisted. Over the next couple of days, Bruce took his turn on picket duty, squinting over the sights of his rifle at the road where it entered a small village below. There were several false alarms, as knots of people and the occasional truck or half-track vehicle came into view through the sheets of water. Each time, they turned out to be Kiwis or Aussies beating a ragged retreat from the action to the north, or Greek families carrying a few possessions and fleeing the fighting.

The weather cleared in the early hours of April 18. Then, at nine in the morning, just as Bruce was gingerly biting into an "Anzac tile"— as the rock-hard biscuits they received in their Army rations were known—it began. There was an unearthly howl from the sky to the south, followed by the crump of a heavy detonation.

"What the fuck was that?" he spluttered through a mouthful of crumbs.

"Dive bomber," said Bluey. "Stuka. Looks like it was attacking Elasson. And mind your language."

There was a whoosh and a thump, and a column of dirt heaved itself out of the hillside several hundred yards to their left. It was followed by another.

"This is it," said Bluey, tightening his grip on his rifle.

Shells fell sporadically, some close to the men, some farther off, as though the guns were some blind creature groping for them. Then, a couple of tense hours later, there was a roaring, squeaking noise from up the road to their right. It grew louder, and still louder, and then a monolith of metal appeared around the bend in the road just north of the village. The long barrel of its gun was inclined toward the slope on which Bruce and the rest of his company were entrenched.

"Shit!" breathed Bruce. Despite all the hours on the parade ground, nothing had prepared him for this. The German tanks presented a fearsome sight as tons of steel rumbled toward the Kiwi troops; Bruce had never seen so much military hardware in one formation. Five tanks appeared, although shortly after one came into view it paused, wheeled around, and went back the way it had come. It was almost as though it had sensed what was to come, as a moment later there was a flash and a terrific bang close by the leading tank. Rock and dirt began flying as shells landed thick and fast. It was horrifying, but also exhilarating to be this close to the action.

"You bloody beauties!" Bruce yelled, encouraging the gunners miles away to the south. "Stick it up them! Show the bastards!"

The tanks halted in their advance and actually began to reverse along the road, the artillery fire pursuing them. The foremost was hit, its offside track snaking off. The others left it stranded there at the mercy of the big guns.

There was cheering from the rifle pits, but it faltered. A throbbing hum was heard beneath the visceral pounding of shellfire. High in the blue sky to the northwest, six dots appeared, flying unhurriedly in formation toward them.

"Bloody hell," said Bluey. "Get your head down."

But the planes passed over them, intent it seemed on attacking the artillery batteries to the south. Their diving assaults could be heard—the nerve-shredding wail of the sirens mounted on the wings—followed by the tremendous explosions of the aerial bombs.

Huge and black, a Stuka roared over the ridgeline from the direction in which the planes had disappeared. Rocks, stones, and vegetation were flung into the air, and the staccato hammer of the aircraft's cannons came a second later. Bruce heard an agonized shout from somewhere close by. Another plane ripped overhead, and this time Bruce saw a man hit. The soldier pitched forward, blood spurting from his shoulder. It dawned on Bruce that this was now for real. Mates would die—or be injured, maimed, and mortally wounded. It was pandemonium. Men were yelling. Some were running down the hillside; some were running up it. Planes periodically tore across on strafing runs, and Bruce had no doubt that they were inflicting heavy casualties. In the absence of any order to do otherwise, he stayed put, trying to melt into the stony Greek soil every time the roaring whine of an aircraft engine was heard.

The day passed in a blur. Every now and then, there would be a lull, where the guns would fall silent and the skies would be empty of aircraft. The tanks hadn't reappeared. Bluey decided he would use the disabled tank—still otherwise unscathed a thousand yards away—for target practice, in case any of its crew were still inside. Eventually, a corporal appeared and told him to stop. Bluey muttered, but Bruce found it highly reassuring. It was the first indication he'd had since breakfast that anyone was still issuing orders.

Several more flights of Stukas passed over during the afternoon, but only one plane bothered to strafe their position. The Germans were clearly more interested in trying to suppress the artillery. And, while Bruce half expected a rush of gray uniforms to appear from the north, it didn't happen. In the early evening, a story swept through the trenches that they were about to be withdrawn again. When, just after nightfall, they heard the sound of engines approaching from the south, Bruce and his mates knew it was true. The trucks were there to take them away from the scene of their first-ever battle.

———

By noon the next day, 25 Battalion was encamped in a stony stream bed under the cover of a dense olive grove. Everyone was weary from the fight, and from the arduous truck journey overnight. The previous few days' rain had turned some stretches of road into a quagmire, and more often than not Bruce's transport arrived at the bad patches to find motorbikes, trucks, or even Bren carriers stuck fast. It took time to clear the blockages. At midnight, they had passed through a large town that was mostly ablaze. Behind them, there was a huge explosion as the engineers blew the Alamanas bridge just to the north.

They had some respite over the next day or so, the thick canopy of the trees affording them some protection from aerial attack. All the while, they wondered and worried about the military situation. Rumors were rife. They were going to be ordered to launch a counterattack. The Germans had made a marine landing south of them and they were caught between two advancing armies. They were going to fall back on the beaches and evacuate. They were shortly to be moved to another position where the brass had decided they would fight to the death.

After hurried preparations, the troops boarded their vehicles and traveled the 170 miles to Molos. Following an exhausting overnight journey, navigating treacherous mountain roads peppered with potentially lethal slips and bomb craters, they arrived just southeast of Molos around dawn and settled in.

The company sergeant told them that they were now in the vicinity of Thermopylae.

"Mean anything to any of you ignorant sods?" he said.

"Sparta," said Bruce. "The Spartans fought the Persians here."

"Very good, Private. Go to the top of the class. This is a good bit of dirt to fight on, boys. This is why they've pulled us back here. This is where we decide who gets to keep Greece."

Soon concrete intelligence reached them from the units of 24 Battalion that had been tasked with watching the Alamanas bridge. Two German motorcyclists had appeared, and they had been shot up. One was dead, the other wounded. They were, it turned out, a reconnaissance party for the 5th Panzer Division, which was massed ready to launch an assault just to the north.

And then definitive word came from high command. The New Zealand divisions were to stage a rearguard action to hold the enemy at bay long enough for the Allied forces to be evacuated. They were surrendering Greece, after all.

The news didn't go down well.

"Bloody hell. What happened to 'hold Greece at any cost'?" Bluey said. "We were doing the job back there. We could have held them at Olympus. We could have held them back there at Elasson."

Several people muttered their agreement.

"Didn't you hear?" someone else said. "It's a lost bloody cause. The Krauts have got past the Greeks on the western side of the mountains. They'll be in Athens any day. There's nothing left to defend."

"Oh, shit," said Bluey.

———

They began taking fire from German heavy guns. It went on for hours, until suddenly there was a series of colossal bangs from close at hand to the south. One of their artillery units had moved up and started counterbattery firing. But this seemed to be regarded as a provocation by the Luftwaffe. Stukas appeared and began remorselessly hunting the New Zealand guns.

"Where in God's name is *our* air force?" Bluey said. "I haven't seen a single Brit up there since this show began. We do have an air force, don't we?"

"Yep," someone replied. "But as far as I can tell, RAF stands for Rare As Fairies."

Even with shells dropping all round them and planes circling like furies in the sky, the men laughed.

———

Tanks came into view in the late morning of April 24. They were immediately engaged by the guns, and three were destroyed. Stukas appeared and, as before, went after the artillery. There was somehow a different intensity about the response. It was clear that the Germans meant business today.

More tanks were seen in the afternoon, and D Company's position began to receive machine-gun fire from the high ground to the left. With the sun low over the hills, they couldn't see exactly where the fire was coming from.

The distinctive whine of a Stuka pierced the air, then another, and another, until they were coming wave after wave like an aerial orchestra of wailing violins. Bruce immediately looked skyward and saw swarms of the swastika-emblazoned planes fanned out across the sky and coming at them relentlessly. Again and again they hurtled down, dispensing carnage on each earthward run.

The dive-bombers kept on coming. On the third wave—or perhaps it was the fourth—Bruce felt a searing pain in his left forearm. He looked down and saw a ragged slash in the khaki fabric of his tunic, which was already soaked with dark blood.

"Shit!" was all he could utter. "Jesus, Bluey, that was a close one," he shouted to his mate above the roar of the gunfire. "Bastards nearly knocked us for a six there."

"Keep your bloody head down, ya silly bugger," Bluey yelled back. "That big snout of yours will make an easy target."

When Bruce had a moment, he pushed up his sleeve. An ugly gash ran diagonally across the muscle of his forearm, but he was lucky. It didn't seem that deep, even if blood was welling steadily from it, and the bone didn't appear to be broken. It was just a scratch by wartime standards, he told himself. He rolled his sleeve down again and took up his rifle. With the Luftwaffe hammering them incessantly—unchallenged by Allied aircraft—it seemed pointless, but he kept firing back anyway. It was rather like being blindfolded in a fairground shooting gallery: Bruce could only point and hope.

"When will these buggers ever give up?" he muttered to no one in particular. "When we're all dead?"

There was no respite. Bruce had never felt fear like he did that day, but it was also fear that kept him going. He began to feel faint from blood loss, but he carried on mechanically: load, cock, aim, shoot. Load, cock, aim, shoot.

Antiaircraft guns pounded away monotonously, inflicting little damage on the aerial predators but doing their best to keep them at bay. The Stukas were too fast and too easily maneuvered to present clearly hittable targets, but every now and then the gunners struck a wayward plane with a well-aimed hit, excitedly high-fiving one another as if they had won an Olympic shooting medal.

At one point, as drifting smoke obliterated the world, a projectile of some sort screamed past Bruce's face, leaving a hole in the air that his head sagged into. It felt as though someone had boxed his ears.

"Fuck, Bluey, did you see that?" he said, his own voice sounding oddly remote. He turned to his mate just in time to see Bluey Watkins' luck run out. He was twisting and leaning to sight at something when he copped a bullet—perhaps a round from an aircraft cannon—square in the forehead. His head burst apart in a crimson spray.

Bruce blinked once or twice. Then he dropped his rifle and reeled toward his friend.

"Jesus, Bluey," he yelled. "Not you! Please, God, not you!" But Bluey was dead and there was nothing Bruce could do but mouth a silent prayer and get back to his position.

The shock from seeing Bluey go down, the ringing in his ears, and the blood loss from his wound dulled reality to the point where it seemed he was in the midst of a surreal dream, one in which everything was happening in slow motion. But the feeling faded. They say that when adrenaline kicks in, fear subsides. And so it was for Bruce. As he was forced to confront the reality of war and the inevitability of battlefield mortality, an unnatural calm came over him and, from then on, he concentrated on winning this personal war and surviving his second battle.

In the twilight of the late afternoon, dozens of tanks appeared on the horizon. It was a sight to strike terror into the heart, but the New Zealanders—fighting for their lives—were undaunted. Despite the Stukas dealing death and terror from overhead, the Kiwis met fire with fire. The tanks could make no progress under the withering attack of the artillery, and by day's end several were burning like torches and the others were limping away. The evening was heavy with the acrid smell of gasoline-fueled smoke.

Still, it was obvious even to Bruce that the tanks were a sideshow in what had become an infantry battle. 25 Battalion was outflanked. As night came on, the enemy on the higher ground above Bruce's position attacked with a vengeance, sending a storm of bullets pelting down on the largely unprotected soldiers. The hollow clanging of metal on metal reverberated as the fiery missiles ricocheted off tanks, trucks, jeeps, helmets. Curling and curving tracer fire lit up the battlefield, the colorful trails crisscrossing the night sky like a fireworks display on Guy Fawkes Night. It was a frantic scene—officers barking orders, then sometimes countermanding them almost as quickly. Bruce clearly heard the command for D Company to hold firm, but several men scrambled past him heading down toward the road.

"Where are you going?" he asked.

"We've been told to fall back," one of the soldiers said.

Bruce began to wonder if he'd heard the order correctly, but decided he felt safer where he was for the time being. About twenty minutes later, he heard the sound of someone scrabbling up the slope behind him.

"Who's that?" he asked.

"We've been told to come back and sit tight" came the reply.

Darkness brought with it some respite, most notably from the constant aerial assault. The gunfire began to peter out, and the pathetic cries of wounded—English and German—could be heard. Someone came along the line and whispered, "Prepare to move. We're falling back at ten thirty."

"Really?" Bruce asked.

"Really," the man replied, and he was gone with a sound of rattling scree.

It was over, for now.

Chapter Eight

—

Josefine, Maribor, January to March 1942

Jožef is wrong," Dejan was saying. "Women are some of our best operatives. Men are under constant suspicion, but women and girls have a little more freedom. We have many young women in our ranks. Some even younger than you."

Dejan—which wasn't his real name—was the area commander of the Narodna zaščita, the National Defence, which was the unarmed wing of the Slovene resistance. Their role, as Dejan had explained to Josefine, was primarily gathering intelligence, couriering important documents, disseminating anti-Nazi propaganda, transferring armaments, and helping Allied escapers. The Osvobodilna fronta or OF, the organization that carried out sabotage and waged guerrilla warfare, had started out in the early days of the occupation as a ragtag outfit, with rudimentary equipment and little discipline. With the return of veterans of the International Brigade who opposed the Fascists in the Spanish Civil War, however, it had been transformed into an effective fighting force.

The National Defence, by contrast, mostly comprised ordinary Slovenes—people like Josefine—who were united by their determination to liberate their beloved country. Both were communist organizations, but the partisans welcomed anyone who opposed the Nazis. The Lobniks had little interest in politics and no interest in communism.

"It's not just the Nazis we're fighting," Dejan had been quick to remind Josefine. "We're fighting three enemies. The occupier, his servants, and the national traitors. His servants are the collaborators. They're bad enough. But they can be ordinary people who are just trying to find an easy way through. The worst of the worst are the traitors—the Ustaše, who are Croatians, the Styrian Homeland Union." He paused, and spat. "And the Chetniks."

"The Chetniks. Those mongrels."

"Thugs and hooligans," Dejan continued. "Scum the Nazis have armed to do their dirty work for them. Against their own people. Against their own homeland."

In Limbuš, Josefine and her family had to be secretive, discreet, and extremely cautious. While the isolated, partisan-dominated villages could rely on the protection of their patrons, Limbuš, in the heart of German-occupied territory, could not. Dejan especially warned Josefine about the dangers from collaborators. The Volksdeutsche—many of whom were friends and neighbors before the occupation—understandably sided with their home country. But many middle-class and conservative Slovenes actively backed the Nazis—greedy, self-interested politicians and church officials who saw the opportunity to protect their wealth and position by siding with the occupiers. And soon after the invasion, both the economy and rates of employment improved and there was a feeling among some that support for Hitler's regime was justified.

There were also scores of young girls who enjoyed the privileges and gifts that they received in return for amorous liaisons with the Nazis. Silk stockings, chocolates, fine dining, and the best champagne were all on offer from the skirt-hungry occupiers—the occasional fuck being the only thing expected in return. Josefine even knew some who claimed to have fallen in love with their Nazi suitors. For a few this may have been true, but for most it was no more than a love affair with power and privilege.

And worse by far were the mercenary opportunists who traded information for cash; the capricious conspirators who could be bought for favors and the cowardly informers who offered up names and incriminating details to evade punishment. For those with elastic loyalties, it was hard to turn down the luxuries on offer when most of their friends and neighbors struggled to put a decent meal on the table and provide adequate clothing for their families. They were lurking everywhere, in the hard-to-detect guise of ordinary citizens pretending to be above suspicion. It was hard to know who to trust.

As Dejan had been briefing Josefine, an older man had arrived who had shot her a look of darkest suspicion.

"Who's she?" he asked. "How do we know we can trust her?"

"Hush," Dejan replied. "She's the sister of our liaison officer. She can be trusted."

The man had nodded, but he sat in the corner listening. When Dejan had told Josefine that she would be a courier, the man had made a scoffing noise.

"She can't be a courier," he said. "She's too pretty. The Švabi will be all over her like flies."

Dejan had looked at her appraisingly and her cheeks burned, as much with indignation as anything else.

"Marco has a point," he said. "You might need to find some kind of disguise. Something to make it less likely you'll draw unwanted attention."

———

A few days later, Josefine knocked on Dejan's door. After a pause, Dejan opened the door a crack.

"Yes, old woman?" he said. "What do you want?"

Josefine, leaning on a hickory walking stick, stooped over and with her head in the shadow of a shawl, raised her face so that the light caught it. Surprise registered on Dejan's face, followed by a grin.

"Well?" she said. "Will it do?"

"Yes," he replied. "Yes, I think it will. From now on you'll be known as Grandma."

And so her codename was *Baca*.

The instincts that had inspired her choice of disguise proved correct. As she hobbled about the streets and alleyways of Limbuš and Maribor, pausing often as if for breath, it was as though she were invisible to the Nazis. She could pass within a pace of German soldiers and they didn't spare her a second glance.

Her vital work began.

———

Polde wrote regularly from Krieglach, and despite the danger he even made visits home. It was Josefine who answered the quiet knock the first time, in early January 1942.

"Dear God!" she said, as the door opened and Polde's wide grin appeared in the frame. They embraced, but then Josefine thrust him away and struck him hard on the chest.

"What was that for?"

"It's too dangerous. You can't come back to Maribor," she said.

He was greeted with the same mixture of incredulity, delight, and outrage by the other members of the family, too. "Fool. You'll have us all killed," Jožef said, but his eyes were leaking.

Over dinner, they caught him up with the news. Most of it was somber—friends missing, or known to be dead. Although they hadn't written to tell him of Anica's and Roman's ordeals, he had heard most of it from Srečko, who wrote to Polde regularly. All the laughter had gone from his eyes as they talked about it.

"He tells me you've joined the partisans, Ani," he said gravely. "You know, when the Švabi first arrived, I thought there was nothing we could do, it was futile to try to oppose them. Now." He stopped. "Now, after all that they've done to our family, to our country, even if it's futile, I think we have to oppose them with every means at our disposal. I'm proud of you, Ani."

Anica hung her head to hide her pleasure.

And a day later, when she was hugging him farewell, Josefine whispered in Polde's ear, "I've joined the partisans, too, Polde."

He gave her a squeeze. "Good for you, Pepica. But promise me you'll be careful."

"You're the one who needs to be careful," she replied. "Please be safe."

———

Polde surprised them with another visit, scoffing at their protests that it was too risky. He was more concerned with the cost. Prices were always rising during wartime. It cost him the best part of half a day's wages to buy half a kilo of butter. When Jožef asked him, he admitted that he had used up nearly all his money on the fares. Jožef gave him some, although his own resources were stretched enough.

On Polde's second visit, Josefine wasn't there. She was with relatives in Radkersburg, in Austria. Her close relationship with her wider Austrian family was an asset to the National Defence, because Josefine often went back and forth across the border.

Polde left a note for Josefine when he left on February 2, 1942, to walk the four miles across the Drava to Maribor to catch a train for Graz in Austria. As usual, despite his reassurances that it was perfectly safe for him to visit, he didn't allow any of his family to come with him to the station.

The first his family knew of what had befallen him was when Srečko burst through their door. Srečko, too, had deemed it safe to return to Limbuš.

"Polde has been arrested," he said breathlessly. "I was at the station, and I saw it all. He bumped into an SS officer, one of Hitler's golden-haired, blue-eyed arseholes, and the Švabi decided he'd make something of it."

He'd accused Polde of hitting him with a closed fist, and called on his comrades to confirm they'd seen it.

"I could have you shot," he'd said to Polde. "Perhaps I should have you shot."

Srečko didn't tell them about the insults the Nazi had flung at Polde—he had called him a lowly dog, a piece of shit, and told him that he was worth less than nothing—or how abjectly Polde had taken it all and apologized; how the brave, carefree spirit that Srečko knew him to be was reduced practically to kissing the Nazi's boots in an effort to try to avoid trouble.

"The Švabi asked for his papers, and went in to use the station telephone to do a check. When he came back, the smug bastard looked like he had been awarded the Iron Cross. It made me sick to my stomach to see him. Just by being a bully boy, he'd found a wanted fugitive. You would have thought he'd captured Tito himself by the way he was bragging to his friends."

"What did they do with him?" Jožef asked.

"They took him away in a car. I'm afraid I don't know where."

They all knew this was serious. Polde was the third Lobnik to be arrested. The other two had been lucky. Anica was a young woman, and despite their suspicions they had nothing on her. Roman was just a boy. But Polde had already been declared an enemy of the Reich, and he'd been on the run. It didn't look good.

Jožef wrote to Josefine in Austria and asked her to travel to Krieglach to see if Polde had turned up there. If, for any reason he'd been allowed to go free, he would have continued his journey. It was a faint hope. And when Josefine's reply arrived—she wrote that she had made the three-hour train journey north only to find Polde hadn't been seen and hadn't returned to his job—it was no surprise. Josefine asked the work supervisor to let her know if Polde showed up. She returned to Radkersburg to wait, and when after two days no word had arrived, she traveled back to Limbuš.

She arrived just over a week after Polde's arrest. He had left her a note:

> *Darling sister, I thank you for your letter that I read with much pleasure. I am now on holidays for two days in Limbuš and will go back to Krieglach on Monday, back to my hard work. Please, do send me the package because I can warm things here and also cook. We have a big oven and enough coal. Krieglach is very beautiful and the landscape is beautiful too. I earn 60 pfennigs and work 9 hours per day. I earn just enough and will send you the money for the jacket. Loving greetings from Polde.*

It was dated January 31, two days before his world had collapsed.

Soon after her return, Josefine witnessed the massacre in Glavni trg, the town square. And, two days after that, she wrote the note that she passed to the English soldier at the prisoner-of-war camp.

———

A little over two weeks after she had crawled and limped her way five miles from the camp back to Limbuš, Josefine received another letter, brought to the door of her house by a man who wouldn't give his name or explain how he came to have it in his possession. It was addressed, in German, "To the Lobnik girl who dresses as an old woman."

Josefine eyed it warily, then thanked him and took it. She closed the door and made her way back to the kitchen, supporting her weight on the hickory walking stick she used for her disguise. Her knee was still swollen and very painful—the doctor had said it was badly sprained. Because of it, she hadn't been able to keep her promise to return to the camp the week after she'd passed the note. She'd sent Jelka in her place, but Jelka had been scared off by a guard as she'd tried to approach.

Josefine sat heavily, and with trembling fingers unfolded the note:

> *I waited on Sunday but there was no sign of you. I hope nothing terrible has happened. I have made inquiries with the Slovene prisoners here and I'm sorry to have to tell you that your brother Leopold is not being held in this camp. I have been unable to find any further information about his whereabouts but I will keep trying just in case something turns up.*
>
> *I will walk along the perimeter fence every Sunday between 10 and 11 in the morning. I would like it very much if I could see you again.*

Along with bitter disappointment, she registered with faint bewilderment the soldier's declaration that he would like to see her again. She recalled the gesture he had made—as if to tidy his hair—that was so at odds with his generally unkempt appearance. She snorted in irritation. Then she put him out of her mind.

Over the next month, she beseeched Jelka to do anything she could to find out what had happened to Polde, but her friend came up with nothing. Josefine pushed her partisan contacts for information, but they had no further news, either. She tried everything, but came up empty-handed. Her knee was on the mend; she even considered venturing back to Stalag XVIIID herself to search out the unknown soldier who had looked for her brother. Perhaps he might have something more to tell her. But when she weighed the risk and contemplated the ten-mile round trip on her sore knee, she decided against it.

There was nothing to do, it seemed, but wait.

————

Josefine's fears for Polde's safety escalated when Anica came home one night in tears.

"This is heartbreaking. Those Švabi pigs have no heart, no feeling," she said, clutching a sheet of paper. "I've just copied the note the Milavec boys wrote to their parents before they were shot." Her duties as liaison officer included communicating with families of slaughtered partisans and innocent victims of Nazi reprisals, and she would copy various papers and letters as a permanent record of Nazi atrocities.

Anica had learned that, through the compassion of an older guard who slipped them a pencil stub and a scrap of paper, Albin and Marjan had been allowed to write to their family to say their farewells.

Memories of Glavni trg came flooding back and Josefine could hardly bring herself to take the paper from her sister's hand. Trembling, she read the notepad on which Anica had copied the letter:

Dearest Parents, our last greetings go to you, dearest dad and mum and brother France. Forgive us and may you be happy, give our love to the boss, the Kral boys and uncle. Marjan and I must die. Today it will be all over. Ivan has already been killed in action. Dearest Parents, God be with you! A hug from Albin and Marjan.

Josefine looked up at her sister with tears in her eyes. She knew Anica was thinking the same thing: had Polde suffered the same fate? What sort of brutes, she wondered, could inflict such pain and suffering in the name of military justice?

"When will this end?" she asked.

Chapter Nine

—

Bruce, Greece,
April to May 1941

In the light from still-burning fires, torches, and headlight beams, Bruce looked upon a scene from a nightmare. He watched his comrades as they slowly came to terms with the fact that they had survived while others had fallen. Hastily bandaged injuries made the clearing to which they had withdrawn more reminiscent of a hospital ward than a battlefield, and many uniforms were in tatters. One soldier had a sleeve torn off, another had lost his tunic altogether, and others were wandering around with rucksacks, rifles, and bayonets missing. Bruce, his helmet abandoned long ago and his battle fatigues ripped in several places, was simply glad to have a break.

Some of the men were clearly battle-shocked, jabbering incoherently; others seemed unscathed, wandering around nonchalantly as if the whole terrifying experience had been all in a day's work. They were different ways of coping. For his part, Bruce couldn't quite grasp the enormity of what had just happened. He had seen men die. He had seen a mate die a violent death no more than ten feet away. For all he knew, he had killed people—he had certainly tried, shooting in the direction of the enemy until the barrel of his rifle was too hot to touch. Both the memories and the possibilities were too terrible to contemplate.

As his nerves calmed, Bruce's main concern became finding Blackie and Logie. Both were in C Company, which had been badly shot up. He feared the worst as he asked around and no one seemed to know anything about them.

Finally, he found a staff sergeant who told him he thought they were "probably all right." Bruce needed to know for sure. He hunted around until he spotted Blackie. That wasn't quite true; he heard Blackie long before he saw him. That laugh of his couldn't be mistaken, and Bruce knew Blackie was fine.

"Bloody hell, Bruce," Blackie shouted. "Ya made it, ya lucky bastard. Knew ya would. You always were a lucky bugger."

"Take more than some cross-eyed Kraut to do me in," Bruce yelled back with a veneer of bravado. "Glad to see you made it in one piece, Blackie. Jerry probably wouldn't bother with an ugly sod like you. Fritz would run a mile if he saw a mug like yours."

He paused, and his grin faded.

"Old Bluey copped one, though," he said. "Poor bugger's gone."

A few minutes later, Bruce saw Logie. He'd been wounded—a bit more seriously than Bruce—but nothing life-threatening.

"Thank God," they both said as soon as they saw each other.

"I was worried about you, Logie," Bruce got in first.

"Me too. I mean, about you," Logie corrected himself. Logie had always been the gentler of Bruce's two best friends. "What's the damage?" Logie inquired, pointing to Bruce's wounded arm.

"It'll be fine. I'll get the quack to have a look at it shortly. And yours?"

"Nothing a few stitches won't fix."

They slapped each other on the back, just like they would have done at the Midland Hotel on a Saturday night, as though nothing had happened.

———

Once he knew Blackie and Logie were alive and well, Bruce washed for the first time in several days, taking comfort in the mundane ritual. He tried to shave with a blunt razor he had borrowed from someone who could no longer see the point in personal grooming. His head felt lighter and clearer afterward.

Then he turned his attention to his forearm. Gingerly, he removed the dressing that had been hastily applied to the wound. The flow of blood had more or less stopped, but the ragged edges of the gash had flared outward, exposing flayed flesh and what he thought might be tendons. He did his best to clean the wound and then dressed it again with some recycled bandages, still faintly stained with blood, that he'd scrounged from the medics.

To the north, burned-out tanks littered the bomb-ravaged landscape. Trees had been uprooted by shellfire and the ground was pocked and pitted with craters, some big enough to swallow a tank. Lorries destroyed by machine-gun or mortar fire lay capsized by the roughly rutted tracks that served as roads; and, in the distance, a sole Stuka downed by the antiaircraft boys was still smoldering. Bruce felt the first stirrings of pride. They might not have been able to follow through on all those lofty promises to defend Greece, but they had delivered on their second goal: to give Jerry enough of a fight to slow him down while the main body of the force was withdrawn.

Thoughts now were turning to the evacuation. The usual rumors were flying about where and how it was to be accomplished, and all the dangers that lay in their way.

The 25th had been ordered to make its way to Monemvasia, where the plan was to use small *caiques*—traditional Greek fishing boats—to ferry them to ships anchored a safe distance out from the bay. They were being sent back to Cairo. Bruce was pleased to be on his way out of this hellhole.

Late at night on April 24, the evacuation convoy was ready to leave.

"Thank God it's over. For now, at least," Bruce said to Blackie and Logie, as they were about to climb aboard their separate trucks.

"Let's hope Fritz doesn't drop a big bugger on us and splatter our guts from here to kingdom come," Blackie half jested.

Logie knocked his fingers on the timber of the tailgate.

"I wish you wouldn't say things like that," he sighed. They all knew that the possibility of an aerial attack on the way out was very real.

"See you back in Cairo!" Blackie yelled as his truck moved off.

"First stop, Mannering's Bar. Your treat!" Bruce called back.

Then it was Logie's turn. He waved and gave a thumbs-up as his lorry started.

It was a slow, stop-start journey along narrow, twisting mountain roads, more like alpine tracks at the best of times. In places, the carriageway had been wiped out by bombs and what was left was badly damaged, with the hooded headlamps picking up potholes that might as well have been bottomless, so deep and dark were they. Broken-down or bombed-out lorries and tanks frequently blocked the way, requiring the attention of overworked road maintenance crews to clear them. The waiting wore on the nerves almost as much as the hair-raising driving. Bruce pitied the drivers, who were totally exhausted but who still had to remain alert and focused.

The dawning of Anzac Day, April 25, 1941, found them bivouacked in a dense area of woodland, where—bloodied, bone-weary, and now battle-tested—they were able to snatch some sleep. Reconnoitering parties surveyed the way ahead. While they were encamped, word came through that the Germans had made a landing on the coast to the north. On April 28, 25 Battalion rushed across the last stretch to Monemvasia, arriving in the early hours. There, they were set to work wrecking anything they couldn't take with them; they didn't want to leave anything for the Germans. Trucks were pushed over cliffs; tires were slashed; engines immobilized; petrol tanks contaminated with sand or water. To the men, dispirited and demoralized as any retreating army is, it was soul-destroying to look upon the coastal fields strewn with wrecked machinery, for all the world like a military junkyard. What was left behind or lost in combat could have equipped a small army. Over two hundred planes were gone, eighty-two of which were deliberately destroyed; thousands of trucks were abandoned; almost two thousand machine guns and hundreds of anti-tank and field guns were disabled; and over a hundred tanks were discarded—all now lost to the Allied war effort. It was hard not to think about the valiant Greeks, who had put so much faith in the Allies' military superiority, to say nothing of their commanders' hollow promises. To a man, the soldiers felt they had failed them. Waiting in the darkness, they strained to look for lights in the distance, fearing that the ships may not have made it. They needn't have worried: the ships were there.

But Bruce wasn't.

———

D Company's sergeant's much-vaunted grasp of Greek geography deserted him at a crossroads a little after one in the morning on the night of April 26. They sat for five minutes or so, while the sergeant in the cab of the lead truck and the driver pored over their map and peered through the filthy windshield at the roads forking in front of them.

Finally, the sergeant made up his mind.

"That way," he said, pointing to the right-hand fork.

"You sure, Sarge?" the driver asked.

Sarge was sure. So, with a grinding of gears, the pair of trucks holding Bruce's platoon rolled off in the wrong direction. Some time before dawn, those in the back of the hindmost truck saw the lights of a vehicle bearing down on them from behind. Rifles were cocked and aimed, but as it closed the gap they realized it was one of theirs. Someone banged on the cab of the truck and the driver pulled over.

"You're going the wrong bloody way," the driver of the pursuing vehicle yelled. "Monemvasia's that way. How many trucks are ahead of you?"

"Just one," the truck driver replied. "You better chase him down."

The other man checked his watch.

"We'll never catch him and get back to the beach before it gets light. Nah, we'll just let him go. He'll work it out."

Miles to the south, Bruce's truck pressed on toward Kalamata.

When they arrived, Bruce and his comrades saw what they were expecting to see: masses of men and machinery jammed at the end of the road adjacent to the beach. But the markings on the vehicles and the insignia on the uniforms were unfamiliar. They realized they had fallen in with one or more English units.

Finally, they saw someone directing the vehicular traffic.

"Morning, gents," a jovial Englishman with a corporal's stripe greeted them. "You're a bit out of your way, aren't you?"

"Are we?" their driver replied.

"Your lot are meant to be catching a boat at Monemvasia. That's bloody miles away. This is Calamity Bay."

"Where?"

"Kalamata Bay. But we call it Calamity Bay because it's total chaos here. Now, you'll have to get this truck out of here. We've got wounded to bring along the road. We're leaving ours as a present to Jerry. Full of sand, of course."

They drove on and pulled over.

"What do we do, Sarge?" the driver asked.

He considered.

"We can't risk driving back. We'd be sitting ducks on the road during daytime. And if we leave it till tonight, we'll miss the boat. Nah, we'd better take our chances here."

After abandoning their truck, Bruce and his comrades tried to find someone who could tell them how they set about being allocated a place on the evacuating craft. Dawn broke over a chaotic scene. Soldiers were scrambling to find their units; officers were struggling to restore order; there were agonized cries from the wounded, who were being handled as gently as possible by their stretcher-bearers; and the panic-stricken were jostling for front-of-queue priority. Vehicles of all descriptions were parked haphazardly everywhere—on and off the road. Notable by their absence were ships. A few small fishing boats were the only vessels on the water.

Rumors about what was happening were thicker on the ground than the discarded cigarette butts on the beach. Some of the British soldiers were adamant that they were to be taken off by warships that evening. Others maintained that it was to be a flotilla of Greek vessels. Still others swore they had heard that the evacuation fleet had been ordered back to port because the Germans were expected to attack. The one thing that everyone seemed to agree upon was that the Germans weren't far away.

As they sat or milled around, smoking, playing cards, brewing tea, everyone glanced nervously at the sky. All it would have taken was a few Stuka runs and everyone on the beach would be mincemeat.

"Kiwis?" an English soldier said. "Whatchoo doing so far from bleeding home, then?"

Bruce was asking himself the same question.

Toward evening, there was a ripple through the mass of unwashed soldiery. Everyone was suddenly on their feet, and there was pushing and shoving as they pressed forward.

For a time, they made progress, a few shuffling steps toward the water. Bruce could hear the sound of marine engines beyond the crowd. The ships' tenders were quickly loaded and those soldiers— a few hundred, no more—were taken to the vessels anchored in the bay.

They must be embarking us, after all, Bruce thought.

"Stick together, boys," their sergeant said.

The grumbling of the crowd became louder. There were shouts and curses, and word came back from the direction of the beach that there was to be no more loading.

"What?" said Bruce.

"They's worried the ships are going to be attacked," a soldier said sourly. "They's told 'em to bugger off, haven't they. We're on our bleeding tod."

The Kiwis conferred.

"What do we do now, Sarge?"

"Well. Seems to me we've got two options. We can wait here for Jerry and surrender. Or we can run."

"What're you gonna do, Bruce?" asked Terry, a fellow Wellingtonian who had become a good mate of Bruce's.

"I'm gonna run," Bruce said, without hesitation. "Coming?"

Terry looked thoughtful.

"Nah, I reckon it's over for me. Had a gutsful. If they come, I'm giving myself up."

They shook hands.

"Best of luck, Terry."

"You're the one who'll need the luck, Bruce. Look after yourself."

———

Bruce had no plan. He was frightened and his wound was very painful, but surrender smacked of cowardice. By now, he hated the Germans, and would much rather have fought the bastards than give up his arms and become their prisoner. All he wanted was to get as far away as possible and then consider how he might get out of Greece and back to friendly territory, hopefully with the help of some locals.

He figured that the best option would be to head for the hills, away from the German troops. He reasoned that cutting off and capturing the mass of men at Kalamata would be their primary objective, so it made sense to put as much distance between himself and Calamity Bay as possible. He had a vague idea that the German advance was from the east, so he struck out west, across the farmland and olive groves of the Peloponnese. Every so often, he sighted other soldiers, their rifles slung over their shoulders, trudging along apparently with the same plan. He didn't see any Kiwi uniforms, and certainly no one from the 25th.

He knew most Greeks detested the Germans as much as he did, but nevertheless he steered clear of villages. Whenever he saw a Greek civilian—mostly women, working in the fields—he would call out, "Do you speak English?" The answer was always a shake of the head. One old woman beckoned to him, and gave him food—a rag tied around a handful of olives, and the heel of a loaf of dense brown bread smeared with soft cheese. Bruce shook her hand heartily. She pointed to his bloodstained forearm and grimaced. He shrugged and grinned. She made a sign by hugging her arms across her chest, and he understood.

Take care, she was saying.

He bowed his head, and lifted his hand in farewell.

———

When he was a safe distance from Kalamata, Bruce paused to consider his predicament. The plains had fetched up against the kind of mountainous terrain he'd become familiar with in his time on Greek soil. The thought of those steep, rocky mountain passes would have been daunting for anyone considering traversing them on foot. Here he was, hungry, thirsty, fatigued, and in pain. He didn't think he could make it.

While he was sitting on a rock by the side of the road on the outskirts of a village, thinking through his next move, he sensed someone nearby. A young girl, probably no more than seventeen, was standing a short distance away, eyeing him warily.

"You speak English?" he inquired hopefully.

"A leetle," she replied hesitantly in a heavily accented tone. "Jus' a leetle. Whatchou wanna know?"

"I need to get a ride up the hill," he said slowly and clearly, pointing first at a truck parked beside the road and then toward the top of the mountain.

"Aah," she said and, without another word, beckoned Bruce to follow.

He never caught the girl's name. She led him into the village and knocked at the door of a small stone house. A black-haired man with a pronounced five-o'clock shadow opened it. The girl spoke rapidly to him. He looked at Bruce, spoke a few words in reply, and bowed slightly.

"He say honored for help."

"Spiro," the man said, tapping himself on the chest.

"Bruce," said Bruce.

They shook hands.

Half an hour later, they were on the road winding up into the mountains, Bruce lying in the back of the truck among crates that smelled of chicken shit. It was an uncomfortable journey, but better, he reflected, than walking.

Toward nightfall, they passed through a village. Just outside it, Spiro stopped the truck and waved to Bruce to come out.

"Dimitsana," he said, pointing back toward the village. He waved his hand at a stone barn beside the road, pointed at Bruce, and mimed sleeping. Bruce extended his hand, but Spiro drew him into a crushing hug and slapped his back.

In the morning, Bruce removed the dressing from his forearm. The margins of the wound were angry red, and there was yellow pus on the bandage. He closed his eyes briefly.

"Don't you go getting infected," he muttered.

———

From Dimitsana, Bruce hitched another ride and was given the name of someone who might be able to hide him in the partisan stronghold of Kalavryta. He was dropped off about five miles from the town and Bruce covered that distance before dark. A few surreptitious inquiries soon led him to the man whose name he had been given: Costas Papadopoulos.

Costas was a big man. Not only did he dwarf Bruce by several inches, but he was also verging on obese. He had a pudgy, ruddy face dominated by an outsized nose, and his belly suggested an excessive affection for moussaka. The whites of his eyes were crisscrossed by red veins that looked like main routes on a road map—doubtless the result of similarly excessive ouzo consumption. A bristly, dark-brown beard that hadn't been trimmed for years—probably never—completely covered his cheeks and jowls. But what struck Bruce, and probably anyone who had ever met Costas, were those wild eyes, blazing like an out-of-control bushfire.

It didn't take Bruce long to realize that Costas' fierce exterior concealed a much softer soul. He spoke no English, so most of their communication was through hand gestures and facial expressions. The flow of information improved markedly when ouzo was introduced, and Costas also enlisted the help of a local teacher to translate. From this man, Bruce learned that Costas had been widowed just a few weeks earlier. His wife had been the victim of a random strafing by a Messerschmitt while she was visiting her sister in Larissa in the first few days of war. Costas hated the Nazis with the same passion as he had loved his departed wife. He would do anything to destroy these monsters who had taken, however unintentionally, the only thing he loved more than his country. He unhesitatingly welcomed Bruce into his home, promising to escort him onward as soon as the opportunity to flee the country presented itself.

The resilience and resistance of the Greeks never failed to amaze Bruce. In the brief time he was in Kalavryta, he encountered many who were prepared to help not only him but the dozens of other evaders who were roaming the hills. They weren't obviously frightened or concerned about reprisals, even though they must have known their actions would put their lives in danger if they were caught. They were fiercely patriotic, and this translated into a steely determination to rid their country of the Nazi invaders.

His short stay in Kalavryta was a surreal idyll, not unlike the phony war he and the 25th had enjoyed in Athens before their baptism of fire. It was a picturesque place. The grand dome of the church presided over a maze of narrow streets that veered off at odd angles and led to nowhere in particular. Within a couple of days, he had settled into village life: his routine included a long walk along the stone-paved streets, a break at a little café in the square for his daily intake of the sludge-like coffee (a taste for which he was finally beginning to acquire), a stop at the *periptero* to buy cigarettes, and, while he could afford it, the lunch special of the day at the *kafenion* with Costas. Bruce was lucky at first to have enough cash left over from his time in Athens to return some of Costas' hospitality. Many of the other villagers were not as fortunate, and Bruce did whatever he could for them with the little money he had.

It seemed hard to believe that war was raging all around them and across Europe. There were rumors of engagements between the partisans and the Nazis in the foothills of the ranges, but there was no sign in the village itself of any conflict. Bruce didn't feel under any threat of betrayal; even if there were German sympathizers around, he guessed they knew too clearly what the consequences would be if the villagers suspected them of turning one of their Allied guests over to the enemy.

It wasn't human agency that brought his time on the run to an end. Bruce's arm initially seemed to be healing—or at least, if there were an infection brewing, it was held at bay for a time. Perhaps the generous doses of Costas' ouzo helped. But it soon became clear he needed medical attention. The only doctor in the village had recently left—Costas didn't trust him anyway—and he was reluctant to take Bruce to the nearest physician at Skepasto because he didn't know the man. But when Bruce became feverish, Costas grew concerned.

"Costas says he will get you transport to Corinth," the schoolteacher translated. "There's a hospital there."

Bruce was shaking and light-headed as he set aside the clothes that Costas had found for him and dressed in his tattered uniform again. He couldn't afford to be found in civilian clothes, and he certainly couldn't bear the thought of his generous Greek hosts suffering the terrible consequences of harboring a suspected foreign spy. A man whom he didn't know drove him down the long, winding mountain road toward Corinth. They passed signs of the occupation—tanks dug in beside the road, convoys of troop carriers parked in sidings. Just short of the town,

Bruce's driver stopped. He nodded at Bruce, then wordlessly shook his hand. Bruce got out of the car and staggered; he felt weak and dizzy. The car turned around and drove off back the way they had come, leaving him to totter toward the town as best he could. Just short of the outskirts, he threw his rifle down a well. He was so weak he could barely lift the bloody thing anyway. Then he sat beside the road to wait.

It didn't take long. Within the hour, there was the sound of a lorry approaching. It rounded the bend and bore down on him. For a moment, Bruce thought it might drive right by him, but the driver did a double take and it stopped with a squeal of brakes. There were shouts in German, and five or six soldiers leaped from the back and surrounded him.

A man—an officer, to judge from his uniform—motioned for Bruce to stand. When it became plain he could do so only with difficulty, he was dragged to his feet.

"For you," the officer said in very good English, "the war is over."

———

Bruce was taken to the hospital at Corinth. As his health and strength returned, he was plagued by feelings of shame. His freedom had lasted less than a week. He had surrendered, and all this after playing little or no part in what had to be seen as a humiliating defeat. Any way he looked at it, he was a coward. He wondered what his family— especially his dad—would think of him. He wondered what his mates would say. He couldn't imagine Blackie or even Logie ever giving in.

Lying in his hospital bed gave him too much time to brood. He wondered if he would ever get home. How would he be treated in captivity? Would he die a prisoner, starved or ill-treated? Perhaps that would be for the best, considering how badly he had failed . . .

For the first time in his life, he considered suicide. It seemed like the only way he could salvage any honor from his situation, and the only escape from the fear and guilt that he firmly believed would dog him for the rest of his days. He was on powerful medication for relief from the pain of his debrided wound: all it would take was to pop a few too many of the bitter white tablets in his mouth, a swallow of water, and then . . .

But these dark thoughts passed in a few days, when he decided that life was better than a self-administered death.

———

After two weeks in the hospital, he was to be trucked with a group of discharged patients to the Corinth collection center, the first stop for all POWs captured in Greece. He was roughly shoved into the back of a khaki-canopied German infantry truck and sat on a hard, slatted timber bench seat near the back, which looked as though it had been splintered by machine-gun fire. There were twenty of them in the truck and as they waited to move off, he wondered what lay in store. There were two disinterested-looking guards seated near the cab; they weren't exactly advertisements for Hitler's master race. One had a very bad haircut—it looked as though it had been hacked by a drunk armed with serrated scissors—and a lopsided mouth with protruding, tobacco-stained teeth. The other was gaunt and ghostly with a yellowish, pock-marked complexion and straggly blond hair. Buck Teeth had a roll-your-own fag hanging lazily from the corner of his mouth; Crater Face had smoked his almost to the butt and had another tucked behind his ear for later. Neither seemed the least bit interested in the supervision of their prisoners, so—on the spur of the moment—Bruce decided he would make a bid for freedom.

The truck accelerated, bumping and rattling its way along the cobbled, granite-hard road. Just as the driver swerved violently to avoid a deep, bomb-blasted pothole, Bruce made his move. The unexpected turn literally threw him off the truck and he was momentarily unbalanced as he leaped. He tried to land on both feet but fell awkwardly, his left foot hitting the ground first and his body twisting unnaturally as he tumbled onto jagged, unyielding cobblestones, his injured fore-arm taking the full brunt of the impact. The wound, which had not fully healed, split open again. He tried to scramble to his feet, but the searing pain from his left ankle told him he was going nowhere. He made one last determined effort to move, but couldn't. His escape bid was over, seconds after it had started.

The guards were definitely alert now. He was kicked in the guts a couple of times and subjected to a stream of German invective. Then he was thrown unceremoniously back into the truck and shackled to the bench seat.

His military records later stated that he "fell off the back of a truck," but that was because the guards didn't want to admit they had screwed up. They certainly weren't taking any further chances: he remained chained to the seat for the rest of the journey to the Corinth collection center.

On May 18, 1941, the Defence Department sent a telegram to Bruce's parents back home. Many times over the next several months, he would imagine their thoughts on receiving it.

MUCH REGRET TO INFORM YOU THAT YOUR SON 32673 BRUCE GORDON MURRAY HAS BEEN REPORTED MISSING. THE PRIME MINISTER DESIRES ME TO CONVEY TO YOU ON BEHALF OF THE GOVERNMENT HIS SYMPATHY WITH YOUR ANXIETY. F JONES MINISTER OF DEFENCE.

The message didn't say "Presumed Dead," but the family had already made that assumption. Stuck on the other side of the world, knowing only that Greece had been a military disaster, his parents and siblings had given up hope.

They had decided Bruce was gone.

Chapter Ten

Josefine, Hitler's Slovenia, March to August 1942

It was a crisp March afternoon as Josefine strolled into Slomškov trg, a leafy square in front of the Cathedral of St John the Baptist near the old center of Maribor. A young woman seated outside a café on the other side of the square raised her arm in greeting and flashed her a smile. Josefine waved back, made her way through the crowds of people enjoying the sunshine, swung the satchel from over her shoulder, and hung it on the back of a chair. She was dressed in her everyday clothes. Social connections aroused few suspicions so there was no need for disguise. She sat down on a third chair, leaned forward, and clasped her hands on the table.

"How are you?" the other woman asked. "I haven't seen you for such a long time."

"Yes, it must be two years. The last time must have been the day we skated on the Drava."

The other woman lowered her eyes, accepting the code.

"You're looking so lovely," she said. "I would swear you've grown younger since the last time I saw you."

Josefine laughed, a genuine laugh. The only time they had previously met was on the other side of town, where Josefine, disguised as an elderly woman, had pretended to drop her bag as she passed Mara Zlata in a back street. Mara had stooped quickly, picked up the spilled contents, and replaced them along with a package of documents she slipped from inside her coat before handing the bag back to Josefine.

Josefine was about to reply when Mara glanced past her and frowned slightly. A hand fell on Josefine's shoulder. It was a light touch, but she jumped nonetheless.

"*Guten tag, frauleins.*" It was a young German soldier, smiling amiably. "What are two nice girls like you doing on this fine afternoon? My name's Karl." He offered his hand to Josefine, who took it, the shock still registering on her face.

"My name's Alenka," said Mara, whose real name was neither Mara nor Alenka. She extended her hand to the soldier and met his eye long enough to give Josefine time to compose herself.

"And you are . . . ?" The soldier turned back to Josefine.

"Lucija," she replied.

"Delighted to meet you, Lucija," he said. "May I?" He gestured at the empty seat at the table. Josefine's heart skipped a beat. She thought he was asking to inspect the satchel. But the more experienced Mara was quicker on the uptake.

"But of course!" she said. "We would be honored."

With a look of profound self-satisfaction on his face, and a glance toward the far corner of the square, the soldier sat.

"We're old friends, Lucija and me. We used to go skating together. But we haven't seen each other since . . . well, since before the war."

"Oh, let's not talk about the war," the soldier said, waving a hand across his face. "I find it gets in the way of conversation. Don't you?"

"Yes." Mara nodded. "It's very . . . inconvenient."

Even as she recovered from her fright, Josefine had to admire Mara's presence of mind and the way in which, without saying anything untoward, she had managed to inject a note of flirtatiousness into her voice.

"I expect you're a very good skater," the soldier said to Josefine.

"What makes you say that?" she squeaked.

"I was watching you walk across the square," the soldier said. "You have good . . . balance, I think. Very graceful. A skater, Karl, I said to myself. I bet she skates."

The weight of his gaze made her shiver with revulsion.

She forced a smile.

"It's a pity we've met in spring and we can't go skating together," the German went on. "I would very much have liked to show you what I can do."

His words hung there. Josefine was sure he would see her shaking.

"I would have liked to see what you can do," said Mara softly, and the man turned back to her eagerly. Their eyes locked.

"Perhaps we can arrange something," he said. "There are other things we could do together. Besides skate. If you're free."

"Oh, we're free," Mara said. "Lucija and I were just talking about how free we are these days, weren't we, Lucija? The local boys are such pigs. Slovene girls these days must choose between pigs and having far too much free time."

"I have a nice friend," the German said. "In fact, he's standing right over there." He jerked his head toward the far corner of the square, where another man in uniform was lounging against a wall, smoking a cigarette, and staring in their direction. "We could perhaps help you with some of your free time. Perhaps even tonight?"

"What do you think, Lucija? Are we free tonight?"

"I'm free," Josefine said. "Completely free. As usual."

"That's settled then." The German clapped his hands. "My friend and I will meet you at Gostilna Pri treh Ribnikih. Seven sounds like a civilized hour, don't you think?"

"Very civilized," replied Mara.

The German stood and bowed to each of them in turn, his gaze lingering on Josefine. Then he turned on his heel and strolled, whistling, across the square toward his mate. He looked so pleased with himself that Josefine wouldn't have been surprised if he'd skipped or broken into a dance.

"Ugh," said Mara under her breath. She fluttered her fingers at the two Germans, who were looking back at them.

"Thank you," Josefine said earnestly, her voice unsteady. "I nearly panicked. I nearly gave it all away. You saved my life."

"You were better than you think you were," Mara replied. She stood up, and quite naturally plucked the satchel off the chair on which the soldier had been sitting and slung it over her shoulder. It was heavy, stuffed as it was with papers recently stolen from the *Kommandantur*. She and Josefine embraced.

"You are very brave, comrade. Keep up the good work," Mara whispered in Josefine's ear. She stepped back. "And whatever you do, stay away from Gostilna Pri treh Ribnikih at seven tonight!"

They laughed, and went their separate ways.

———

In early April, Anica arrived home distressed and agitated.

"Oh, Pepica, it's too horrible," she said. "They've killed fifty brave men. They captured fifty partisans and now they're all dead."

"Oh, God," moaned Josefine. "Was there anyone we know?"

"Jože Fluks," said Anica, her voice almost a whisper.

"I don't think I know . . ."

"You'd remember him. He came to talk to Papa just after I joined, to reassure him that they would look after me and that the men would leave me alone. You'd remember him by his codename, Andraz."

"Oh, God," said Josefine again. She did remember Andraz. He was a lanky, good-looking young man, a laborer from Maribor and a partisan with a reputation for being recklessly brave. Those who fought with him said he had no fear. On March 30, 1942, almost two months after Polde's arrest, he became another victim of the Nazi reprisals.

Once again, he was allowed to communicate with his parents in a note smuggled out of prison on the eve of his execution. Anica had the awful task of copying his last words to his family, and brought the transcript home for Josefine and Jožef to read:

> *Dear Family,*
> *Today I was sentenced to death! Don't mourn for me, be brave as I am brave.*
> *In my thoughts I kiss you all, Mum, Dad, Majda, Jelka, Tony, my girl Ancka*
> *and all my friends and pals. Think well of me, I will think of you till the end.*
> *In my thoughts I send you my last kisses.*
> *Jože.*

Anica had heard that the group of fifty of whom Jože was one were driven into the countryside. Deep in the forest, they were forced at gunpoint to disembark the truck and to walk into the trees. At a chosen spot, they were ordered to halt. Shovels were thrown to them and they were commanded to dig a trench. Once it was deep enough, the order was given to kneel on the edge. Each was shot in the back of the head, and tumbled into the grave they had dug for themselves.

The news was terrible enough. Jožef and Anica took it all the harder, as they were now convinced that it meant Polde had suffered a similar fate. If Jože Fluks and his comrades were slaughtered so

mercilessly, what hope could there be for Polde? Only Josefine refused to accept he was dead. But even she was visited in the sleepless,
small hours of the morning by images of the body of her beloved
brother blindfolded, lying cold and dead in some lonely pit in the
forest.

All she could do was pray, and she prayed and prayed again.

The close shave in Slomškov trg reminded Josefine of the constant
danger that her work exposed her to. Hers was a round-the-clock
war. There was no escape from the daily surveillance, no way to
avoid the random inspections, no respite from the constant risk of
discovery. As her superiors in the National Defence reminded her
regularly, there was no opportunity to lower her guard. While the
Nazis were easy to spot, collaborators were everywhere, especially as
the brutality of the occupation escalated. More and more Slovenes
were reaching the conclusion that it was better for them and their
families if they threw in their lot with the invader, and even people who had seemed staunchly patriotic in the early days were now
turning. In many ways, Josefine's war—operating right beneath the
enemy's nose—was more fraught with danger than that waged by
the partisan fighters in the hills. Unlike the mountain-based fighting
units, Josefine had no hillside hideaways or rugged terrain to retreat
into. There were no armed reinforcements to back her up and no
quick escape routes if she were discovered or betrayed. And, while
some areas of Slovenia to the east were partisan strongholds, Maribor was firmly in the grasp of the enemy.

But with every day that passed, her determination to resist—and
to resist more actively—only grew. Nazi brutality toward the Slovenes
happened more and more frequently, and practically every aspect of

daily life was affected by their repressive policies. The administration declared Slovenes to be unworthy of anything beyond a rudimentary education, and schools were closed. There had been nearly two thousand pupils in Maribor high schools the year before, when Roman was attending; now there were barely a hundred. Worse, families were being uprooted and displaced for no apparent reason. In August, while she was across the border in Radkersburg, Josefine received a letter from Roman:

On Sunday, we were joyfully swimming in the Drava, without a care in the world. We were all together, the Loburg and Lobnik families, and I don't know if we'll ever be together again.

On Monday morning, on 4 August 1942 at 6.30 a.m. a swine, I can't use any other word to describe it, knocked at Mrs Pavla's door and he asks: "Where are the boys?" "At work," Pavla replies. Rado was lucky, he had taken the 6 a.m. train to Villach. What about Srečko? He was at home and escaped. Pavla was left alone, they took her to devil knows where. She was allowed to take only one suitcase and some money. She was not the only one who was taken away, many others were taken as well, people from Ruše, Studenci, Maribor and God knows where else. Anica stayed on the property with Sanja but they were not left alone for long. The pigs came back and made an inventory of everything and then they locked the doors. But they were a bit slow, so we had managed to take some things away before they came back. Anica took half the food supplies from the larder and this is all she now has to cook. Pepica, if you knew about this shocking incident, you'd be sickened. What is the point of dragging one woman away like that, given that Srečko escaped right under their noses? Could you, Pepica, imagine on Sunday that something like this would happen?

Will we ever be as happy as we used to be again?

The devils have already started to eat and drink as if they were the big shots in Limbuš. Why should I yield to these brutes?

Greetings from Roman, from a sad Limbuš

Josefine was pleased that Srečko had evaded capture yet again, but she was appalled at the plight of his family, especially his poor mother. Pavla had been caught in a purge of partisan families. Between August 3 and 6, 1942, over twelve hundred relatives of slain hostages or known partisans were arrested. Many families were wiped out altogether. Children were separated from parents.

Josefine had also witnessed these despicable acts of tyranny. She had watched, angry and enraged, as other neighbors were given a few hours to pack a single suitcase of personal possessions before being deported—to where, no one knew—and their homes left vacant to be taken over by Germans. She was only too aware that her family might be next, and everyone she knew had the same fear. Their turn could come at any time.

Roman's last words worried her. She knew that mail was being intercepted and what she read amounted to her little brother's declaration of war.

Sure enough, when she returned to Limbuš a few days later, it was to learn that sixteen-year-old Roman had followed in his older sisters' footsteps and joined the partisans.

———

Josefine's own response to the escalation in repression was to insist that she be assigned more active roles in the movement. Dejan readily agreed. Because of the Lobnik family's close connections in Austria and the lengthy spells she spent there, Josefine was very familiar with the regions across the border such as Radkersburg, Villach, and Graz. This cross-border knowledge was an asset to the resistance and she was sometimes called upon to work in these territories. She was fluent in German, both written and spoken, which was a valuable attribute, and she was regularly called upon to transfer (and translate) enemy intelligence. Her memory was excellent, too, so she often memorized top-secret German reports and briefing papers to avoid being caught with them in her possession. Capture with confidential German military documents on her person would have meant a charge of treason and, with it, a mandatory death sentence. At first, most of the work was in her familiar role as a courier, delivering messages and dispatches or smuggling stolen dossiers, money, and medical supplies through heavily guarded checkpoints. But she never knew what she might be ordered to do, and whatever it turned out to be, she never refused. She was frightened often enough—and sometimes admitted to moments of panic—but she always did what was asked of her.

Chapter Eleven

———

Bruce, Greece to Maribor, June to July 1941

Two words," said Shorty Lamont. "Geneva bloody Convention."

"That's three words," Bruce pointed out, but no one laughed.

They were discussing conditions at the transit camp in Corinth, a consolidation point for all soldiers captured by the Germans in Greece.

Bruce hadn't paid a lot of attention when the Army had explained the rules of warfare to soldiers before sending them on active duty, but he definitely remembered there had been something in there about the humane treatment of POWs. At Corinth, the Germans treated them like common criminals—or worse. They were denied blankets or bedding and had to sleep on hard concrete floors, with only their filthy trench coats to keep them warm. There was never enough water, and what there was of it was dirty, probably contaminated. The open ditch that served as a latrine was a breeding ground for disease. The food consisted of some sort of lentil soup and the occasional rock-hard biscuit—not enough to sustain a young child, let alone a grown man. And violence from the captors toward the prisoners was the rule rather than the exception.

Each day was much the same for Bruce. He would wake hoping it would be his last in Corinth. As soon as it became plain that it wasn't, he would resign himself to another day of abuse and hunger.

One day, around two weeks into his internment, there was a change in the atmosphere. The guards were bustling about ensuring everything was shipshape, which entailed a good deal of yelling at prisoners and lashing out with the boot. At the same time, the officers were roving about dishing out similar treatment to the guards. It was conspicuous that everyone had taken great care with their appearance. Boots were polished, tunics were pressed, buttons were done up, and hair was neatly combed and slicked back.

In the early afternoon, a line of cars swept into the camp. Every guard in the vicinity snapped to attention. When they came to a halt, a short, plump man climbed out of one, using the pair of gloves he carried in one hand to dash the dust off his leather coat.

"Who's that?" Bruce asked.

"Search me," Shorty replied. "Who's that, then, Günter?" he called to one of the guards who spoke a bit of English. At first, the guard on the other side of the wire ignored the question, standing ramrod straight, the back of his neck red with the scrubbing it had received in the morning. But when the official party began walking in the other direction, he half turned and hissed a few words over his shoulder.

A buzz went through the crowd of prisoners.

"It's Himmler!"

"Who?"

"Himmler. One of Hitler's top dogs."

"Hey, Heinrich!" someone yelled. "You fat bastard!"

"Heini, you son of a bitch," Bruce shouted at the top of his voice.

"Go back to Berlin and kiss Hitler's arse," screamed another.

Himmler's glasses flashed in the sun as he turned his head at the sound of his name. But as every prisoner began shouting abuse—Himmler was called everything from a dim-witted dolt to a stupid oaf—he faced front and kept walking. A red-faced officer shouted in German to the guards, who all spun to face the prisoners, brandishing their rifles with bayonets fixed. It had no effect. If anything, the torrent of abuse grew in volume and creativity. There was no way of knowing whether Himmler understood any of it but, to judge from the freedom with which boots and rifle butts were swung for a day or two after his visit, it was clear the guards had a pretty good idea.

———

One day, Bruce woke up and got what he wished for. It was a Thursday, as it happened, and his thirty-seventh day in the facility, and it also turned out to be his last. He and the others who were to be moved had been informed the night before. They had been told that they would be marched to a railhead, where they would entrain for another camp at an unspecified location.

The march must have been at least six miles and the searing June heat took its toll. Bruce was exhausted by the time they arrived at the station. There, they were told they were to board a train which would take them to Gravia. It didn't look as though there were nearly enough carriages for everyone and, strictly speaking, there weren't. But they were crammed aboard anyway, and the long, uncomfortable journey began. A brief stop in Athens provided some respite and the opportunity to stretch their cramped limbs and breathe something other than the stale body odor and putrid farts of their fellow prisoners. But the single dollop of tasteless muck they were served for dinner did little to satisfy their hunger. Then it was back aboard the train, and the journey continued into the night. They arrived at Gravia at three in the morning, fatigued and dehydrated.

"You all right, Shorty?" Bruce asked his mate. He had known Shorty Lamont since Cairo but they had become mates in Corinth. Shorty was barely five foot four; even Bruce looked down on him. He was quite handsome in a rugged, craggy sort of way. Had he been a foot taller, he might have made a name for himself in the talkies. He had played halfback for Wellington, or so he reckoned, but Bruce couldn't recall anyone by the name of Lamont playing for the provincial team. Not that it mattered.

"Nah," Shorty replied. "My guts are bad. I'm shitting through the eye of a needle. I don't reckon I'll last much more of this."

Bruce looked at him with concern. He did look drawn and very pale. It was clear he was in a bad way.

"Hold on, mate," he said. "You'll be all right. We can't be far away from where we're going. And the camps can't be worse than this."

Shorty nodded then grimaced, his hands pressed to his midriff.

———

They were ordered to fall in, and word filtered through that they were going to have to march again. A groan went up, but soon they were trudging out of town and up a steep track into the mountains.

"Surely they don't expect us to get over that?" someone said when they stopped for a brief rest. Bruce looked up at the rocky rampart ahead and shot a worried glance at Shorty. If Shorty had heard, he gave no sign. His head was hanging and his breath was coming in short, sharp gasps.

Not long after they had resumed walking, Bruce felt Shorty stagger. He caught his arm.

"Give us a hand, will you?" he asked another soldier. "Me mate's just about done in."

Without a word, the other man slung Shorty's left arm over his shoulders as Bruce did the same with his right. They walked on, Shorty doing his best to put one foot in front of the other. But as the heat of the day came on and they wound their way up the ever-rougher track—it would have been impassable for motor vehicles, and fit only for donkeys—his toes began dragging in the dust.

They passed a man lying by the side of the trail. He wasn't moving. Some glanced at him. Others averted their eyes. Soon enough, they passed another who had fallen by the wayside, then another, and another. Death was to be expected on the battlefield—it was a daily fact of life—but to see soldiers die like this was something quite different.

"So that's the plan," someone behind Bruce said. "They're gonna walk us to death. Bastards."

Bruce wanted to contradict him, but it was hard to see on what grounds.

————

Eventually, they made it over the mountain pass and began descending. The track remained rough and, if anything, picking their way down over the loose, rocky ground, exhausted, malnourished, and dehydrated, was harder than the climb had been.

At last, late in the afternoon, a town came into view on the plain in the distance, far below.

"Jesus, I know where we are," someone said. "That's bloody Lamia, that is. We've just climbed over the Pass of bloody Brassos."

There was a dejected murmur among some of the men. This was ground that the New Zealanders—the 25th chief among them—had recently done so much to defend against impossible odds. Bruce suddenly grasped that this was no coincidence. He felt sure that this death march over the battlefield on which they had so distinguished themselves was a cruel, vindictive trick on the part of the German victors.

They camped short of Lamia—if being forced to sleep on the stony ground could be dignified with the word "camping." Every bone in Bruce's body ached, and the ration of unspeakable food each man was issued was woefully inadequate. Shorty lay where Bruce and the other soldier—Bruce didn't even know his name—let him fall. Bruce feared he might already be dead but his faint, rasping breath confirmed he was still barely alive.

By morning, Bruce's whole body had seized up like a rusty lock and refused to cooperate—his arms and legs resisted any movement he willed them to make. It was only the threat of a German bayonet in the guts that forced him to his feet.

"Still with us, Shorty?" Bruce whispered to his mate.

Shorty shook his head slightly, and his mouth twitched. He might even have been attempting a grin. But when Bruce began hauling on his arm, he gave an agonized groan.

"Fuckin leave me, Bruce. I'm a goner."

"Give us a hand," Bruce called to another soldier, who looked down and shook his head. Bruce called out to another, but he walked past, pretending he hadn't heard. The third man paused, then came and took Shorty's arm. Together, he and Bruce dragged Shorty to his feet and bore him along.

As the day wore on, Bruce occasionally felt a vertiginous desire to drop Shorty, to lie down and wait for his own end to come. But each time, he felt a surge of anger, and in the end it was sheer bloody-minded resolve not to let the bastards get the better of him that kept him going. If anything, the conditions for the last stretch to Lamia were worse, depleted as the prisoners were. Bruce passed a man sitting tying a piece of wood to the sole of his foot, which was clad only in a ragged, bloodstained sock. Some poor buggers, he realized, didn't even have boots. The Germans had no interest in supplying adequate clothes or footwear. Bruce, whose own well-shod feet were killing him, had no idea how they had gotten this far.

They arrived in Lamia in the afternoon. Bruce and the other soldier eased Shorty to the ground as gently as they could. Bruce shook the other man's hand. He was grateful for the help even if, once again, he didn't even know the man's name. They spent another unbearable night in camp, and in the morning they were forced to march to the station, where a locomotive with a line of dismal-looking cattle wagons was standing in wait. If he'd been told a week before that the Germans would force them to travel in conditions such as these, Bruce would have scoffed. But after the death march they'd just endured he wasn't even surprised.

The prisoners were herded into the crowded, unsanitary cattle trucks, at least fifty men to a space no more than fifty feet long and sixteen wide. No one seemed to know how long they were going to have to endure these conditions; most didn't care. They had reached the point where they heard their orders and simply complied, like robots.

There was the shriek of a steam whistle and, with a lurch that sent everyone in Bruce's carriage sprawling against their neighbor, the train was in motion.

———

Several hours later—it might have been as many as five or as few as two, for all Bruce knew—the train drew to a halt. With much shouting, the doors to the wagons were swung open and the prisoners were forced out onto the platform. Bruce half carried Shorty with him.

They were made to march again, this time through the streets of a town. The townspeople lined the street; most watched stone-faced or with open pity as the Allied prisoners limped and shuffled past. This time, there could be no doubt: the intention was to humiliate them in front of the Greek populace and flaunt German superiority. It was like a Roman triumph.

Outside town—Bruce heard someone saying that this was Salonika—they were herded toward a cluster of buildings enclosed within a wire perimeter fence. A gauntlet of German guards was there to meet them, and it was clear from the flurry of kicks and jabs with rifle butts aimed at anyone who stumbled or who made eye contact that they were not about to receive better treatment than they had so far endured.

Sure enough, their time at the Salonika Dulag—short for Durchgangslager, or transit camp—was hellish. Anyone would have recoiled at the filthy, lice-infested sleeping accommodation, but for Bruce, who was regarded by his friends as ridiculously fastidious about his grooming and general hygiene, it was intolerable. In the mornings, they were mustered on the parade ground of what had plainly been an old Greek Army barracks, and . . . nothing. They were simply forced to stand there, whatever the weather. If it wasn't the blistering sun that tormented the men, it would piss down with rain, which left them drenched and their clothes sodden, but at least it helped make up for the lack of showers.

The meals were no better than they had been at Corinth, and mostly comprised the same watery lentil sludge. Every now and again, someone would triumphantly fish out a lump of some anonymous, coarse meat. Bruce supposed it must be goat meat, but others were firmly of the opinion that it was horse or even donkey flesh. The soup—if it could be called soup—was usually accompanied by a hard-as-rock army biscuit or some moldy bread.

On the third day, Bruce heard a voice calling from outside the wire perimeter. An old woman was standing, half concealed by a shrub. Each time she called, there was a commotion in the crowd of prisoners. It took him a moment to work out what she was calling.

"Thank you, English."

She then threw something over the wire. A man standing close by Bruce caught it. He was instantly mobbed by others, but no sooner had the ruck formed than a guard came swinging his rifle butt and kicking his way into the thick of it. He held out his hand for the object, which the prisoner abjectly handed over. With a porcine smile, the guard held the loaf of bread aloft and pointed at the man's wrist and raised his eyebrows. The prisoner closed his other hand defensively over his wristwatch. Then, after a moment's consideration, he slipped off the band and handed it over. The German took it and threw the bread onto the muddy ground, where another, even more desperate ruck formed over it.

This, it turned out, was the deal: the unscrupulous goons demanded one watch for a single loaf of good Greek bread. It didn't matter what make of watch or what condition; a battered 1929 Citizen was worth the same as a mint Rolex. The exchange rate never varied. Bruce was too attached to his prized timepiece—a very nice Roamer—and, even though he was desperately hungry, he chose to starve rather than hand it over.

Meanwhile, people were dying. Many who had survived the march were succumbing to disease. Cholera, dysentery, and even malaria were rife, and Bruce never saw any sign of the Germans supplying basic medications such as quinine or atabrine. The dead and the dying lay covered in swarms of flies and God knows what else. Some begged to be put out of their stinking misery. Every now and then, there would be shouts and a shot or two, and Bruce would glimpse German soldiers dragging a corpse toward the camp gates. He was never sure whether these men were killed for some trifling act of insubordination or whether they had committed Nazi-assisted suicide by making some gesture resembling an escape attempt. Few, if any, had a realistic chance of getting away, such was the generally weakened condition of the men.

Shorty, miraculously enough, seemed to be somewhat on the mend, although he was still weak and plagued with cramps and bouts of bloody diarrhea. He had even begun taking some interest in his surroundings. Around a week after arriving in the camp, Bruce asked him how he was and he raised a thumb. Bruce dared to hope that his mate might make it, after all.

———

As it turned out, they were at Salonika for twelve desperate days. On the evening of the eleventh, they were paraded and names were called out, Bruce's and Shorty's among them. In the morning, those named were told they would be on the move again. There would be another march, to a railhead not far from the camp, and from there the prisoners would be dispatched to their permanent accommodation. They weren't told where this was to be.

The walk in the morning ought to have been easy—it was a short distance over flat ground—but so debilitated were the prisoners that they took twice as long to cover the distance as they should have. Shorty made it under his own steam, but only just.

The scene at the railway station was surreal. On one side of the platform, there was a train comprising cattle trucks, with a few better-class carriages to house the guards and caged dogs—fierce-looking Doberman pinschers—and bringing up the rear, a flatcar on which was mounted a heavy machine gun and a searchlight. On the other side, a German marching band was assembled, the sun glittering on their brass instruments and polished uniform buttons as they stood, waiting. The prisoners were ordered into a line at a table from which women in starched white smocks were doling out food parcels. Men were taking these, standing there agog, and then tearing them open, scarcely able to believe their eyes—there were unimaginable treats inside: tinned bacon, a half loaf of relatively fresh bread, and sweet biscuits.

Many bolted these delicacies as they crouched on the platform, waiting to board the train. Bruce was a little more circumspect. He decided he couldn't risk this being the last decent food they received for a while, and limited himself to eating some of the bread and half of one of the biscuits.

After an hour or so waiting, a whistle blew. The prisoners got painfully to their feet, and the band set the mouthpieces of their instruments to their lips. On the bandleader's signal, they struck up a tune. Bruce and Shorty looked at each other. Bruce shook his head in disbelief, and Shorty shrugged helplessly.

To the strains of "Roll Out the Barrel," the prisoners crammed into the cattle trucks. The German band oompahed its way through a badly orchestrated version of the classic wartime polka as if it were a ceremonial send-off for VIP passengers on a cruise liner. But Bruce figured that whatever lay ahead would be anything but a barrel of fun.

There was barely room to sit, and definitely no space for those who were ill to lie down. And many were ill. Dysentery was the most common complaint. In one corner, a steel milk churn served as a latrine. In the opposite corner, there was an Aral-branded four-gallon tin with its lid crudely hacked off and brimming with dubious-looking water. With fifty-five men vying for one can, there were plenty who shat themselves just waiting their turn. Others used their helmets if they couldn't make it in time, emptying them through the ventilation gaps and often being splattered by their own mess. Those who fought their way toward the solitary latrine bucket were roundly cursed by those they shoved, jostled, and trampled on the way. The can couldn't cope and, not long into the journey, its stinking contents overflowed and piss and shit spewed across the planking floor. Anyone would have found this hard to take, but for Bruce it was intolerable.

At the occasional stops, each at some bleak and godforsaken marshaling yard in the middle of the Greek countryside, the shitcan would be emptied and the jagged-edged water tin refilled. Bruce regarded the hazy, petrol-scented water with profound suspicion, but it was all that was on offer. It was gone soon enough as the temperature in the wagon soared in the heat of the day.

———

Every now and again, someone would try to "jump the rattler," as escaping the train had come to be called. Although all such attempts were plainly futile—most of the prisoners were too frail and exhausted to make a serious dash for it and, to further complicate matters, knew nothing of the geography, language, or military allegiances of the territory they were in—no one blamed the would-be escapers for trying and everyone urged them on, hoping for a successful outcome. It never happened. The machine gun at the back was hardly ever called upon; usually all it took was a few guards and a couple of dogs to mount a pursuit, the happy shouts and barking indicating how much the dogs and men alike appreciated the break in the monotony of the journey. Surprisingly, none of those recaptured alive were punished. They were just shoved back into the carriages again. Doubtless the guards thought that this was punishment enough.

———

Bruce had managed to commandeer a corner of the wagon for Shorty, who lay curled up in the fetal position, retching a little bile every now and again, his trousers soaked in watery shit.

"I'm a goner, Bruce," Shorty whispered, as Bruce tried to get him to sip from his canteen. Bruce waved away a fly that was trying to settle at the corner of his mate's eye, but it merely performed an irritating circuit and settled again.

"Pull yourself together," Bruce chided him. "You've been saying that for bloody weeks."

"Nah, Bruce, mate. I can just feel it. I'm done for. I won't last another day."

"You can do it, Shorty," Bruce replied, struggling to inject into his voice a conviction he didn't feel. Shorty was one of several men who were failing fast. The helplessness of the dying made the plight of the living shamefully insignificant. When the prisoners beseeched the guards for some kind of medical assistance, they just shrugged.

"You'll make it, mate," Bruce urged. "Think about your family and stay strong. Once we get there, you'll be right as rain."

On the third day of the journey, Bruce shook Shorty's shoulder and got no response. He shook it again, a little harder, but his hand registered the change. Shorty was limp in the way a living body never was. Bruce found himself consumed by an irrational fury toward his little friend, whose pathetic corpse looked like that of a child, curled up and emaciated as it was.

"What the fuck, Shorty," he sobbed, punching the lifeless shoulder.

The worst of it was that, as soon as he'd realized Shorty was dead, he'd felt a surge of relief—he was one of the fifty-four in the carriage still alive—followed immediately by a flood of guilt. Others watched him indifferently as he wept. But soon enough, he had composed himself. He knew that it wasn't Shorty but his German captors at whom he should be directing his anger. He swore to Shorty that wherever he fetched up, whatever godforsaken pit the Germans consigned him to, he would make their lives as difficult as he possibly could. He had never felt hatred for another human being as he found himself hating the Hun.

Shorty's body was unloaded onto the platform when they next stopped, some eight hours after he'd died. Bruce and his fellow prisoners milled around it; some joined him as he mumbled the words to "The Lord is My Shepherd"—at least as many as he could remember—and that was as much of a funeral as his mate got. The body remained on the platform as they were ordered to board again, and it wasn't the only one. There were six corpses, and they were still there as the train pulled out. Bruce had no idea whether anyone would take the trouble to give them a decent burial, let alone find out who they were and notify their families waiting at home.

————

After four days of this hell on wheels, it became clear they were nearing the end. The guards were more noticeably relaxed and their mood more buoyant; they were looking forward to a few days' leave. Sure enough, toward the evening of the fourth night, those with a view through the slats reported that they were passing through the outskirts of a city. They drew into a station, the signs proclaiming it to be Beograd. Bruce didn't even know what country Beograd was in, and no one around him could shed any light on the matter, either. They hardly dared hope that the nightmare was over. But when they were unloaded and ordered to line up, it was to find that they were in a proper, sanitary railway station. Better still, there were tables set up with crisp white linen coverings and the Belgrade Red Cross banner prominently displayed. The prisoners were at last issued some decent food—lemon tea and hot soup containing a chunk of real meat. It was half-decent food and they all ate as if it were their last meal. Some thought it might be.

But, when they were ordered back aboard the stock wagons, they were told that they were only a day away from their permanent POW camps. Most of the train was bound for Wolfsberg, Austria, where the occupants would be interned in Stalag XVIIIA. Some of the wagons were to be detached in Maribor, Slovenia. Bruce heard the name of the camp for which he was destined—Stalag XVIIID—for the first time. For four tedious days, the routine had remained unchanged. The only difference was that each day there were fewer passengers. At least the dead no longer had to suffer the agony of their debilitating diseases, the ignominy of capture, or the indignity of imprisonment. They had reached their final destination before they completed the journey.

Now that Bruce knew it was almost over, his feelings were mixed. On the one hand, he was relieved beyond words that the train journey was almost over. But on the other, he was profoundly anxious. Each time he had hoped for better treatment, he had been bitterly disappointed. If the pattern continued, he reckoned, he might even envy Shorty and the others who had died on the way.

———

The first step in Bruce's induction to Stalag XVIIID was delousing. Most hated this procedure, in which prisoners were forced to strip and stand with hands on head as their private parts were minutely inspected and every bodily crevice was sprayed with a rank-smelling chemical. Bruce welcomed it. He was eager to be clean and sanitized, rid of the parasites, filth, and infections accumulated during the torturous train ride, and the spray certainly smelled as though it would do the trick.

Delousing was followed by form-filling. The pen pushers took over, recording date of birth, next-of-kin contact details, postal addresses, Red Cross information, service records, medical details, work history, marital status, religion, physical characteristics—height, weight, distinguishing marks, eye and hair color—and even dietary needs, as if the Nazis intended to prepare vegetarian meals for those who requested them. The Germans were nothing if not thorough with their documentation. Finally, when the bureaucrats were done, Bruce's mug shot was taken.

He was now officially "Murray, B. G. Kg 4257."

He was directed to his accommodation. Stalag XVIIID had been designed to accommodate 2,000 troops back when it was a Yugoslav Army barracks. Now, as a prisoner-of-war camp, it housed almost 4,500 Allied prisoners captured in Greece and Crete. Bruce was one of many who had to live in leaking army tents while flimsy wooden huts were being constructed. Unlike the camps they'd endured on their long journey, there were at least beds to sleep on, although they proved to be bone-achingly uncomfortable. There was also something that passed as food at reasonably regular intervals. It might have been a thick, diarrhea-brown gruel made mostly from fermenting vegetables, but at least it was hot and the servings were generous compared to the starvation diet on the train.

Bruce fell into an exhausted sleep, and he was only hours into the first night of God knows how many he was doomed to spend at Stalag XVIIID when he had already begun to dream of escape.

Chapter Twelve

—

Josefine, Maribor,
August to October 1942

The Slomškov trg incident with Mara Zlata had unsettled Josefine but, at the same time, she couldn't ignore the adrenaline rush that she got from confronting danger and surviving. She pushed Dejan for more and more challenging assignments. It was through this insistence on doing more that she came face-to-face with prisoners of war for the second time.

Escaping POWs almost invariably sought the assistance of partisans—either before they made a run for it or, mostly, after they realized that they had little hope of getting out of Slovenia without local support. The conditions were often extreme, particularly in winter, and the terrain—the mountains, valleys, and rivers—was challenging for the fugitives and waiting partisans alike. Few of the escapees had any idea of the geography and were stranded in remote and unfamiliar territory. Some were arrested, frozen and half starved, and relieved to see German troops, while others were found by sympathetic villagers and hidden in the hills until they could be connected with the freedom fighters. Partisan guides were often called upon to escort these soldiers on their way to freedom.

The first time Josefine performed this kind of work, it was to assist two British prisoners who had fled into the Pohorje forest after bolting from their work camp close by. A search by the guards failed to locate them, and their luck held: they were found by a farmer sympathetic to the partisans and secreted in a cave in the hills behind Hrastje. The National Defence was notified, and Dejan summoned Josefine.

"All you will need to do is take them along the track to this farm," he said, showing her the route on a map.

Josefine nodded. She knew the area well, having spent many a happy summer walking in the hills and foraging for the berries and mushrooms that grew there. The distance wasn't great, although it would be cold and the narrow track would be treacherous in the dark.

"You'll leave them there, and they'll be met by a guide from another district. Your job is then over."

Josefine traveled to Hrastje and, as evening fell, she and the farmer who had hidden the two men walked quietly up a path to the cave. The pair were there, looking drawn and pale. Efforts to communicate were hampered by the fact that Josefine and the farmer spoke no English and the men spoke neither German nor, of course, Slovene. But they managed to convey to her that a German patrol had passed by in the forest below them only an hour before. One of them—a small, intense dark-haired man—performed an elaborate mime, pressing his wrists together and hanging his head, then pointing the forefinger and index finger of his right hand against his temple and making the noise of a shot. His meaning was clear. He would rather die than be recaptured. Josefine found that the men's fear helped soothe her own. She made a palms-down calming gesture and, reaching into her bag, gave them some bread and cheese, which was gratefully received. Once they had eaten, she motioned them to follow her. They picked their way along the track that threaded through the trees on the hillside, pausing every now and again to listen. Apart from the usual woodland noises, they heard nothing, and neither did they see anything to cause alarm. They arrived at the drop-off point on the farm without incident. Josefine showed them to the barn where they were to await their next guide. Then she made to leave.

"Stop," said the dark-haired man. He fumbled with the silver badge on the breast of his uniform jacket and held it out to her. She took it, and he folded her hand closed and clasped it with both of his. There were tears in his eyes.

"*Danke,*" he said. "*Danke.*"

Josefine was deeply moved.

———

It occurred to Josefine, as she basked in the glow of pride she felt in the wake of this mission, that perhaps she had found her calling in the struggle against the Nazis. While she craved more direct action than carrying documents gave her, she was honest enough to admit to herself that, unlike Anica, she didn't have the stomach for armed combat. But perhaps, by helping the men who were helping her people, she could strike a blow.

She helped several other escaping prisoners of war in the following months, mostly from Stalag XVIIID or from the work camps associated with it. Because she was most familiar with the immediate vicinity of Maribor, this was the area she was most often called upon to work in. Since it also had the highest concentration of Germans, it was also the most dangerous. She never really knew where those she helped were bound. Some, she supposed, were bustled toward Switzerland. Others went to Italy, or even through Austria to Germany.

The escape routes varied constantly, both to baffle anyone trying to trace them, and also because they had to be repaired each time they were traced and disrupted.

Those soldiers who had made carefully considered escape plans were usually the easiest to move, although "easy" was a relative term. They often had civilian clothes, counterfeit documents, and could speak reasonable German, so they could be escorted through town centers, right under the noses of the Germans, and evacuated on normal scheduled rail services. The threat of exposure was ever-present. A random inspection of work permits would quickly uncover forged identity papers; a few words of English spoken inadvertently under questioning would immediately reveal the offender's nationality. Other escapees were taken through the hills and onto the back roads, where German patrols or pursuits might be encountered.

One feature of the escape lines is that they were highly fragmented. After Josefine had passed the men under her care to the next group, her involvement ended. She had no idea who was involved in conducting them after that. This was a deliberate strategy. If anyone was arrested, there was only a limited amount of damage they could do to the wider organization if they cracked under torture.

The other consequence was that Josefine never knew if those she helped made it to safety. She was sure plenty didn't, but she hoped and prayed that others—perhaps even many others—did win through. All she could say is that with only one exception, and this due to circumstances beyond her control, she had successfully passed every one of the men she'd been asked to help up the line.

At worst, a recaptured prisoner faced a few days or weeks in the cooler. The risks for Josefine were much greater. She faced the prospect of execution; the best she could hope for would be spirit- and body-breaking torture.

———

Helping fugitives from the prisoner-of-war camp was possibly the most dangerous branch of her activity. Sometimes she and her comrades had the luxury of a head start, when it took several hours for an escape to be discovered and the camp Klaxon to sound. More commonly, it was a matter of an hour or two, and sometimes only a matter of minutes. As soon as a breakout was detected, security in the surrounding district was ramped up. Snap searches were more frequent, checkpoints were stepped up, all roads in and out of town were heavily guarded, low-flying spotter planes buzzed through the skies constantly, troops scoured every possible hiding place, and suspected escape routes were carefully monitored.

The dangers were brought forcibly to her one day in early October when she was informed that three prisoners of war had made a run for it from a work party and were hiding in the forest near the camp. "There's no time to lose," said Dejan. "They'll be missed any minute, if they haven't been already. Can you go?"

Josefine borrowed a bicycle and pedaled furiously to the vicinity where the escapees were supposed to be hiding. Her nerves were on edge as she walked into the trees. A hundred yards into the shadowy forest, she heard soft voices, and took cover behind an ancient oak tree. Then she saw them: three men in Allied uniforms hiding in the undergrowth.

She stepped out.

The reaction to her appearance was less than rapturous.

"What the fuck? It's a bloody girl!" said one of them in English. He held up a placating hand. "Pardon my French."

"Where are the partisans?" a stocky, completely bald man asked in German.

"*Komm,*" she said, and beckoned to them.

"We were expecting partisan soldiers, not a bloody schoolkid," the man said, reverting to English.

Josefine only smiled in reply.

"*Komm*," she said again, slowly, in German. "I'll take you some-where to hide. You'll have to wait there until it's safe to move you."

The bald man seemed to understand, although his face was a mask of skepticism. The three men followed Josefine to a place she knew in the forest where it was possible to see anyone approaching without being seen.

"Here you must wait," she said.

Because there had been no advance notification of the escape—it had been purely spontaneous, in response to maltreatment by one of the guards on the work detail—there was no plan to shift the men. So when Josefine went back that night, it was to bring the three back to Limbuš, where they were installed in the hut in the vine-yard where Srečko had been living. Jožef, who seemed pleased to be able to do something concrete for the cause, really turned on the Slovene hospitality, and plied his guests with the local spirit, slivovitz (plum brandy). It turned out that the bald man—whose nickname, thanks to some untranslatable joke, was "Curly"—spoke reasonable German. He proudly told Josefine and Jožef that the escape had been his idea. He'd had a gutsful, as he put it, of the rough treatment from the guards, so he decided he was going to shoot through. Of the rest of the detail, only his two companions were game to come along, although others were happy to provide a diversion.

"How did you contact the partisans?" Josefine asked.

"There was a Slovene supervisor there who we saw steal a pistol one day. Well, I didn't think he wanted to use it for a doorstop, so we asked if he had contacts in the partisans. I suppose he did, the way it's turned out."

The man who had reported the escape to Dejan did indeed have partisan contacts. He was deeply afraid that the three apparent pris-oners of war might turn out to be part of some plot with the Germans, but he was even more afraid that they might shop him for stealing the pistol if he refused to help.

"So anyway, in the afternoon, on the way back to the prison camp, we made a run for it. The rest of the boys started singing 'Hitler's Only Got One Ball'—do you know that one?"

Josefine didn't, so Curly gave them a swift rendition in English:

Hitler has only got one ball
Göring has got two but they're small
Himmler has something sim'lar
But poor old Goebbels has no balls at all . . .

With his limited German, translation proved difficult.

"Anyway, it really riled them," he said. "By the time they'd finished booting people up the backside, we were in the trees."

"Where are you from? What country?" Josefine asked, thinking of the prisoner to whom she had handed the note inquiring about Polde, and his unfamiliar uniform.

"Australia," Curly replied. "You heard of it?"

"Of course I have," Josefine lied.

———

The men were obliged to lie low the next day, but they were thoroughly reconciled to this by the aftermath of the slivovitz. In the evening, Josefine led them into the forest, where they rendezvoused with half a dozen armed partisan soldiers.

"This is more like it," said Curly.

The band made its way along little-known, well-hidden trails through farmland, swamps, and streams to a remote farm about ten miles from Limbuš, where Josefine's responsibility ended. They would stay overnight and then be passed to another team.

The group arrived at the farm at midnight as planned. They gave the agreed signal—three torchlight flashes in quick succession.

No response.

The signal was repeated several times, but there wasn't a flicker of a reply from the lightless farmhouse.

"Are you sure this is the place?" Josefine asked the man in charge of the National Liberation Front detachment.

"Yes. Something's wrong."

No sooner had he said the words than there was a roar of gunfire from one of the outbuildings. Somehow the Nazis knew they were coming; they must have been betrayed. Twigs snapped and fell around them.

"Švabi!" the leader of the fighters yelled. "Švabi! Get down! Now!"

Josefine had frozen, standing in full view of the Germans.

"Take cover!" the leader commanded. "Get out of sight or you'll be shot!"

One of the escapees yanked her to the ground while the partisan militia immediately took up defensive positions.

Her paralysis faded. She saw a mound of stones and rubble that would provide some protection and she slithered across to it on her belly. "*Hitro! Hitro!*" she hissed in Slovene. "Quick. Over here!" One of the partisans loosed a few shots at the Germans to provide cover as the Australians joined her.

The fact that they were returning fire seemed to cause general consternation among the Germans. It quickly became plain that they hadn't been expecting armed resistance, and their fire was ill-disciplined and poorly directed. Their bullets whistled harmlessly by the bunkered-down partisans, who fired only when they could see a target. Bullets were too precious to waste. Several Germans were seen scurrying into the barn from which the initial burst had been fired. The partisan leader sent some of his men to work their way into areas of dead ground from which they could safely approach the building. The rest directed fire at the windows and at the planking beneath them. There were shouts from within, whether from pain or fear, it was difficult to tell.

This was the first pitched battle Josefine had seen, and it terrified her. The night sky lit up as the muzzle flashes blazed through the blackness. After half an hour or so, the German fire gradually petered out.

"They're out of ammunition," the partisan commander said with satisfaction. He waved at one of his men to spray the barn with sub-machine-gun fire. The result was instantaneous. There were shouts of "*Ich ergebe mich!*" from within. "I surrender!"

"*Raus,*" the partisan called. His men flanked the door, rifles cocked and trained, then it was opened and the Germans filed out, hands held high. They outnumbered the partisans, but their numerical advantage had counted for little. Two of them were being supported by their comrades.

As soon as they were out and encircled by partisans, the barn was searched and their abandoned weapons brought out with much satisfied chatter.

"Go back to the road and find somewhere to hide. Wait for us there," the partisan leader instructed Josefine. "There's one more thing we have to do."

Josefine and the Australians made their way back into the trees. They hadn't quite reached the road when there was a prolonged rattle of gunfire and then silence. Josefine crossed herself.

"You jokers don't muck around, do you?" one of the horrified Australians said.

"Please, God. End the violence," Josefine prayed.

Chapter Thirteen

—

Bruce, Stalag XVIIID, August 1941 to April 1942

Stalag XVIIID was in the Pobrežje district of Maribor, around five miles from Limbuš and on the same side of the river. "Stalag" was short for *Kriegsgefangenen-Mannschaftsstammlager*—"main prisoner-of-war camp"—and the prisoners were known colloquially as "kriegies." The Stalag camps were for noncommissioned military personnel—footsloggers like Bruce. Officers were sent to the Oflag camps, and aircrews were imprisoned in the Stalag Luft compounds. There were numerous smaller *Arbeitskommando*, or work camps, attached to the main camp and POWs spent lengthy periods at both the base and the associated outposts.

Around a month into his stay, the new huts were commissioned. They were basic and crowded—there were roughly two hundred men to a hut with a washroom in the middle and latrine buckets for night use when the POWs were locked in—but they were relatively weatherproof and the straw mattresses on the bunks were luxurious compared with everything Bruce had experienced since leaving the hospital in Corinth. The bunks were arranged in blocks of four and Bruce was lucky enough to score a top one, farthest away from the farts and snores, and offering a modicum of privacy.

Bruce became part of what the POWs called a "combine"—a small group of ten or so men who looked after one another, shared food, discussed personal problems, and generally helped make life more bearable. Frank Butler was another member of the combine. He was a short, dapper bloke, rather rotund, with a generous crop of thick, black hair that he did his best to slick back with spit in the absence of Brylcreem. He was a saddler and harnessmaker before the war and had plied his trade in the small Lincolnshire village of Swallow. His love for animals saw him posted to the RAVC, the Royal Army Veterinary Corps. His number was 4177, indicating he had been captured and processed very shortly before Bruce. Frank's grin lit up his ruddy, roundish face. He had a booming voice that could be heard from almost anywhere in the camp compound, although it took Bruce a while to adjust to his broad accent. He and Frank hit it off almost immediately, and became inseparable in the way that Bruce, Blackie, and Logie had been.

With decent shelter, life was bearable. It didn't take long to get into a daily routine. The hardest thing to cope with was the tedium that threatened to drive men mad. "Barbed Wire Barminess," they called it, and it got to them all in the end. To combat it, sports contests of every sort—football, baseball, volleyball, cricket, rugby—and concerts, stage shows, and festivals helped relieve the monotony. The arrival of Red Cross parcels was a major event. The parcels, which arrived every few weeks, were kept in a separate storehouse in the *vorlager*—the camp administration center—and Bruce was like a two-year-old in a toy shop when they were handed out. Tins of jam were treasured, bars of chocolate were hoarded as if they were bars of gold, and, of course, fags—the camp's preferred currency—were prized above all else. The contents varied, but there were always staples like canned meat, sugar, biscuits, coffee, soap, and powdered milk. Sometimes there would be a bit of butter, some dried fruit, a block of processed cheese, and, on rare occasions, a tin of salmon. Clothing was a regular and welcome addition. Bruce looked forward to the days Red Cross parcels were distributed.

Education was also offered, by the pooling of prisoners' resources. Shortly after his chance encounter with the Lobnik girl, Bruce took a crash course in German to help fill in his spare time. Immersing himself in the language meant he quickly became competent. He could have attended lectures on law, architecture, history—a variety of subjects was on offer—but he knew that, if he were to escape, fluency in German would greatly enhance his chances of success. A fringe benefit was his ability to harass and abuse the guards in their own language. Some of the guards seemed to enjoy it as much as he did, and hurled abuse back in mangled English.

To his own amazement, Bruce even found himself becoming pals with some of those on the other side. One day, as he was passing one of the guards, the man stepped to intercept him. Bruce leveled the cool, hostile stare at him that he reserved for the Germans. He was met with a big, open grin.

"New Zealander?" the guard asked.

"*Ja*," Bruce replied hesitantly.

"Then you must know . . . Jack Sullivan? Charlie Saxton?"

It was a time before Bruce realized his mouth was hanging open.

"Only two of the greatest All Blacks ever," he replied, pulling himself together.

"*Ja*, All Blacks," replied Ulrich Hutmacher. "I play! In Heidelberg. Rugby."

"The Krauts play *rugby*?" said Bruce, aghast.

"*Ja*," said Ulrich. He thumped his chest. "Wing forward."

Bruce could only shake his head in disbelief. Rugby, Ulrich told him, was big in his hometown. He had played for RG Heidelberg in their glory days, when they were twice runners-up in the national German rugby championships in 1937 and 1938. He had an astonishing depth of knowledge about prewar All Blacks and was keen to learn more. Bruce, who had never been shy about talking rugby, was happy to fill him in. He began looking for Ulrich, and found himself looking forward to the times he knew this surprising German was on duty.

Soon nothing was off-limits. They talked about politics in Germany (Ulrich had once supported Hitler, but not now), the likely outcome of the war (Ulrich felt the tide had turned against Germany), the other guards (most of them, Ulrich felt, were good men, but there were some bad apples), the camp commandant (Karsten Neumann, whom Ulrich regarded as a stickler for the rules but basically decent). They talked about everything, just as old mates would having a beer back home. Bruce learned about Ulrich's marital problems, his kids, his upbringing, his hobbies, his aspirations. It surprised Bruce that Ulrich was far from alone in despising Hitler and what he was doing to "our Germany."

Bruce told Ulrich about his own war experiences, his old life in New Zealand, and the state of his marriage. His life with Doreen, he explained, was all but over.

They did good turns for each other with no favors expected in return. Bruce gave Ulrich Red Cross cigarettes, chocolate, and canned meat but waved away Ulrich's offer to give him wine or schnapps in return. Ulrich respected that. Both sensed it risked changing the relationship from one of mutual trust and respect to one of exploitation and extortion. Their unlikely bond was too important to compromise for a few fags or a case of wine. On the other hand, when Bruce was sent to solitary confinement for disciplinary reasons, which happened rather a lot, he didn't decline the odd tin cup of grog that Ulrich brought him. Ulrich also got Bruce out of a few scrapes, intervening with the camp commandant to prevent Bruce being transferred.

Ulrich wasn't the only guard whom Bruce came to respect and whose company he came to enjoy. There was Matthias Baumgartner—"Matte" for short. Before the war, Matte had been a production manager for the famous Dresden-based Anita lingerie and corsetry manufacturer. His role was the equivalent of Bruce's at Prestige and they spent many hours discussing technology advances, branding, and packaging. It was a revelation to Bruce: not all Germans were Nazis, and not all Germans were bad.

———

Nonetheless, he was true to his vow to Shorty to make life as difficult for his captors as possible. Sabotage was his usual recourse, but escape was his ultimate goal. The satellite work camps, or *Arbeitskommando*, provided the best opportunities for disruption and escape. The work camps were often miles away from the main camp; they were generally lightly guarded and poorly supervised. POWs were assigned to work in mines, sawmills, factories, on roads and railways, and—the job of choice for most—on farms. Previous work experience was a key factor and, since there wasn't a big demand for lingerie and hosiery specialists, Bruce was posted to several *Arbeitskommando* to tackle a diverse range of tasks.

Bruce's first chance to strike back was on a railway working party while he was repairing tracks through an alpine pass. The partisans had blown up the lines in several places, preventing the movement of troops and supplies. Bruce's crew was tasked with making urgent repairs to restore the vital transport link. On the second day, he came up with a plan to torpedo the remedial work.

"Hey, Jonesy," he said to his mate when he was sure the guards were well out of earshot. "Let's bugger up the works here. We'll lay the tracks as they ask, but if we don't properly tighten the bolts that connect the tracks to the sleepers, the little blighters should shake loose in a few days and, whammo, a train will be off the rails and in the bloody ditch. We'll screw them just tight enough to pass the daily check—if they bother to do it. Whaddya think?"

"I'm in. Let's have a go. I'm not sure it will work but it's sure as hell worth a try. As long as the goons don't twig to it, we'll be fine. The stupid pricks probably won't bother inspecting the bolts anyway, lazy buggers that they are."

Bruce and Jonesy were right: the guards took a cursory look at their shoddy workmanship and left. Bruce tried this ruse several times, always hoping to derail a German troop train or armaments shipment. He would never know if his efforts succeeded but at least he had the satisfaction of knowing he had tried.

On road reconstruction work, Bruce had devised various sabotage methods. He would put loose stones in huge potholes and, without compacting them, cover the pebbles with cement, so that the fill would eventually collapse, leaving another huge crater to repair. He made weak concrete mixes by adding too much water and too little sand and gravel, so that the concrete broke up the first time a heavy truck rolled over it. Where he could, he would pour water over cement bags so that they hardened and were rendered useless. He cut power cables, stole tools, put sand in machinery. He did as little work as possible, which wasn't difficult because the idle guards spent more time eating and talking than supervising, or he would "pull a *kranker*," feigning illness or injury to avoid work altogether. He soon prided himself on his ability to mimic a range of alarming symptoms: vomiting, shaking, even a high temperature—usually faked by holding the thermometer close to a light bulb while the doctor was distracted. More than once, he presented with a kidney infection, which was verified in the laboratory: all it took was to borrow a urine sample from a real sufferer. Bruce was far from alone in deriving tremendous enjoyment from pulling the wool over the eyes of the pompous camp doctor, and every day off work felt like a little victory over the Hun.

It was at bribing guards and bartering for normally unobtainable goods, mostly using paraphernalia filched from the guards themselves, that Bruce excelled. Most of the goons were of Austrian rather than German descent, so few had deep loyalties to Hitler or the Reich. They were generally unfit for front-line duties, either too old or physically weak, and had been assigned to the camps because there was nothing else they could do. The ancient, the infirm, the incapable, and the incompetent were left to guard the POWs. Many were indolent or just plain greedy, and more interested in personal gain than anything else. That meant that most were susceptible to bribery. And then, of course, as soon as they had once succumbed to temptation, they were open to blackmail.

Bruce found he could rely on the Austrians to pilfer virtually everything he wanted from the camp stores or buy hard-to-get merchandise in Maribor in return for a packet of fags—two if it was something important. They would do anything if the price was right. And if something couldn't be obtained through commerce, it was simply stolen. Guards often left tools and implements lying around, either too slack to pick them up or too dumb to realize their worth to the prisoners, and Bruce never wasted an opportunity to filch whatever he could. He amassed an impressive inventory of stolen objects: several hammers, a hacksaw, three German Army tunics left hanging on pegs (trousers were more difficult to come by), a box of Austrian Stiegl beer, a few rolls of canvas, a cooked ham, even a few rounds of ammunition. They were all put to good use—shared among his fellow POWs or bartered for other necessities.

His prize catch was a camera, a chrome Leica IIIc. It belonged to one of the most hated goons in camp, Wenzel Schneider, known to all as "Weasel." Weasel was swaggering around one day brandishing it, proud as punch.

"I reckon the escape committee could do with that," Bruce said to Frank.

"Bet you can't," said Frank, his eyes alight with mischief.

"Bet I can," Bruce replied.

Frank organized for three of their mates to start a brawl. Weasel, known for his no-nonsense disciplinary methods, set his camera down tenderly on a bench and ran toward the fracas. The fight broke up quickly, and Weasel was back within two minutes to pick up his pride and joy—only to find it was gone. It had taken Bruce all of fifteen seconds to secrete it inside his coat and hurry off to his hut, proud owner of a new Leica. Weasel searched high and low and threatened all manner of dire consequences, but none of the POWs would let on what happened. And it was a measure of the regard in which Weasel was held by his fellow guards that the search for the missing camera was lackluster at best.

Bruce regarded the camera as the jewel in the crown of his criminal career. But others rated another of his feats more highly. When Bruce first arrived at the camp, there was an illicit radio operating. The set had been built out of scavenged and smuggled parts and was housed in a biscuit tin with schnapps corks serving as knobs. But the tin was inadequately ventilated, and four of the valves burned out. The radio was vital for morale: loudspeakers on poles throughout the camp blared bulletins proclaiming Nazi triumph after triumph, and while the prisoners did their best to drown these out by shouting, laughing, and banging on the walls of the huts, they had an impact.

Everyone knew that the camp commandant kept a radiogram in his office. That meant there were four replacement valves for the taking. Bruce and Frank volunteered to have a go.

Sometimes bold and brazen triumph over careful and cautious. Bruce decided that the best option was a daylight heist on a Sunday, when the administration building was deserted save for a single, sleepy-looking guard. He woke somewhat as Bruce and Frank approached, and he looked fully alert when Bruce flashed a handful of cigarettes and Frank took three cans of meat from his tunic.

Their accomplice, "Cracker Jack" McCafferty—a locksmith before the war—had the door unlocked before the goon had finished counting the fags. Cracker Jack then stood guard while Bruce and Frank sauntered into the empty office and removed the four valves from the radiogram. They were back outside in less than a minute.

———

Sabotage, theft, and larceny helped relieve the boredom and gave Bruce a sense of purpose. But his number-one preoccupation from the day he was taken prisoner was escape.

Being meticulous and methodical by nature, Bruce promised himself that he wouldn't risk an escape attempt unless the odds of getting away were good. This meant having a plan, along with the necessary accoutrements—identity papers, maps, money, food.

But sometimes good sense surrenders to irrational impulse. Soon after he arrived at Stalag XVIIID he had spied the opportunity to fly the coop, and he couldn't resist. He was with a work party. The only goon in sight had found a pleasant spot in an alpine meadow and was fast asleep. Bruce simply walked away.

His problems started when he reached the bottom of the hill and virtually stumbled into an SS camp. Fearing he'd been seen, he took cover in the first place he could find: a swamp. He cowered there, with soldiers going about their business only yards away. He planned to make a run for it after dark, but another group of soldiers set up camp on the other side of the swamp at dusk. He was now surrounded with no way out. Once, a pair of soldiers came straight for him. He listened to their approaching footsteps, and was on the point of standing up and surrendering when he heard the unmistakable sound of running water. They were almost pissing on top of him. How they didn't see him he would never know.

Bruce had some food in his pocket. He decided to sit tight, confident the soldiers would pack up and move on the following day. They didn't. Nor the day after that. His food was soon exhausted, so he was reduced to eating some sort of watercress and a palm-like weed that grew nearby. These and the swamp water that he was forced to drink tasted like cow dung, but they kept him going. He had to listen to the Krauts drinking, laughing, and singing while he languished in a stinking bog.

He could handle the cold and the hunger, but Bruce was not temperamentally suited to unsanitary conditions, and he could never abide creepy-crawlies. When he noticed a black thing hanging from his arm, he nearly shouted. Lifting his leg from the water, he found it was festooned with leeches. He swatted and scraped and scratched as quietly as he could, but nothing did any good. He experienced a spasm of horror.

Nor was that the only spasm he endured. With an ominous growl, his bowels began to churn. Soon he didn't dare fart, in case he soiled himself. His head began to pound and he threw up, gouts of thick green slime tinged with blood that floated on top of the water. He was sure he'd poisoned himself, and when, by the fifth day, the Germans showed no sign of shifting, he could take no more. Half delirious, he walked into the campsite. The merry conversation among the Germans faltered as he appeared in their midst. Bruce raised his arms. They stared at the bedraggled creature that had dragged itself from the marsh. Someone said something in German and there was laughter. The laughter grew. They were still laughing when they delivered him back to the camp, and there was general amusement among the guards of Stalag XVIIID as well—not that it stopped them from giving him twenty-one days' solitary after he'd recovered from his illness. This was no *kranker*. It took days to recover from the severe gastroenteritis he'd contracted from the swamp.

———

His second attempt was no better planned.

In April 1942, on an unseasonably cold spring day, Bruce was on a work detail where the only guard to be seen was huddled over a coal-fired brazier in his hut trying to keep warm. His greatcoat was hanging on a peg outside, out of sight. It was too tempting to ignore. Bruce made a spur-of-the-moment decision. He quietly removed the coat and walked off the roadworks site and into the distance. The guard was a big, corpulent man and the greatcoat hung off Bruce's slight frame like a sack on a broomstick. But it was too late to turn back now. He had no plan to speak of and only the vaguest idea of where to go, but he was engulfed with euphoria.

His best option, he figured, was to head for the hills, which were rumored to be partisan territory. It was only as he walked deeper into the forest in the foothills of the mountains that it occurred to him that the German Army overcoat he was wearing might get him shot on sight by the partisans. Likewise, if he were to encounter an SS patrol, he might be executed for impersonating a German soldier.

But it was too late to turn back and too cold to jettison the coat. He would have to take his chances.

Bruce made his way up the slopes of the Pohorje range. It was a steep climb, and he was soon breathless and lay down to rest. He was sitting with his back against a rock and considering his next move when there was a sharp crack next to his ear followed by the sound of a gunshot. He rolled over and pressed himself into the earth, wondering if he was being shot at by partisans or by Germans. Slowly, he raised his head and peered around the rock. It took a moment to discern the gunmen: there were at least three of them and they weren't dressed in any kind of uniform. They must be partisans.

"*Ingleski, Ingleski!*" he shouted, and held his arms up where they could see them. "*Partisanski, Partisanski!*" he yelled for good measure.

There was a volley of shots. Bruce heard the slugs slapping into the damp earth on either side of the rocks. He kept his hands where they were. Suddenly he was staring into the pitiless black eye of a rifle barrel, with a pair of equally hard eyes scrutinizing him over the sights. The gun remained trained on him as two men appeared and dragged him to his feet. Bruce kept his arms in the air. With the muzzle of a rifle in the small of his back, he was marched higher up the slopes of the mountain.

When they finally stopped, Bruce was surrounded.

A man who looked like he might have been their leader barked something in almost unintelligible English.

"What you are?"

Bruce shot him a puzzled look.

"Who you are?" the man corrected himself.

"*Britisch Kriegsgefangener*," Bruce replied.

"*Britisch?*" one of the others demanded.

"British prisoner of war," Bruce replied, nodding. He decided it was too difficult to explain that he was a New Zealander. "From Stalag XVIIID at Maribor. I've escaped."

There was a hurried exchange between several of the men.

"What do you here?" the leader asked. "This not bladdy good place here be." He sniggered at his use of an English swear word.

"How can you prove who you are?" the man who had spoken in German said. "You spoke German before. How do we know you're not a Nazi?"

"*Ich spreche Deutsch*," Bruce explained, "because I'm learning it in the POW camp. Here, look at my dog tag."

The leader grabbed the tag and inspected it. "Not say British here," he said as he pulled at the metal disc. "No bladdy say British."

He'd probably never seen a POW ID, and Bruce doubted that his understanding of written English would be any better than his command of the spoken word.

"Look here," Bruce emphasized, pointing to the stamped letters. "It says Stalag XVIIID. It doesn't say British because it's a prisoner-of-war identification."

They quizzed Bruce for half an hour and, after a thorough interrogation, they decided his story was true. It was more likely to have been the POW work clothes underneath the greatcoat than anything Bruce said that finally convinced them. They couldn't help him, they told him, because they were on a mission. They explained as best they could that they were preparing to ambush a convoy of German trucks. They had supposed Bruce was a lone German soldier sent ahead on surveillance duties.

But they gave Bruce a couple of large shots of slivovitz, as much food as they could spare, and directions to the nearest train station at Pragersko, where they thought he might be able to get a train to Austria. From there, he could make his way to the Swiss border. Switzerland, as the only neutral country bordering Austria, was as good an option as any for Bruce. He hadn't thought that far ahead anyway.

The leader embraced Bruce, slapped him on the back, and wished him luck. Then they parted. Bruce made his way toward Pragersko. He made slow progress and, just after dusk, he realized he wouldn't make it much farther before nightfall. He settled down behind a copse of trees and had a little of the leathery sausage and rock-hard black bread that the partisans had generously given him. He reckoned he had enough to last for a day, if he was careful. Who knew what would happen after that.

It wasn't the prospect of starving that made Bruce reconsider the wisdom of his escape attempt. It was the cold. He wrapped himself in the greatcoat and heaped tree branches, moss, and tussock clumps over himself, but even so he was sure he would freeze to death. It was a godsend when the first frigid rays of the sun poked through the trees.

Bruce felt the relief flooding through his almost icicled body. He had made it through the night.

There was no point in lingering, so he made his way stiffly down the hill to a village, where he ditched the greatcoat and prowled around the houses for clothes he could steal. His best chance was to take clothes left overnight on a washing line before the owners were awake. His first attempt was interrupted by a barking dog so he retreated quickly. He found washing hanging in the foggy dawn, but no men's clothing. Either the locals didn't do their washing regularly or the diligent wives took it in at night. More likely, he thought, the men were away fighting for the Nazis or the partisans.

It was getting later and Bruce could see a few flickering candles alight in some of the windows. He was about to withdraw to the hills when he finally spotted a peasant's jacket, shirt, and trousers hanging on a line partially hidden by an outhouse.

He looked for any sign of life and, seeing none, unpegged the garments and ducked into the shed to change. The clothes were still slightly wet, probably from the overnight dew, and were too small, even for someone as slight as Bruce. They might have belonged to a boy, not a man. But they would have to do. The shirt buttons strained the well-worn fabric, and he couldn't do the trousers up properly so had to tie the top buttonholes together with some string he found hanging on the wall of the shed. The jacket was a reasonable fit—a bit short in the sleeves but, apart from that, it was fine. He dumped his POW clothes under a pile of sacks in the corner of the hut and walked the few miles to Pragersko. He arrived at the station shortly before the early-morning train was due to depart for Graz, from where he hoped to catch another to somewhere near Switzerland. He would try to cross the border where it was lightly guarded or, better still, unguarded altogether. But that was a problem for later. First, he had to get there.

He strode up as confidently as he could to the ticket office. His German, although still far from fluent, was good enough to buy a ticket without arousing suspicion, or so he thought. The ticket seller looked him up and down before finally—and reluctantly, Bruce felt—handing over the ticket. He waited for what seemed like an eternity, even though the train was only minutes away, and, just as he was about to step onto the carriage, a German soldier tapped Bruce on the shoulder. He had been sprung by the ticket seller.

"Your papers, *bitte*," the soldier demanded.

Bruce did his best to bluff, fumbling in his pockets for his non-existent papers and feigning surprise when he couldn't find them. "I must have lost them while I was working on the farm," he explained hesitantly, searching for the right words. "Probably fell out of my pocket."

"Where are you going?" the soldier demanded.

"To see my brother in Graz."

"What's his name?"

"Günter Fuchs," Bruce replied, giving the soldier the name of one of the guards at the camp.

"Where does he live?"

Bruce had no idea what to say. The best he could do was, "Near the railway station. He's going to meet me there because he's just shifted."

The guard raised an eyebrow. Bruce could see the guy wasn't at all convinced by his lame explanation and, after another, more vigorous interrogation, Bruce eventually had to admit he was an escaping POW. He was roughly bundled into the back of an aging Mercedes and taken straight back to the camp, where a twenty-one-day stretch in the cooler was awaiting him.

For all that effort, he had managed to travel only eight miles from where he broke out. As he was being driven back to Maribor, Bruce realized that his amateur escape attempt had been doomed to fail from the outset. He wasn't familiar enough with the geography of the region, had no food, no money, no documents, and no plan. He cursed himself for being so stupid. To have any chance of success, he now knew he needed prearranged help on the outside, the right papers, suitable civilian clothes, enough food to last a week, reasonable maps, a reliable compass—and more good luck than anyone was entitled to expect. Help on the outside was critical; he was chillingly aware that he might have been shot on sight by either the partisans or an SS patrol.

He only ever told a couple of his best mates, but Bruce had to concede that recapture was a relief. After hiking up the hills of Pohorje, where he almost froze to death, the relative comfort of Stalag XVIIID wasn't so bad after all. Even if he had to spend time in the slammer.

Hope, he realized, was not an escape plan.

Chapter Fourteen

Josefine, Maribor to Radkersburg, October 1942 to February 1943

In mid-1942, enlistment in the Wehrmacht was made compulsory for many Slovenes and the persecution of families with real or imagined partisan links increased. The proclamations posted around the streets of Maribor stated that the penalty for refusal to fight for Germany was "imprisonment," which was clearly understood by the populace to mean deportation or execution. Some of the Lobniks' friends were caught up in this. The fate of one of them was unknown—his family hoped he was safe in hiding somewhere—but the other had been shot dead. Meanwhile, families of suspected partisans—whether actively involved in the resistance movement or not—were persecuted by the Germans and by their stooges, the *Steirischer Heimatbund*. Stones were thrown through their windows, their livestock were shot, thugs dogged their steps when they left their houses. Jožef Lobnik was one such target.

One afternoon in late October, there was a forceful knock on the Lobniks' door. Jožef answered it—and was pushed back into the house by a pair of German soldiers.

"We know you're one of them—*der Partisanen*," one of the soldiers snarled, gesturing toward the Pohorje hills, a known hideout for resistance fighters.

Jožef started to protest but, realizing the futility of challenging two Nazi brutes, squared his shoulders, faced his attackers, and spat on the ground. The soldier who had spoken nodded at the other, and Josefine watched, horrified, as they advanced on her father. Jožef made to struggle. One of the soldiers drew his pistol and struck him on the head with the butt. Jožef swore, but the fight went out of him. The Germans frog-marched him to the door while Josefine clawed uselessly at their arms. There was a German staff car outside, and Jožef was jabbed in the back with a rifle butt and forced into the car. Josefine knew he would be interrogated—or worse—until he gave up the names of those partisans he knew, or until the Nazis tired of torturing him for information when none was forthcoming.

"Papa!" screamed Josefine as the car drove off.

"Pepica." Jožef shouted back through the open window, speaking in Slovene so the Germans wouldn't understand. "Somehow we'll make these bastards pay for what they have done to our family and our country."

———

In January 1943, with her father still under constant scrutiny, Josefine was called upon to help three Allied prisoners who were being sheltered in a small hut near Limbuš while an attempt to smuggle them to the Italian border was arranged. It was the pit of one of the harshest winters Josefine could remember, and it was vital that the soldiers were given bedding and warm clothing. In ordinary circumstances, Josefine could have carried everything herself, but snow lay in heavy drifts. She decided she needed another pair of hands.

It had been drummed into her that the first rule of survival in the partisan movement was to trust no one—"not even your best friend," as Dejan had put it. But Josefine had no hesitation in confiding in Jelka that she was a member of the partisans, thus breaching the second rule of survival: tell no one.

Jelka had willingly agreed to help. Between them it had been an easy task to get the supplies to the soldiers. Jelka had even shared a joke with the fugitives in her broken English before they returned to Maribor. The plan was that the men would be moved in a few days.

Three days later, there was a soft knock at the door. Josefine opened it to find Jelka standing on the doorstep, hunched over as though in pain, her face bruised and swollen and streaked with tears.

"Jelka! My poor Jelka! What has happened to you?"

Jelka stumbled into her arms, sobbing uncontrollably. Josefine led her to the kitchen, sat her down, and put her arms around her.

"Tell me what happened," she said.

At first, Jelka only shook her head.

"Pepi," she said at last, in a voice so hollow with grief Josefine could hardly hear it. "Pepi. I'm so sorry," she wept.

"Why are you sorry?" Josefine asked. "What have you got to be sorry for?"

Jelka's face contorted.

"I'm so sorry, Pepi," she repeated. "I've put your life in grave danger."

Josefine was taken aback. She thought she was beginning to guess what Jelka was about to tell her, but she could hardly bring herself to believe it. Jelka hated the Nazis. It was Jelka who had passed on the information about Polde, to say nothing of other pieces of information that had been useful to the partisans. It was Jelka who had gone in Josefine's place to rendezvous with the soldier at Stalag XVIIID and it was she who, not three days before, had helped Josefine to carry the supplies to the escapees.

"What are you saying, Jelka?" Josefine asked, keeping her voice as steady as she could.

It was a long time before Jelka could answer.

"Pepi," she said. "I'm pregnant. And I've done a terrible thing."

Josefine saw it all. She unwrapped her arms from around her friend and stood slowly. She walked around the table and stood with her arms folded.

"Who's the father?" she asked.

Jelka buried her face in her hands. Josefine waited. Finally, Jelka's heaving shoulders steadied. She dropped her hands and took a deep, shuddering breath.

"His name is Gerhard," she whispered.

"A German," said Josefine, incredulously.

"A German," replied Jelka.

Josefine nodded slowly. "Tell me everything," she said.

Jelka told her everything. Oberleutnant Gerhard Schreiber was a junior administrator at the *Kommandantur.* He was handsome, and he had made little secret of his interest in Jelka. She had resisted, for a while. He had a bit of a reputation among the other female staff. But he persisted. He seemed, Jelka told Josefine, different. When she finally allowed him to take her for a drink, he had talked about how terrible he found the war and what it was doing to ordinary people who just wanted to live ordinary lives. He had talked about his family in Germany and he had cried a little.

Soon after that, they became lovers. He was good to her, Jelka told Josefine. He assured her that he was in love with her, and that as soon as the war was over he would take her to Germany with him and they would be married.

"You believed him," Josefine said.

"I believed him, Pepi," Jelka replied, and began weeping again.

She missed a period, she said. Then she missed another. She had consulted a doctor two days before Josefine had come knocking to ask her to help with the supplies for the soldiers. The day after their mission to the hut, she had confirmed that she was pregnant. She immediately went to tell Gerhard, whom she expected to be overjoyed at the news.

Josefine guessed what happened next, and Jelka tearfully confirmed it. Jelka's Nazi was anything but pleased. He ordered her to "get rid of the bastard child." He told her that he knew of a local doctor, a friend of the Reich, who could be relied upon to perform the procedure and keep it quiet. When Jelka told him that she wanted to keep the child—their child—he became angry.

"He said the most awful things, Pepi. About me. About my . . . baby. He sent me away. He told me he didn't want to see me again."

Josefine stared at her best friend, her sister, her beautiful complexion mottled beneath the bruising, those lustrous eyes now red and puffy, her nose running. How many times, she wondered. How many times had she and Jelka talked about girls they knew who had fallen into precisely this trap, bedazzled by the youth and charm of some Nazi officer or another, or seduced by the trappings of privilege— good food, silk stockings, fine wine. Jelka knew what Josefine thought of such women. Yet here she was.

"How does any of this involve me?" Josefine asked, although she was beginning to understand.

"I was desperate, Pepi," Jelka said. "I loved him. I thought he loved me. I thought he would want our child, I really did. But when he said those things . . ."

She looked as though she were about to be sick.

"When he said those things, I realized what a fool I had been. And then I realized that my life was over unless I could get him to help me. I thought I could get him to send me away to Austria or somewhere safe. You know what the locals do to anyone who's pregnant to a Nazi. I'd be beaten, or worse, and I was desperate to get away. So I went to see him again. It was as though I had been blind but now I could see. He never loved me."

She stopped again.

"He never loved me. I realized that. He was looking at me as though he hated me. He told me that I had to get rid of the baby, and when I asked him if there was no future for us, ever, even when the war was over, he told me—"

She choked on the words.

"He told me he has a wife. He has a wife and children. Oh, Pepi. What a fool I've been."

"I still don't see what this—"

"I told him about the British. I told him I had information that I could give him if he promised to help me."

"You betrayed men who have been risking their lives so that Slovenia can be free? How could you?"

"Don't, Pepi. Please, don't."

"Tell me the rest."

Gerhard Schreiber had listened as Jelka described the hut and how to find it. Then he had become interested in where she had come by the information.

"I told him I had been approached by a man I didn't know, who offered me money to take a package to the hut. Gerhard didn't believe me. He . . . he hurt me. He hit me. I fell on the floor and he kicked me, here." She laid her hand on her belly. "He told me he would keep kicking me until the baby was dead unless I told him."

"Told him what, Jelka?" Josefine asked, surprised at the ice in her own voice.

Jelka just looked at her, her eyes pleading. "I had to, Pepi. The baby."

"So you gave this Nazi my name?"

Jelka nodded.

Josefine turned her head away so that Jelka wouldn't see the disgust on her face. She couldn't altogether keep it out of her voice. "You'd better go, Jelena," she said. "There's no place for you here. Not now. I'm sorry for your predicament, but you must go."

"What will you do?" Jelka asked. "You can't stay here. They'll come for you."

"I can look after myself," she said, but she was wondering the same thing.

———

After Jelka had gone, Josefine tried to think. She was on the verge of panic. The only person she had left to talk to was Anica, but Anica was out. Josefine wasn't sure if she could afford to wait for her sister to return.

Nevertheless, she decided it was the best thing to do. She spent an anxious hour listening for the sound of Anica's step on the path outside—and half expecting the sounds of engines, doors, jackboots. When finally she did hear noises, it was the welcome sound of the return of her beloved big sister.

"What is it, Pepica?" Anica said as soon as she saw Josefine's face.

"Ani, I'm in trouble," Josefine said. "Big trouble. I need your help as I've never needed it before."

She explained what Jelka had done.

"Traitorous bitch," Anica spat, but when Josefine described the circumstances she softened a little. "Stupid bitch," she said. "Forget about her. We've got to get you out of here. Pack what you can and we'll leave right away. We'll go to the farm in Radkersburg. You'll be safe enough there in the meantime. There's also Uncle Josef and Aunt Agatha, if necessary."

Anica instructed her to pack as little as possible, and to dress for a long walk in the snow. Normally, Josefine would have traveled by train to Graz and then on another train to Radkersburg, where she would have been picked up by her cousin Mitzl Rossnegger and Mitzl's husband, Gustl. But Anica considered it too dangerous to use public transport in case Josefine's name was on a watch list. They had to assume the authorities were on her trail.

Instead, they would walk to the Austrian border near Gornja Radgona, where Josefine would cross the Mura on the lightly guarded—and sometimes unguarded—rail bridge on the Ljutomer–Radkersburg line. Once she was safely across, Josefine would make her own way to the farm. She knew the area well and would have no trouble getting there, provided she could avoid German patrols. She was traveling with Slovene papers in her own name—arranging false identity documents took time—and, if she were intercepted, there would be no escape.

Roman came in while she was stuffing belongings in a small suitcase.

"What's happening, Pepi?" he asked.

"I have to go away, little man," Josefine told him, although Roman was nearly as tall as she was. "Look after Ani for me."

"Where are you going?"

"I'm going to Radkersburg. I'll be back soon. I promise."

Roman knew better than to ask why.

———

In good weather, it would have taken Anica and Josefine eight hours to reach the border. But parts of their route lay through deep snow, and they were obliged to give one section of road a wide berth when they saw a German checkpoint on it. Even though most of the roads had been cleared of snow, it took them twelve hours to reach the banks of the Mura. They found a position among the trees on an embankment overlooking the bridge, but in half an hour of watching they saw no sign of any guards.

"Best you go," said Anica. Then her face—so calm and stern these days—crumpled. "Oh, Pepi."

The sisters embraced fiercely.

"We will all be together again, Ani," Josefine said. "We'll beat the Švabi, and our family will be together again. Even Polde. I promise."

"Even Polde," echoed Anica sadly. "Take care, Pepica. Until then."

Josefine scrambled down the embankment onto the railway line and walked briskly across. On the far side, she looked back, but if Anica was still there she was impossible to make out in the shadow of the trees, made dim by a flurry of snow.

It was almost midnight when Josefine reached the Rossnegger farm. She was exhausted, and worried about how she would be received. She was fond of her cousin Mitzl, but less certain of Gustl. On previous visits, she had found he had a way of making her feel unwelcome. And here she was, turning up unannounced in the middle of the night; there had been no time to warn them that she was coming.

She rapped loudly on the door and waited. There was no response, so she knocked again. Finally, Mitzl, sleepy-eyed but wary in her flannel nightdress, opened the door.

"Pepi!" she said, startled to see her young cousin so late at night. "What are you doing here? Sorry, what's got into me? Come in! You'll freeze to death out there. I'll go get Gustl."

Gustl and her two second cousins, Wilhelm and Gerda, were roused from their slumber and soon they were all sitting around an open fire, which Mitzl had stoked. Josefine wondered how much to tell them.

Trust no one, she thought ruefully. Tell no one.

But she decided she had to put her faith in her family. Omitting a few details, she explained what had happened.

"Poor Pepi," Mitzl commiserated. "My dear, you'll be safe with us. And don't worry. You can stay as long as you need to. We could do with an extra pair of hands to help around the farm."

Gustl just grunted. Josefine could tell he wasn't happy. Mitzl caught the same inflection.

"Pepi can stay in the spare room, can't she, Gustl?" she prompted.

"If she must," he replied.

———

Whether it was because Mitzl had talked to him, or because he had come around to seeing how useful Josefine could be, Gustl was in a better temper the following morning. The Rossneggers had employed four farm laborers before the war. Those men—along with every other able-bodied male in Austria—were off fighting. Gustl was desperately shorthanded.

"You can milk the cows," he told her, handing her a steel bucket. "One of them usually does it." He jerked his head toward the pair of prisoners of war whom the Rossneggers hired through the local German commandant. "But he's useless. Worse than useless." He spat. "He knocks the bucket over more often than not, or gets shit in the milk if I'm not watching him like a hawk. He probably does it deliberately. Not that I blame him. I'd probably do the same thing if I was in his shoes. But I have to get rid of him and get a replacement from the Wolfsberg camp."

As she observed them during the course of the day, Josefine saw what her cousin meant. The two men moved unnaturally slowly, and seemed to be more accident-prone than was quite credible. One of them opened a gate, sauntered through, and somehow managed to mess up the simple task of relatching it. If Josefine hadn't been on hand to do it, the cattle would have escaped into the lane leading down to the house. The other was set to work pitching hay into the yard. He somehow bent a tine on the fork. When Gustl fetched him another fork, he bent a tine on that one, too. Josefine saw the same man toss the match he had used to light a cigarette into the hayrick. Only good fortune meant it didn't go up in flames.

"They think I'm a Nazi, or that I'm a Nazi lover," Gustl said, and spat again. "How do I tell them that we're part of the Slovene-speaking population near the border and that we're more Slovene than Austrian? How do I tell them that I hate the Švabi as much as they do? But I have mouths to feed. I have a family to take care of."

He shot Josefine a look that reminded her that her presence was putting his family in danger. But then he shrugged and walked away.

Now that she was safely away from Limbuš, she had permitted herself to grieve for Jelka, and to feel the pity that she had been unable to express to her friend's face. As she observed the POWs, she was aware that they were also observing her. She felt the weight of their gaze whenever her back was turned.

Men, she thought. Everywhere, they're all the same.

Chapter Fifteen

Bruce, Stalag XVIIID, April 1942 to April 1943

Not only did Bruce swiftly acquire a reputation as a serial escaper, but he also became known as a recalcitrant. There was a good reason for this. His attitude to his capitivity—and to his captors—hardened after he received news from home in April 1942.

Bruce was always apprehensive when he opened mail from New Zealand. He had had his share of good news and bad. For this reason, he was nervous when he received four letters at once. He could tell from the handwriting that one was from his parents and another from his sister Betty. The writing on the other two was unfamiliar. He opened the envelope from his folks, ignoring the sections blacked out by the censor, and read the short letter. They addressed him using his family nickname:

Boy, Nothing much to report at home. Norm's broken leg is on the mend and he gets the plaster cast cut off next week. Jo has had the flu quite badly but is over the worst of it and she's coming right, too. We haven't heard from Alan for a while but we think he's okay. One never knows what's happening in this war so we're a bit worried about him.

There wasn't much else apart from a few snippets of gossip about wartime life in New Zealand. It ended with:

We hope you're well and that your life in the POW camp isn't too harsh. We think of you often.

The envelope with Betty's handwriting contained two letters: one from her and one from his other sister, Jo. It was much the same gossip, but it was good to know that, minor ailments aside, everyone was well.

He opened the next letter:

Dear Bruce,
I don't know how to break this to you, but our dear son Cecil was killed in action on 23 November 1941. I know how close you were to Cecil. You two were best pals so I know this news will hit you just as hard as it has hit us. We're told he died bravely so that's some consolation. He was our only son so Doris and I have taken the news very hard. We're doing our best to cope but we're not dealing with it at all well. Blackie White was killed on the same day in the same battle so that was a double kick in the guts. Sorry to break this to you while you're holed up in a POW camp but we knew you would want to know.
Yours sincerely,
Cliff Logan

"Jesus Christ," Bruce croaked.

"You right, Brucie?" Frank looked up from reading his own mail.

Bruce couldn't answer. His throat had closed up. He had to re-read the letter before he could begin to believe it. He opened the fourth envelope with shaking hands.

It was from Alf White, Blackie's father, who repeated the bad news. Both Blackie and Logie had fought bravely but died within minutes of each other in the same battle at some place called Sidi Rezegh. Bruce vaguely recalled hearing about the heavy casualties the New Zealand Division had suffered there, thanks to the German propaganda that circulated around the camp. But he always took these bulletins with a grain of salt, and it hadn't occurred to him for a second that his mates might be among those killed. There was a fair chance he'd have been among them, too, if he hadn't been captured. As he sat there, mourning his mates, Bruce almost wished he had been.

While Bruce was no saint when it came to his vocabulary, "fuck" was a word he kept in reserve for specially trying circumstances. With his world in tatters, now was the hour.

"Christ, is there no justice in this fucked-up world?" he moaned.

The thought of reuniting with Logie and Blackie after the war was one of the few things that had kept him sane and gave him a purpose in life. There was little emotion in the letters, but Bruce knew the parents well and knew their grief would be overwhelming.

———

As POWs from the North Africa campaign trickled into the camp, Bruce was there to ask them if they had known Blackie or Logie. Finally, a man named Rusty Hayhurst nodded and said that he had fought alongside them at Sidi Rezegh. Logie had taken one in the chest and had died some hours later after the medics had done everything they could to save him. Blackie's death was more puzzling. Rusty saw what happened, and heard others talking about it afterward.

"We were behind this ridge, and we were taking heavy fire. Blackie just upped and ran over the top, firing his rifle like a madman. He didn't get far. He muttered something before he did it. I thought he said 'Fuck the Boche,' but some of the blokes who were closer reckoned it was 'Fuck the bitch.' S'pose we'll never know. He'd only just found out he'd copped a dose, so it could have been the second one."

Bruce closed his eyes upon hearing this. He remembered as clear as yesterday Blackie saying "I'd rather die" when Bruce had asked if he was worried about venereal disease.

The next few days were the blackest Bruce had known, including the spell in the hospital during which he had contemplated suicide. Those in his combine were worried about him, especially Frank.

"I wasn't there when they needed me, Frank," Bruce mumbled one day. "If I'd been there, they'd still be alive."

"How d'you reckon that?" Frank replied.

Bruce shrugged. "I could have done something to stop it. I've failed my best mates."

The camp doctor prescribed a cocktail of pills, but nothing made much difference. Bruce lay in his bunk for five days straight. He couldn't work, he hardly ate, and he wouldn't talk.

The only thing that got through to him was when Frank, as exasperated as he was concerned, finally said to him, "These mates of yours. They don't sound like the sorts who'd admire the way you're carrying on. Is this how they'd want you to remember them?"

Bruce glared at him from his bunk. "Fuck you, Frank," he said.

"That's more like it," Frank said, relieved.

But even at the end of that time, when he snapped out of it, Bruce recognized that something had changed in him. He could never forgive himself for not being there alongside his mates at Sidi Rezegh.

———

His grief brought a hard edge to his confrontations with the guards, particularly his regular run-ins with a bumptious little Hitler clone known to all and sundry as "The Skunk," thanks to his surname, Schunke. His given name of Dieter meant he was sometimes called Dirty Skunk. But mostly it was just The Skunk. Bruce's relationship with him was toxic from the outset, but around the time he learned of the tragic loss of his mates it descended into open, mutual hatred.

The Skunk had put Bruce in solitary more often than all the other guards combined. Known variously as the cooler, the slammer, the dungeon, the bunker, and the hole, even the best of the solitary confinement cells were hovel-like. The Skunk invariably dumped Bruce in the worst in the block, right next to a broken sewage pipe. It was a dark, dank shithole, with moldy, suicide-gray concrete walls and a caked-mud floor. Bruce was given one torn blanket, a grimy cup, a spoon, and a towel. A bucket sat in one corner for ablutions and he usually created a makeshift screen from the blanket to give himself some privacy. Worst of all, he was only allowed to shave twice a week, a form of torture for Bruce.

Goon-baiting or run-of-the-mill abuse earned up to seven days in solitary. Obstructing a guard could fetch anywhere from seven to twelve. Escape was a mandatory minimum of twenty-one days, and it might be followed by a transfer to a *Strafe Lager*, a disciplinary camp. Striking a goon attracted the harshest punishment of all: the maximum time permissible under camp rules. Even accidentally bumping into a guard might be enough to have Bruce thrown into the slammer, although few such collisions were accidental. Bruce had been in the hole so often that he sardonically called it his home away from home. He often wondered why he retaliated as he did, knowing what the punishment would be, but in the end it felt like earning a badge of honor: it signified he had done something to strike at his captors. While he was serving his time, though, he wished he were somewhere else. Anywhere else.

One unseasonably hot day in September 1942—it was close to eighty-two degrees—Bruce was working with a crew repairing tracks near the main Maribor railway station. The station was close to the town center, so The Skunk had brought his mistress along, doubtless to show her off to the POWs. She was a knockout, way out of The Skunk's league, and obviously enjoying the benefits that went with a Nazi liaison. She paraded her wares with the sensuality of an exotic dancer, plainly aware of the effect a show of cleavage would have on the sex-starved prisoners. Evidently she was enjoying herself, but The Skunk didn't seem to be. He was noted for his short fuse, and today something was definitely niggling him. It wasn't even lunchtime and he'd already used his rifle butt to send one POW to the infirmary to have an ugly wound stitched. He'd also forced another prisoner who was complaining of feeling faint to carry on working in the full heat of the sun. When the inevitable happened and the man collapsed, The Skunk had kicked him in the stomach. The prisoner had vomited, and Bruce had lost it.

"Stop it!" he shouted at The Skunk. "That's enough. Treat us decently or we'll down tools."

There was a murmur of agreement from the others in the work detail. The threat of a stop-work was a dangerous tactic to use with any guard, but much more so with The Skunk.

"Get back to work now, you lazy bastards, or I'll shoot every one of you," he said in German. To show that he wasn't bluffing, he unslung his rifle, worked the bolt, and fired a shot dangerously close to Bruce's head.

"You maniac!" Bruce shouted, his ears still ringing. "*Verrückter!* You'll kill someone if you shoot that thing off again!"

The Skunk sneered at him.

"That's it!" Bruce said. He threw down his shovel. "We're not taking any more of this. Come on, guys. Let's show this German prick he can't mess with us."

There was a clatter of metal as first one, then another, then the entire gang dropped their tools and folded their arms, glaring at The Skunk.

The Skunk had gone white with rage. He worked the bolt on his rifle again and fired into the air.

"Work!" he shouted in English. "Back to work now!"

No one moved.

As his girlfriend watched him with interest, The Skunk ejected the spent cartridge, slammed home the bolt of his rifle and leveled it at Bruce.

"Work," he ordered.

Bruce shook his head.

The Skunk's girlfriend looked from one to the other like a spectator at a tennis match.

"Work, or die!" shrieked The Skunk, gesturing with the rifle at Bruce's shovel.

Bruce shook his head again.

The Skunk aimed a little to the left of Bruce's temple and fired again. Without pausing to think, Bruce rushed him, knocking the rifle aside and landing a decent punch flush on the German's jaw. His girlfriend screamed. The shots and her shout brought the other goons rushing from the shed, one of them still holding the hand of cards he'd been playing. Bruce was grabbed by both arms and shoved face-first against the concrete wall.

The Skunk scrambled up from the ground. He grabbed Bruce by his collar and bashed his head against the wall. He did it again, once, twice. Bruce could feel blood trickling down his neck. The Skunk released him and was about to kick him in the back when he spotted the bars of Red Cross chocolate Bruce had stashed in his canvas bag, which was now lying on the ground with its contents strewn all over the gravel. Chocolate was a precious commodity, rarely available to rank-and-file soldiers. The Skunk's eyes lit up.

"Give me those," he demanded.

Bruce said nothing.

"*Jetzt!*" The Skunk commanded. "Pick the chocolate up now and give it to Gretchen." He knew Bruce understood German. "Get down on your knees and pick it up before I blow your brains out!"

Still Bruce said nothing and looked defiantly at The Skunk. It was a standoff.

"You think you can disobey a German officer and get away with it?"

"A German pig, more like it."

Ignoring the insult, the apoplectic Skunk roared at Bruce, "Get that chocolate right now or you're a dead man."

Bruce bent down, picked up the Red Cross chocolate, and turned toward The Skunk. "I'd rather toss it in the crapper than give it to your whore," he said calmly as he shoved it back in the canvas bag.

The Skunk grabbed a rail fork and lunged at Bruce, who tried to twist aside, but the weapon tore his tunic and pierced his midriff. Bruce connected with another wild uppercut. But he was outnumbered. A pistol butt was brutally slammed into the side of his face. He nearly fell, but he was dragged upright and the blow was repeated. This time, they let him fall, and The Skunk laid into him with his boot. Bruce saw stars, and something in his jaw cracked. Several more blows connected, then The Skunk was ripping the chocolate from his bag. Bruce opened one puffy eye to see the German standing speechless with rage as the chocolate, by then melted by the sun, oozed through his fingers onto his uniform jacket. It looked for all the world as though he had fished it out from the very place Bruce had threatened to toss it. Bruce managed a wry smile before he lapsed into unconsciousness.

The Skunk forbade anyone to move Bruce. He lay in a pool of his own blood in the blistering sun until the day's shift was over, and only then were his comrades permitted to help him back to the camp. They made to take him to the *Lazarett* but Bruce refused. The camp infirmary was no place for the sick, anyway, and he didn't want to give The Skunk the satisfaction of seeing him hospitalized. Instead, a Canadian vet cleaned and stitched his wounds as best he could.

He ended up in the camp hospital anway. By morning, he was babbling incoherently, and seemed unable to recognize his mates. It was hard to say whether he was suffering more from sunstroke or from the head injuries.

It took him two days to recover from the worst of his confusion. On the third day, while he still lay on the bare boards of his bed in the *Lazarett*, Bruce was informed he was to be transferred to another camp "for disciplinary reasons." First, though, as soon as he was well enough to be moved, he was to go to the main regional hospital camp at Stalag XVIIIB at Spittal an der Drau, where better medical facilities were available. Although he was now mostly lucid and intelligible, he was still suffering frequent dizzy spells and blackouts.

"Getting rid of you at last, are we? Thank Christ for that," Frank said as Bruce was being prepared for his transfer.

"Yup. Can't wait to get something better to look at than your ugly mug," Bruce replied.

They shook hands.

"Well, you know where to find me till the war's over," Frank said. "After that, you'd better write to me here." He handed Bruce a piece of paper with his English address on it. Bruce borrowed a pencil and paper and returned the favor.

"Thanks," said Frank. "Now piss off, ya silly sod."

————

Bruce was in the hospital at Stalag XVIIIB for almost three weeks before he was given a clean bill of health. He was well looked after, and almost sorry to be discharged. After his release he was placed in one of the huts until details of his transfer were finalized. He was informed that he was being sent to the main regional camp at Wolfsberg, Stalag XVIIIA.

The transfer from Spittal an der Drau to Wolfsberg was a straight-forward drive, a pleasant enough diversion for Bruce after the tedium of the hospital camp. He was, however, furious with himself. He had been about as comfortable at Stalag XVIIID as it was possible to be: he had good mates, a good rapport with some of the guards, and he knew whom it was best to avoid. He was a fool, he told himself, to have thrown all that away on account of The Skunk. But, when he was honest with himself, he didn't regret standing up to the bullying bastard; he would do it all over again if the same circumstances arose.

It was November 1942 when he was processed into Stalag XVIIIA. He was told that he would be in the main camp for a week before he would be sent out on work detail. Beyond a warning that any resistance shown to the guards would be severely punished, there didn't seem to be any particular ill will shown toward him for the incident that had led to his transfer.

Soon after he had unpacked his kit in his new accommodation, Bruce spotted a familiar and unexpected figure walking across the compound.

"You, ya lazy bum," Bruce yelled. "What's a slob like you doing in a classy joint like this?"

"Bloody hell, it's Murray." Frank Butler beamed. "Talk about a bad penny. I thought I'd got rid of you."

It turned out Frank had been transferred around the same time as Bruce. He knew Bruce was bound for Spittal an der Drau and perhaps another, unknown camp after that. Neither of them had expected to end up at the same place. The happy reunion was cemented with more illicit wine than was healthy for either of them.

Frank was due to leave for an *Arbeitskommando* at Radkersburg a few days later. He sipped his hooch and winced.

"Why don't you just ask the guv'nor to send you to Radkersburg with me?" he said. "The Jerries couldn't care less where you go as long as they get you out of their hair. Give it a go, me old china. You never know. It might just bloody work."

"All right. I'll give it a go," Bruce muttered, not convinced the plan had any merit.

After Frank left for his new work camp, Bruce made the most of his free time. He got to take in a concert, watch a fiercely contested football match, and enjoy a brass band recital. It also transpired that he had arrived just in time for the opening of a brand-new, prisoner-built 250-seat theater, with all the bells and whistles that might be expected on the West End—a grand stage, proper orchestra pit, and a projection booth. Bruce saw *Mississippi Showboat* staged there.

———

When he was informed that he would be sent out to work, Bruce did what he had promised Frank: he asked to be assigned to the Radkersburg work camp. It wasn't like asking for a promotion at Prestige Hosiery or applying for a new job. You went where you were told. But as he had always said, "If you don't ask, you don't get."

He didn't get, anyway. He was dispatched to Workcamp 1971/L near Weinburg am Saßbach, where he spent a very unhappy three months. One day, for no apparent reason, he was told to pack his gear and get ready to move. Perhaps someone in the hierarchy had finally acted on his request. More likely it was just good luck. Whatever the reason, Bruce found himself on a truck bound for Radkersburg.

Work camp 296/L in Radkersburg housed twenty-four men. The "L" stood for *Landwirtschaft,* or farmwork. It was a former oil mill and the POWs were rostered to work on various farms in the district.

The men all slept in one large room with two iron stoves for cooking and heating. The conditions were tolerable and the facilities decent enough but there was one guard who was neither tolerable nor decent. Günter Jercke represented everything that was bad about Nazi Germany. He derived his pleasure from bullying others, and Bruce pitied his wife, if he had one. With a surname like Jercke, he might have been nicknamed "The Jerk," but he was called "Psycho" by the POWs for no other reason than that was what he was. He was evil, manipulative, arrogant, and sadistic, and he had beaten, bashed, and abused just about every prisoner in the *Arbeitskommando*. Each night, he confiscated the boots and trousers of all the POWs, ostensibly to prevent escapes but more likely just to embarrass and inconvenience them. Bruce loathed this practice, not just because he missed his clothes but because it denied him the opportunity to fold and press his trousers under his mattress as he had done every night since he first arrived at the Maribor POW camp, and his normally mirror-shined boots were returned to him each morning still covered with mud.

Bruce was assigned first to the Wagner farm. No one else wanted to work there, and, being the new boy, he had drawn the short straw. He soon found out why. Kurt Wagner was a Nazi-loving hard-arse.

"I hate you Tommy bastards," were the first words he spoke to Bruce, emphasizing the derogatory term for British soldiers. "I'd stick a bayonet up your arse, given half a chance. So far up you'd feel it ripping your guts apart. By the time you leave here, you'll be wishing you'd been shot and killed, not captured."

Bruce had no doubt he meant what he said and, sure enough, Wagner was determined to make life hell for any POW unlucky enough to be sent to his farm. Bruce wondered whether some whisper of the reason for his transfer from Stalag XVIIID had reached Psycho and Wagner, because between them they seemed hell-bent on provoking a repeat performance. With insult piled upon insult, it was only a matter of time before they succeeded.

Bruce was shoveling shit when he lost it. More accurately, he was lugging buckets of the stuff from the cesspit by the barn out into the fields. There were two of them manning the buckets—Bruce and a chap called "Hoppy" Hopkinson—and every time the rancorous Wagner chastised either for moving too slowly, Psycho, who was the supervising goon, shoved the offender in the back with the muzzle of his rifle, causing the stinking mess to spill out over the sides of the fully loaded pails and onto his clothes. Within an hour, their trousers, tunics, and boots had crap smeared all over them. Bruce was seething.

"You can't force us to do this," he told Psycho in no uncertain terms. "It's against the rules. You know bloody well POWs don't have to *schaufel scheisse*. We can refuse to do this sort of work."

He had no idea whether the Geneva Convention supported his stance. It was academic, anyway, as Psycho hefted a shovel and cracked him in the ribs with the blade.

"Get back to work," he ordered.

Bruce made it through the day, and as soon as he got back to 296/L he set about washing his clothes. He scrubbed them until he had almost worn through the fabric and still he wasn't satisfied they were properly clean. He was wringing them out when a shadow fell across him.

"Give me those," Psycho demanded. He leaned over and grabbed the trousers and dumped them in the corner in a pile with everyone else's, still stinking of manure. Bruce protested, asking for them back so that he could hang them out to dry.

"They'll stay here until I say you can have them back. *Verstanden?* I make the rules here. I'll decide what you can and can't do. If I don't like you—and I've already decided I don't—I'll make your miserable little life even more miserable. Mark my words. Now get back to your bunk before I break every bone in your useless kriegie body."

Bruce's clothes lay there all night, sopping wet. When he put them on the following morning they were still sodden and, to Bruce's sensitive nose, had a distinct barnyard odor. It was uncomfortable working in soggy clothes, particularly on a cold morning, and Bruce was in a dark mood before he even started. His mood didn't improve when he drew bucket duty again.

It wasn't just the stench that got to Bruce, although God knows that was bad enough. It was all the sloppy crap covering his clothes that caused him to lose his mind. By early afternoon, he'd had enough.

"I'm done, Hoppy," he said. "I can't take any more of this crap. Literally."

He set down his wooden pail. Psycho, who appeared to have been waiting for this moment, prodded him with his rifle barrel. Once too often as it happened. Bruce stooped, picked up the bucket, spun, and, with a sweeping motion, sent the contents in an arc over Psycho and Wagner, who was close behind.

"If you dish out the shit to others, you've got to be prepared to take it yourself," he shouted at the slime-covered Psycho.

Wagner swore and cursed as he hurried toward the farmhouse.

"Pump the Tommy bastard full of lead!" he shouted over his shoulder to Psycho. Psycho needed no encouragement. After he had swiped the worst of the muck from his uniform, he laid into Bruce with boot and fist. Bruce barely lifted a finger to defend himself, his satisfaction making him partially immune to the pain.

And, when the authorities at Stalag XVIIIA came to consider the matter, Bruce was amazed to receive a mere seven days in the cooler. It turned out that Psycho was as despised by his comrades as he was by the kriegies, and he had been the subject of a very unfavorable Red Cross report into the treatment of prisoners at *Arbeitskommando* 296/L. By the time Bruce had finished his stint of solitary, Psycho was gone, demoted and transferred. Nor did Bruce have to return to the Wagner farm. He received word he was to be sent to another in the area, this one belonging to a family named Rossnegger.

Chapter Sixteen

———

Bruce & Josefine, Radkersburg, March to August 1943

Good God!"

Josefine paused. She didn't understand the words, but she caught the inflection. She was pouring coffee for the new farm laborer, a British prisoner of war who had been assigned in place of one of the pair her cousin had recently sacked. Now he was staring at her, a look of mingled shock and delight on his face.

"It's you!" he said, then switched to German. "It's you! It's really you!"

She considered him. So far as she could tell, she had never seen this man before in her life.

"I'm afraid I don't know what you mean," she said coolly, and resumed pouring. The fragrant steam wreathed her face.

He opened his mouth as though to speak, then closed it again.

He glanced around at the others: his POW workmate, the elderly guard, who was sipping his coffee with a look of rapture on his face—it was the real thing, not the ersatz variety—and Gustl, the sour-faced farmer, who was watching the exchange closely.

"*Danke*," he said, when she had filled his cup.

Josefine busied herself stacking the bowls from lunch, and when she was sure everyone else was preoccupied she covertly studied the man who had spoken to her. Perhaps there was something familiar about him, but she couldn't possibly have met him before. She was sure she remembered the faces of all of the foreigners whom she had helped along the escape lines. And the only interaction she'd ever had with prisoners of war beyond that was with the scruffy man to whom she'd passed the note back in Slovenia, miles away from here. This man, in his polished boots and trousers with their sharp creases, and with his immaculately combed hair, was not him.

He had plainly mistaken her for someone else.

———

Bruce had often thought about the young woman wearing an old woman's clothes who had passed him the note through the wire. It was her eyes, he supposed: clear, sea-green, utterly captivating. And now, here she was. For his part, he had no doubt that it was her, as unlikely as it might have seemed.

He took his mug and stood at the door of the barn to smoke a cigarette, resisting the temptation to simply sit and stare at her. He remembered her surname—Lobnik—but he was trying to remember the name from the note. Paolo, Poldo . . . Polde, that was it! Polde. Leopold.

Just before he had finished, he heard Gustl give the order for the return to work. Bruce ground out his fag, took his empty cup to her, and placed it on the tray.

"Have you any news of Leopold?" he asked in a low voice.

She started, and stared at him. Her gaze was ferocious, intense.

"How . . . ?"

"Back to work," growled Gustl.

The girl dropped her eyes, picked up the tray, and walked away.

———

It had to be the POW from Stalag XVIIID to whom she passed the note. How else would he know about Polde? But how could he look so different?

Caution had become a habit for Josefine, so she was analyzing the fleeting exchange she'd had with the man for any possibility that it might have looked suspicious to the guard or, she admitted to herself, to Gustl. The guard was a harmless old fellow whom she felt inclined to like, despite the uniform he wore. At mealtimes, he regaled them with stories about the First World War, and lost no opportunity to express sorrow that his country found itself embroiled in yet another war. He seemed content to sit this one out on a hay bale and dream rather than to actually supervise the prisoners. Gustl was probably more of a concern. He made no secret of his disapproval of Josefine and the danger her partisan activities had brought to his farm.

Josefine remembered that day at the camp. The man—it had to be this man—had deliberately moved to block the German guard from shooting at her. He must have continued to obstruct him, because no shot was fired. He could have been shot himself.

He had also done as she asked and made inquiries about Polde, which would have put him in more danger. And it was both brave and unusually determined of him to have sent the note via the plumber. She must thank him for taking so many risks on her behalf.

She remembered the note, with its strange last lines, and she felt her usual, reflexive distaste for the way men always seemed to react to her. She had been propositioned countless times by the German swine, but also by some of her fellow partisans, and even by one or two of the escaping prisoners she had helped. It dismayed her that men seemed intent on chasing women for their own satisfaction regardless of the circumstances. There was a man named Kramer in Radkersburg—he had been a neighbor of the Rossneggers for as long as she had been coming to Austria—who had begun blackmailing young women with the threat of denouncing them to the Nazis as traitors unless they gave in to his demands for sex. He had tried this ruse on Josefine, who had spurned him. And, of course, Jelka's tragedy had cemented her conviction that men were heedless of anyone's interests other than their own.

She remembered that gesture of the POW's—trying to smooth his hair, as futile in the state it was in as putting a coat of paint on a shipwreck. It made slightly more sense now that she had seen him as she supposed he normally was.

She caught herself smiling slightly. That made her frown.

———

It was late in the day before Bruce had another chance to talk to the Lobnik girl. She was scouring out the milk pails, ready for the morning milking, and Gustl had sent him to the barn to return the pitchforks and the shovels.

She glanced up as he approached and then looked away without acknowledging his smile. But, as he passed her, she spoke.

"I must thank you for everything you did for my family," she said rather formally. "You put yourself in danger for us. We are very grateful to you."

"Have you had any news of your brother?" he asked, thrilled that she was talking to him.

She shook her head.

"A very close friend saw him arrested by the Nazis. That is all we've heard of him."

Bruce noted her reference to a "very close friend." How close, he wondered.

"My family believes Polde is dead, but I refuse to give up hope."

She looked up at him, her expression defiant, as though daring him to voice any doubts.

"Anyway," she said. "Thank you."

"It was nothing," he replied and shrugged as if to say "It's what I would have done for anyone," but they both knew the guard might well have shot him for interfering.

"When you ran from the wire, you fell. Did you hurt yourself?"

She grimaced. "Yes, I hurt my knee. I couldn't walk properly for several weeks, which is why I didn't come back. I sent a friend, but she was scared off by the guards."

Bruce remembered the other young woman he had seen, how sure he'd been that it was not her.

"Thank you for sending the message with the plumber."

"I hoped you'd come back," Bruce said. "I was worried when you didn't."

She said nothing more. She stood, took the pails into the barn, and then, without another word to him, walked off in the direction of the house. He gazed after her, congratulating himself on having learned to speak German. He was also reflecting that the chance encounter—the odds of ever seeing her again must have been millions to one—was the best birthday present he had ever received. The date was March 3, 1943. Bruce had just turned twenty-seven.

———

Bruce liked life on the Rossnegger farm. Gustl was a tough boss, but Mitzl was kind to the prisoners when she had no need to be. Food was plentiful and she served up generous helpings of local favorites such as Gulasch, Leberkäse, Tafelspitz, and a variety of wurst. She was a good cook and Josefine helped her most days when she was not out on the farm herself.

Bruce knew he was onto a good thing, so he did his best to ingratiate himself to Gustl. Although he was a soft-handed city boy who made his living from silk stockings, he did his level best to master every task he was given. The Rossnegger farm mostly grew barley and wheat—by now, in June, the new stalks were rippling in the breeze—but they ran a few dairy cattle, planted potatoes, and raised chickens as well. He tugged on cows' teats and scattered wheat and grit for the madly pecking birds and, all the while, kept one eye open for Josefine, whom he hardly ever saw.

But one day he was in the potato field scratching ineffectually at the dirt with a hoe when she suddenly appeared beside him.

"Here," she said. "I'll show you how."

In her hands, the hoe caused the rich brown earth to crumble readily. Bruce watched her work appreciatively.

"I'm not much good at farmwork," he confided. "Although I'm better at farmwork than I am at railways or roadwork. I'm a production manager back home, in a factory making . . ." The German word for "lingerie" eluded him, so he pointed at her ankle and mimed rolling a pair of stockings up his leg.

"Ah," she said. "We have no use for this kind of thing these days."

She gave him a wintry smile and held out the hoe to him.

"A pity. After the war, perhaps," he said.

"Perhaps then," she replied.

"Bruce," he said, taking the hoe.

"Sorry?"

"My name is Bruce. Bruce Murray."

She stared at him. Her expression softened slightly.

"Lobnik," she said shyly, then shook her head. "Of course, you already know that I'm Lobnik. Josefine."

"Josefine," he said. "Nice to meet you again, Josefine."

"Nice to meet you, too, Bruce," she replied.

She pronounced his name "Brooz." He didn't correct her. Instead, he grinned like an idiot. He was still grinning like an idiot when he resumed hoeing.

"She told me her name, Frank," he said as soon as he got back to the *Arbeitskommando.* "I think she likes me."

"Who? What?" Frank replied, although he knew full well. Bruce had been bending his ear about Josefine every day since he'd started work at the Rossnegger farm.

"The Lobnik girl. The girl from Maribor."

"Be sensible, Brucie. Nothing'll come of it, you mark my words," said Frank, anxious to make sure his friend didn't raise his hopes too high.

———

"Spring," she said.

"What's that?" he replied, startled. He hadn't even heard her approach. He was scything tall grass in the hay meadow, enjoying the sun on his back and whistling while he worked.

"You were whistling 'Spring,'" she said. "Vivaldi."

"Was I?" he said, and whistled another bar. "I know the tune but I have to admit I know little about the classical composers."

"You whistle well. Do you play a musical instrument?" she asked.

"Sadly, no. I wish I had learned when I was younger," Bruce replied. "But I love to listen to music."

"So do I," she said. "I miss music most of all from the time before the war."

It was the most he had heard her say at any one time, and it was information about her life, freely given. He was desperate to keep her talking.

"What's your favorite music?" he asked.

"Bach," she said. "I love Bach. Even if he is a German."

"I think I know some Bach," Bruce offered. He whistled a snatch of the Goldberg variations. "That's a piece my mother used to play on the . . ." He groped for the word for "piano."

"*Das klavier*," she supplied for him.

"That's it," he said. "*Das klavier*."

His German was improving, but he still found it a barrier to easy conversation. There was his inadequate vocabulary to start with, and a slightly stilted formality to the sentence structure.

They were smiling at each other. Her smile, he thought, was like the sun breaking through clouds.

———

Little by little, in this way, he learned more about her, and she about him. Snatched conversations in German, their common love of music, working alongside each other, and the occasional shared meal slowly brought them closer together.

A chance comment she made one day indicated that she had a source of information about how the war was proceeding.

"Where do you hear the news?" he asked.

She shot him a look. He understood he was asking for far too much information.

"Sorry," he said, holding up his hands placatingly.

"A radio," she said after a while, and quietly. "I know people who listen to the radio. To the BBC news. I sometimes visit them and listen, too."

He knew that, for her, telling him this was a leap of faith. Because of the day they first met, he knew she was prepared to take risks. But he sensed that she would not lightly risk the lives and fates of others, especially if they were dear to her. He felt humbled, as though he had been handed a precious thing.

"You can trust me," he said. "I won't tell anyone."

She didn't reply.

———

Bruce was marched back to the *Arbeitskommando* every night. He went cheerfully. He was no longer concerned about being locked up because he knew that he could leave any time he liked. Bruce had noticed the loose bar next to his bunk shortly after he arrived at 296/L. When the old oil mill had been converted into a work camp three bars had been fitted to each window for security, and Bruce had been leaning against the middle one by his bunk when he felt it give a little. Closer examination revealed that it was a little too short to reach from the top sill of the window to the bottom, so it was free to move up and down in the metal sockets that were screwed to the sills.

"Bugger me," he said to himself. "I can take this little beauty out."

One night, he unscrewed the bracket and gouged out the sill beneath with a penknife he had stolen from Psycho. He filled the cavity with Plasticine—traded with a guard for chocolate—and replaced the bar and the bracket. Now, whenever he wanted, he could pull the bar downward and it would come free of the bracket at the top. He could now come and go pretty much as he pleased, so long as he was sure the guards were asleep and he was back by dawn. He shared his secret with Frank, of course, but no one else. He thought about making a run for it and getting away for good, but he had learned his lesson from his two failed escape attempts. He had satisfied himself that any further bids for freedom would be futile without outside support from the partisans or friendly locals. Nor did he abuse the privilege—apart from a couple of trips to steal fruit from the Wagner farm. It was amazing how good it was for the soul to know that he could fly the coop if he wanted to.

———

So far as he could gather from Josefine, the tide in the war was turning. The Allies were inflicting defeats on the Axis forces.

"According to the BBC," she told him one day, "the Allied Navy has sunk a whole lot of U-boats in the Atlantic and they say that this might be the beginning of the end for the German Navy."

"That's wonderful news," Bruce replied. "I'll spread the word around the boys at the camp. Please tell me about anything else you hear. We're starved for news here and everyone's anxious to know how the war's going. All we get is one-sided Nazi propaganda, which would have you believe the war for us is as good as over."

Josefine did keep him posted. The news continued to be positive. Late that summer, as they were baling straw amid the sweet scent of the hay, she told him that the BBC had reported a victory to the Russians on the Eastern Front at a place named Kursk. The Germans had launched a major offensive and had been beaten back. It was the first significant reversal of fortune for the Nazi war machine that Bruce could remember.

"Do you think I could come and listen to the radio one night?" he asked Josefine.

She looked at him sharply. It was plain she thought he was joking.

It was Bruce's turn to entrust her with a piece of information that would have cost him dearly had it fallen into the hands of the camp authorities. He told her about the loose window bar, and about his raids on Wagner's orchard. She was the only person apart from Frank whom he told.

"It's too risky," she said. "If you were seen, my aunt and uncle would be shot."

It was the first time she had mentioned her relationship to the owners of the radio. But it was understood between them: she and Bruce now trusted each other.

"And if you were caught, you'd be punished. Perhaps even sent away."

He glanced at her.

"I wouldn't like that," he said. "To be sent away."

She didn't answer, but she realized that she wouldn't like it, either.

———

A week later, Josefine found an excuse to be near Bruce out of earshot of any of the others. "If you really can get away as you say, I could meet you at ten tonight just down the road where Altdörflweg meets Webersiedlungsweg. You know where I mean—right by the Gasthaus. My uncle and aunt will allow you to come and listen to the radio."

He stared at her, dumbfounded.

"I didn't think you'd ask them," he said. "You said it was too risky."

She shrugged. "If they're willing to take the risk, then so am I."

Bruce could hardly wait for ten o'clock to come around. Frank told him he was mad, but when the time came he pretended to be nonchalant.

"Go on, then," he said. "Mind you, make sure you listen to the news while you're gazing at your sweetheart."

"It's not like that," said Bruce. Trouble was, it felt like that. He hadn't felt this nervous since he'd first plucked up the courage to ask Doreen out, all those years ago. The butterflies had nothing to do with the danger of being caught.

Bruce wriggled out of the window and used the Plasticine to

secure the bar in place. Treading as softly as he could, he made his
way to the rendezvous point. Josefine was there, just as she had said
she would be.

"This is foolish," she said.

"I know," he replied. "And wonderful."

As they walked, they talked in low voices. Josefine told him about
Agatha and Josef Hamler, her favorite aunt and uncle. They had no
children of their own, she told him, and treated her like a daughter.
They were relatively wealthy; Josef was a master stonemason who
sculpted headstones. War was good for business. They were careful with their money: heating was considered an unnecessary ex-
travagance, even in winter, and hot water was reserved for special
occasions. But they were as generous with their love as they were
parsimonious with their pennies and Josefine adored them.

They approached a large house. Josef Hamler answered the door
at Josefine's soft knock.

He was a tiny fellow, barely up to Bruce's shoulder and as thin as a
spindle. His skin was wrinkled like a crumpled sheet, and he sported
a bushy moustache out of all proportion to his impish face. The rem-
nants of several meals clinging to his overgrown whiskers would have
fed a large colony of ants.

"Welcome, welcome," said Josef. He shook Bruce's hand
warmly, and kissed his niece's cheek with his bristling whiskers.
"Please come in."

He showed Bruce into the kitchen. A large dining table sat in the
middle, covered with a crocheted tablecloth—for decorative rather
than everyday use—and three ornate barley-twist chairs were lined
along each side with a carver at each end.

"This is my wife, Agatha," Josef said.

Agatha was a plump woman of average height and well above average weight. She had a kindly face but something of a bad-tempered
twist to her mouth. Josefine had told Bruce she was fearsome when she

was riled. It was odd seeing how deferential she was to her diminutive husband.

"This way, this way," she said, and bustled them into a large living room with a few nondescript paintings adorning the walls. A huge, elaborately carved French dresser dominated the room. There were two portraits from an earlier generation hanging above the fireplace. Bruce thought they looked like Agatha's parents. Bookcases completely covered one of the walls and the only other furniture was a couch and two armchairs. Josef couldn't see the point in spending money on furniture unless it had a purpose.

Josef came in carrying a mahogany Radiola, which he plugged in and turned on. It was a while before the valves warmed up, and, meanwhile, he and Agatha quizzed Bruce about his wartime experiences.

Josef produced a bottle of brandy. "This," he said, "is strictly for special occasions and honored guests!"

They all settled in to listen: Bruce and Josef on the armchairs, Josefine and Agatha on the couch.

The radio began emitting a swirl of static. Josef assured them that it just needed tuning in correctly and minutely adjusted the dial, but the only reward was the usual cacophony of whistles and squeals. Then they caught the sound of a voice and some reedy music. The familiar BBC theme broke through the hissing and screeching of the wireless set and, as if deferring to the war's most credible news source, most of the background noise miraculously disappeared.

A booming, baritone voice announced, "This is the BBC Overseas Service."

The news covered all the major war events, including a couple of Allied setbacks, but the item that excited the group huddled around the set was a report that the Allies had established a beachhead in Sicily—a critical breakthrough. They toasted this news with brandy. Buoyed with both the liquor and renewed hopes that the war might yet go the Allies' way, Bruce made his way back to the camp and slithered through the window.

"Well?" said Frank. "What news from the front?"

"The news is all good. I think things are finally starting to go our way, Frankie boy," Bruce replied.

"Spare me," said Frank. "Forget your love life. I was talking about the bleeding war."

———

The late-night visits to listen to the radio became a habit. Soon Bruce was visiting Josef and Agatha Hamler with Josefine once a week, sometimes twice. But as much as he enjoyed the evenings with the Hamlers, Bruce treasured the time spent alone with Josefine far more. Walking and talking with her, or simply sharing a companionable silence, he felt like the luckiest man alive. He wondered what she was thinking, how she felt. He noticed that they took longer and longer to cover the short distance from the crossroads to the Hamlers' house, and it wasn't him dragging his toes. He supposed she also enjoyed the walks.

She seemed fascinated by details of New Zealand. She had never heard of it, she admitted, and couldn't begin to think where it was on the globe. She declared herself puzzled as to why men would travel such a great distance to fight someone else's war. When he asked, Josefine explained how it was that she was Slovene but with relatives in Austria. He hadn't previously had the foggiest idea about the complicated geopolitics of the place in which he had ended up.

They talked about their families—their parents, their siblings. Josefine didn't tell Bruce about her family's partisan connections nor that her sister and brother had been tortured by the Nazis. Not even that her father had been terrorized by the invaders. Bruce didn't tell her about Doreen. He could imagine how it would sound to her if he told her he was in a loveless marriage, and that his wife didn't understand him, and so on and so forth. He supposed she had heard those lines, or lines just like them, from every German soldier she had ever met. And worse than risking her forming a low opinion of him was the possibility that, when she learned he was married, she might not show any signs of disappointment. Confirmation that she wasn't interested in him at all.

———

One night, while Bruce and Josef were enjoying a whisky after the BBC bulletin, there was a pounding on the door.

Josef threw his head back. "Bloody Nazis. Will they never leave us alone?" He got to his feet and groaned as he bent to unplug the radio.

"You need to hide now," he said to Bruce and Josefine, without a trace of fear in his voice. "Go, Pepi. You know where to go." This was the first time Bruce had heard Josefine referred to as "Pepi" and he was puzzled.

Josefine lit a candle and led Bruce down a set of steep, narrow stairs to a basement. In the house above them, they heard the tramp of boots and loud voices.

"What's this?" Bruce whispered to Josefine, who was fiddling with a wooden panel.

"You'll see."

To all appearances, the four wooden panels along one wall of the cellar were identical, but Josefine actuated some kind of catch and one of them swung open to reveal a small cavity behind it, no larger than a cupboard, with shelves stocked with wine and brandy and enough food and water to last a few days. It had originally been built as a wine cellar, but the crafty Josef had made sure it could double as a secure refuge. He had never trusted the Nazis. Bruce and Josefine squeezed into the alcove, and the door refastened with a click. Josefine snuffed the candle and they were plunged into darkness.

They listened to the sounds above. There was shouting, the noise of doors banging and furniture being roughly shifted, and much indignant shrieking from Agatha.

Soon they heard the sound of boots on the basement stairs. Bruce heard Josefine catch her breath.

"Look everywhere," a voice commanded. "Don't leave a corner untouched. Smash everything if you have to and tear the place apart until you find them. They're here somewhere. I know it."

There was the sound of demolition. Glass broke, wood splintered, metal rang on the stone floor. There was a thud, and then another. One of the soldiers was walking along the wall, attempting to smash the paneling with the butt of his rifle. Bruce felt Josefine's hand grope for his in the dark. He took it, and squeezed it.

The rifle struck the wood right by their heads. The panel buckled but showed no signs of splitting. Nor did the soldier seem to notice anything unusual about the noise. The next blow was farther along. It seemed they had escaped detection.

The noise of destruction slowly petered out, but the soldiers were still there. Bruce and Josefine could hear their lowered voices. They heard the sound of a cork drawn from a bottle, and the clink of glass. A bottle suddenly bounced off the false wall, hit the floor, and smashed. They both jumped, but managed not to cry out.

After another five minutes—it seemed like an hour—there was the sound of boots ascending the stairs. There was further shouting from above, and another flurry of banging and crashing. Then all fell quiet.

"Do you think they've gone?" Josefine breathed.

"I think so," Bruce replied.

Her hand was suddenly on the back of his head and they were kissing. She kissed him fiercely, her soft lips open. Bruce's neck was twisted awkwardly to one side, but he dared not move, in case they were heard, and especially because she might end the embrace. At length, she broke away. Bruce heard her sigh.

———

Afterward, Josefine wasn't sure why she had done what she did. It was completely out of character, but the heart is its own master. Perhaps it was the relief, the profound relief that they had survived. Perhaps it was because, with Bruce beside her in the cupboard, she felt protected—she, who had looked after herself every day since the war began. Or perhaps it was a kind of celebration, an expression of her love for life in defiance of the death that the Nazis had brought. The fact was that it was all of these things. And, although she dared not admit it to herself, it was an acknowledgment that this man from the other side of the world had come to mean something to her.

———

The luminous dial on Bruce's watch showed that it was after three in the morning when Josef's voice finally called them out of hiding. They looked about themselves in horror at the destruction the thugs had wrought, but Josef simply shrugged.

"To hell with them," he said. "They didn't find what they wanted, they didn't find the radio, and we're all safe. That's all that matters. This is all just stuff. We have too much stuff."

"I want to help you clean up," Bruce offered. "I have time before I'm due back at the camp."

"No, no," Josef said. "They seemed to know that my niece came here with a prisoner of war, so the next thing they do will be to check at the camp. Some busybody must have spotted you and reported seeing you here. You must go."

Radkersburg was a small town and 296/L was a small camp, so the POWs were well known to the locals. It was no surprise that someone had recognized Bruce.

Upstairs, the scale of the devastation was worse. It seemed that every drawer in the house had been pulled out and clothes were strewn everywhere. Cabinets and wardrobes had been pushed over. Books had been dragged from bookshelves and pages torn out—wilful vandalism that served no purpose. Even the crockery and cutlery had been hurled all around the place.

"Ach, it's nothing," Josef said. "It's not the first time, and it won't be the last. But I see the price has gone up. It cost two bottles of brandy to get rid of them this time instead of one."

Bruce thanked Josef and Agatha. He faced Josefine, and they were suddenly awkward with each other. He leaned in and gave her a chaste peck on the cheek. Then he hurried off. He was back in his room just before morning wake-up. Less than an hour later, there was a general muster. An SS sergeant had arrived, inquiring about a missing prisoner. He was told all were present and accounted for and went away disappointed.

"Looks like your luck's in, me boy," said Frank.

"You don't know the half of it, Frankie," Bruce said. "Not the bloody half of it."

———

Josefine arrived at the Rossnegger farm around midday. Bruce was wondering how he should approach her when she approached him. Her manner had changed. Her old demeanor was back; it was as though the winter freeze had returned. Bruce didn't dare mention what had happened only hours before.

"Bruce," she said. "Brooz. I must say goodbye. I must leave Radkersburg. After this morning, it's no longer safe for me here."

"What?" Bruce was dumbfounded.

"I'm not who you think I am," she confessed. "I'm a Slovene partisan. I'm on a Nazi death list. Someone has betrayed us. I think it was a man called Kramer. I saw him hanging around Uncle Josef's. He's on the German payroll, so if he finds out who I really am they'll arrest me and there will be trouble for Josef and Agatha and perhaps Mitzl and Gustl, too. And for you. I must leave now."

"Where will you go?" he asked.

She gave him a considering look.

Trust no one. Tell no one, she was thinking.

"I'll return to my family in Maribor," she said. "Enough time has passed so I should be safe there now."

"Will I see you again?" he asked.

"I'll come when I can," she said. "*Ich verspreche*. I promise."

His heart, heavy in his breast, leaped. Something in her eyes told him she meant it.

Chapter Seventeen

—

Bruce & Josefine, Austrian–Slovene Border, August 1943

Halt."

The young guard was typically Aryan: tall, blond, blue-eyed. He might have been considered handsome, Josefine thought, were it not for rosettes of acne marring his face. He didn't look much older than Roman—barely out of school.

That, of course, didn't make him any less dangerous. On the contrary, the young soldier was probably fresh to the uniform and, unlike most of the tired and bored old hands, seemed intent on doing his duty by the book.

"What are you carrying?" he asked her.

She stood and waited as he approached, setting her basket carefully down on the ground, and nervously adjusted the matronly shawl that covered most of her face, camouflaging her youthfulness. Her heart was pounding.

Just before leaving Radkersburg, Josefine had made a rendezvous with a partisan contact in Hauptplatz. He had asked her to make a delivery.

"Eggs," she replied. "I have eggs. See for yourself."

It was true. The basket was brimming with eggs. But beneath the straw lining at the bottom were two German Lugers, a document detailing the movements of two armaments trains from Vienna to Belgrade, and a highly confidential report listing the names of partisan suspects about to be arrested. All had been stolen from Gauleiter Uiberreither's office by an Austrian partisan supporter. The rail timetable was the sort of intelligence the partisans could only dream of. It pinpointed when and where they would need to strike to successfully bomb the railway lines and destroy the arms shipments. The information on proposed partisan arrests would save many lives; it meant that suspects could be warned and evacuated before the purges took place. And the pistols? Well, their purpose was obvious.

The checkpoint had been set up at the Radkersburg end of the Mura bridge. Usually the red-and-black sentry box was empty, and the barrier arm raised. But when Josefine came around the bend in the road her thoughts were still in the Hamlers' cellar, and she noticed too late that the arm was down. There was also a soldier stationed on a guard post perched on top of a high wooden platform. She couldn't retreat without being seen.

The pimply-faced guard walked toward her with the arrogant swagger of a schoolyard bully. "Over here. Now," he ordered and beckoned her to a search zone set up on one side of the checkpoint.

She complied, slowly. Her whole body was shaking. Her false identity papers, supplied by local partisans, were well forged—virtually indistinguishable from the real thing—and her local knowledge and fluent Austrian German eliminated any real risk of detection from a document inspection or cursory questioning. But a search of the basket would be a different matter.

"Let me look in here," he demanded, pointing to the basket.

"You can see what's in there," she said, her fear giving her voice an authentic quaver to go with her old woman's rags. "Just eggs to sell at the market. Please, I'm in a hurry."

"I don't care if it takes all day. I want to look at what you've got in the basket," he replied.

"It's taken me half the day to get here. If I'm too late to reach the market, I can't sell my eggs. Then my family goes hungry," she said. "Take some if you want. I need to be on my way."

"I'm a soldier of the Reich," the boy said loftily. "Please don't imagine I can be bought off. Besides, if I want eggs, I can take them anytime I want from the peasants around here. I don't need yours. Now hand over the basket."

"Do you know Fritz Mueller?" Josefine said desperately. "He's my grandson. Poor little boy, his leg was blown off when he stepped on an unexploded land mine. Probably left by those damned partisans. I need to sell these eggs so I can feed his family. His poor mother and father have to stay home to care for him, so they can't work and earn money."

The youth held out his hand for the basket.

"I'm not interested in your family, you old hag. The basket. Now!"

"Watch your tongue, young man. Have some respect for your elders! What's your name? Do I know your family? I live here in Radkersburg so perhaps I do. They won't be happy to hear how—"

"The basket," he repeated.

Josefine staggered and leaned heavily on her stick, but this was no act. She felt faint. This was far from the first time she had been stopped by German guards or patrols, and she had become used to living by her wits. Now it seemed she had reached the end of the line.

Then, on a sudden inspiration, she hoisted the basket. As the soldier reached for it, she dropped it just as his fingers were closing on the handle. It fell to the ground, and there was a loud, wet crack. With a howl, Josefine dropped to the ground and plunged her hands into the slimy mess of yolks and broken shells, breaking any of the eggs that had survived.

"*Mein lieber Gott!*" she cried. "*Ach, mein Gott!* You clumsy oaf! You have broken all of my eggs! You did this deliberately!"

She made a show of struggling to her feet, yolk running down her wrists.

"You saw this," she shouted up to the soldier on the guard post, who seemed to be enjoying the show. "You saw what he did. My family will starve. *Dummkopf!*"

She dropped to her knees again, and began sobbing as she pretended to search through the mess for anything unbroken. There was no need to feign it; the tears were an outlet for the adrenaline.

"Fritz! Fritz! Fritz!" she wailed. "*Mein liebling*, forgive me. Oh, my poor little Fritz! What do we do now? There'll be no money for food."

"I'm sorry," the guard said, his bluster all but gone. "It was an accident. My duty—it's my duty to search everyone. I didn't mean to break the eggs."

He crouched beside her, but his determination to search the basket had altogether evaporated. Josefine scooped up a handful of the broken eggs and thrust it toward his face. He recoiled, doubtless anxious to avoid besmirching his uniform.

"Look what you've done," she raged, and then launched into a fresh bout of sobs.

He stood and stepped away from her.

"If you had obeyed my orders," he said stiffly.

"Orders!" she spat. "What kind of country has this become when a child will give their elders *orders*."

She made a great show of struggling to her feet, leaning on her stick. She snatched up the basket and limped away from the checkpoint and onto the bridge, muttering to herself. She forced herself to maintain a slow, labored pace, but with every step, she was certain the guard would call her back and ask what business she now had across the border, if she no longer had anything to sell.

———

When she judged she was a safe distance away and unobserved, Josefine stepped off the road and blundered a short way into the forest. She sank to the damp ground and wept. She had escaped death by the narrowest of margins. Had the basket tipped over when it hit the ground, had the soldier insisted on searching it even though the eggs were broken, or kicked it over with his foot . . .

She had never previously feared discovery so much. She had always managed to keep her cool. She had never really feared arrest, or torture, and certainly not death. But now something had changed. It was as though her life were a treasure that had suddenly become much more valuable.

With this realization, she was calm again. It was a surprising and baffling discovery. She had always felt that her country was a cause she was prepared to die for, and that had made her fearless. Now, since she had met Bruce, this man from the other side of the world, she had something else she wanted to live for.

She delivered the basket to her contact and hurried off. She needed to get home to her family, and most of all she needed to think.

———

Back in Limbuš, a weary Roman opened the door to her. He was the only one at home—Anica was off on one of her partisan missions and he was just back from one of his.

"Why have you come back?" he asked. "It's too dangerous for you here."

"It's dangerous everywhere," she replied. "I was nearly arrested in Radkersburg. They smashed up the Hamlers' house looking for me."

"Again?" Roman said, his face lighting with a smile. "Aunt Agatha won't have liked that! I almost pity the Švabi!"

Josefine didn't tell him about what had happened at the checkpoint on the Mura bridge. Roman already had more weight on his shoulders than anyone his age should have to bear.

———

Anyone who had kept track of Bruce's career as a military prisoner would have been struck by the change that seemed to have come over him. Whereas he had once been a noted recalcitrant, unafraid to abuse his Nazi captors or to call a German soldier's girlfriend a whore to his face, he was quiet as a lamb for the Rossneggers. He knew that keeping his job at Radkersburg was his best—perhaps his only—chance of seeing Josefine again.

Ever since she had left hurriedly after their near-disastrous encounter with the SS, Bruce couldn't stop thinking about her. He relived that one precious kiss in the cellar until he could almost taste the sweetness of her lips, and wondered what it had meant to her, if it had meant anything at all. He remembered how cool she had been when she came to tell him she was leaving. Perhaps she had felt nothing. Or perhaps she already had a lover. Bruce could only wonder. But he knew how he felt.

At least she *had* come to tell him, he tried to reassure himself. And there were her final words: "*Ich verspreche.*"

Beneath it all, he was nagged by guilt. He was a married man—

not happily married, but married nonetheless. He, too, had made a promise: to Doreen.

To start with, Doreen's letters had been regular since he had departed New Zealand. And at first, at least, she had said the right things: she said she missed him, felt sorry for him in the POW camp, wanted him back, and so on. But this kind of sentiment had dried up. Bruce had been aggrieved that she had never expressed any kind of condolence to him for the death of his two best mates. She knew they didn't like her, and it was mutual, but all the same . . . It was hard to believe she hadn't heard.

The regularity of her letters had fallen away, too. This didn't altogether surprise Bruce, as the fact that mail managed to cross the war-torn world and find its way to him where he languished in enemy hands had always seemed little short of miraculous. He had always imagined that when the war was over he would return to Doreen and they would resume their awkward but more or less functional marriage. He would often remind himself of how badly she had treated him, how she had threatened to throw him out of the house, how she had practically announced, in front of the entire 25th Battalion as they embarked at Wellington, that the mouse intended to play while the cat was away. He remembered two occasions where she had stormed out of the house and not come home for days, without ever having said where she had been all that time . . .

None of it made any difference. He was married to Doreen, for better, as their vows had put it, or for worse. That much was in plain English.

He tried to imagine how Josefine might react if he were to tell her he was married. The scenes never played out well in his mind. In most of them, she merely shrugged and walked away, without so much as a backward glance. In the worst of them, she merely frowned at him as though he had taken leave of his senses, and inquired politely what this information had to do with her, exactly. But he also imagined the alternative, which was not telling her. Despite the flair he had shown for dishonesty toward his captors as a prisoner of war, deceit was not in Bruce's nature. That scenario wouldn't do, either.

He decided he needed to sort his thoughts out before Josefine returned, if she ever returned at all.

———

In the end, it wasn't his deliberations but the *Kriegsgefangenenpost*—the POW postal service—that put him out of his misery.

Ever since the terrible day on which he had learned of the deaths of Blackie and Logie, Bruce had had mixed feelings about mail. He generally looked forward to letters from home, although his gut always tightened in case the envelopes carried more bad news. Most contained tiresome gossip about daily life in Wellington, wartime rationing and food shortages, news about family and friends, and tittle-tattle on the latest scandals. Bruce sometimes wondered if the writers realized he was in a POW camp in war-torn Europe. But the rest of the time, he was grateful for the lifeline to something resembling normality. They were a reminder that there was a world beyond the wire and the war, and that one day he would return to it.

A month after Josefine had left, Bruce received two letters. He didn't recognize the writing on the first, but the second was from Doreen. He opened the first with a twinge of fear, but a quick scan revealed no bad news, and only the usual small talk from a mate who had only just learned that he was a prisoner of war. He set it aside to read in more detail later, and opened the one from Doreen.

Dear Bruce, it began. Not *Dearest Bruce* or *My Darling Bruce*—one or two of the early letters had opened that way. It was a one-pager and, scanning to the foot, he saw no expression of love or tenderness, not even a couple of XXs:

Dear Bruce,

I know this will be hard for you, and I hate to do it while you are so far away in a POW camp. But I decided that it would be fairer if I told you now.

I want a divorce. We both know things weren't good between us when you left, and I'm really sorry to tell you, but I've met someone else and I'm in love with him. I intended to wait for you, but it didn't work out that way. I hope you can understand.

He's an American soldier who was posted here on his way to fight the Japs. All you really need to know is that he's a lovely man, and that we're very happy together. After the war, he's promised to take me to America to live.

So a divorce would be the best for both of us. I can get on with my life and you can do whatever you want. I'm not really sure how these things are done, but I believe it works best if the husband (you) admits fault. I suppose there are forms and things to fill in. I'll send them to you to sign once I have them.

You'll probably think badly of me, and that's fair enough. But I really think we'll both be happier this way. I'm not sure we could ever have been truly happy together.

I'll write again when I know what the next steps are. Don't be too sad. We did have some good times together.

Doreen

Just like that, the entire future that had been laid out before him like a path that he must dutifully tread was gone. This was the woman he had courted, loved, cared for, and planned to raise children with. She was leaving him for some fancy-pants Yank who was no doubt loaded with money, silk stockings, and chocolate. He felt a pang of indignation. Silk stockings! Bruce had kept Doreen supplied with the finest hosiery from Prestige right up until the start of the war.

Still, he knew she was right. Their marriage had been rocky and it was only being held together by the brief reconciliations—at his instigation, not hers—that occurred after each of their flaming rows.

He should have been upset by this news, but he wasn't. Not really. And he wasn't completely surprised, either. The infrequent letters and lack of affection meant he had had his suspicions for some time and was relieved now that he knew the truth. The marriage had seemed moribund. Now it was dead.

That was how his head reacted to the news. His heart surprised him by registering the blow to his pride. Bruce had never tolerated failure that well, and his marriage—like his war—was now a confirmed disaster. Plenty of others had received similar letters, so Bruce found solace in the company of a couple of POW friends who had been through the same thing. He got rotten drunk that night, shedding a few tears, but when he woke in the morning he was remarkably calm. Certainty was better than anxiety.

And, naturally enough, his thoughts returned to Josefine.

Chapter Eighteen

—

Bruce & Josefine, Radkersburg and Gornja Radgona, December 1943 to July 1944

Josefine did keep her promise. In late December 1943, she returned to Radkersburg. After four months in Limbuš, hardly leaving the house, she was keen to get back to the Rossneggers', where she could at least be outdoors.

She tried to tell herself that her restlessness had nothing to do with Bruce. But the surge of joy she experienced when she saw him—his neatly combed hair, his shining workboots, the trousers of his shabby fatigues with their sharp crease—told her otherwise. And when Bruce looked up and saw her, his face lit up with a grin of pure, undisguised delight.

"You're back!" he said, when they finally managed to be alone. "I was worried I'd never see you again. Are you sure it's safe?"

"It's not safe," she said. "But nowhere is safe."

They stood awkwardly, both remembering the kiss, neither quite sure that it meant for the other what they hoped it did.

"I'm glad you're back," Bruce said.

"I'm glad to be back," she replied.

———

"The thing that I don't understand," Josefine told him one day, as they walked companionably along the road from the barn, "is how you look so different from the day when I first saw you."

Bruce laughed, and explained. Josefine laughed, too, but then her smile turned to sadness.

"There's been no word of your brother, then?" he said.

She shook her head.

"My family is sure he's dead," she said. "The Švabi murder anyone who opposes them."

She told Bruce about the massacre in Glavni trg and how afterward she felt compelled to do her utmost to rid her homeland of the Nazi intruders who had robbed her country of its freedom.

"So you became a partisan," he said.

"I became a partisan," she agreed.

"What kinds of things do you do?"

She hesitated—trust no one; tell no one—but he already knew more than enough to do her harm if he wanted to.

"I'm not a fighter," she said. "I carry messages, documents, information, sometimes weapons. But mostly I've been a guide helping soldiers and prisoners like you escape from Slovenia."

Bruce shook his head in wonder. "It must be bloody dangerous," he said. "Was that time in the Hamlers' cellar the closest you've come to being caught?"

She didn't look at him. She blushed ever so slightly at the mention of the cellar.

"No," she said. "I've been through worse."

She told him about Jelka's betrayal.

"That's why I came here," she said simply. "And what about you? How did you come to be working on my cousins' farm?"

It was Bruce's turn to recount his experiences in the POW camp, his unsuccessful escape attempts, and his severe beating at the hands of The Skunk. He also explained how shoveling shit at Kurt Wagner's farm had got him transferred to the Rossneggers'.

Josefine laughed, and Bruce's heart leaped in his chest. It was the first time he had heard her laugh freely and without reserve.

"I've never liked Wagner," she said. "I'm pleased you gave him what he deserved!"

———

Over the next few months, they talked whenever they could steal time alone together. They imagined no one noticed, but it was probably more obvious to others than it was to them that they were falling in love. The glance that lingered a second too long; the momentary contact when none was needed; and the furtive look behind when they passed were all telltale signs. Bruce's fellow prisoners, and even the old Austrian guard, found ways of making themselves scarce to allow them precious time together. Only Gustl looked on sourly, muttering to himself whenever he saw Bruce and Josefine lock eyes or not-so-accidentally touch while they were walking side by side.

Two events brought them closer together. One was a tragedy; the other might have been.

One day in late April, Bruce returned to the *Arbeitskommando* from the Rossnegger farm to find a letter waiting for him. He could see from the writing that it was from his parents. So light was his mood after spending the day close to Josefine that he didn't think twice before opening it. It was only after he had read and reread the opening lines that he sank down onto his bunk.

Frank noticed at once. "What is it?" he asked.

Bruce glanced up at him, a dazed look on his face. He opened his mouth to speak, but nothing came out. His eyes were blind with tears. He handed the letter to Frank.

It was in his mother's handwriting.

Boy, it began. His parents never addressed him any other way.

We're sorry to have to tell you but your sister Jo passed away on the 5th of March. She was seeing an American soldier and it seems the poor girl got herself in the family way. The Yank shot through, of course, and Jo must have decided to end the pregnancy. The doctors tell us that she must have gone to one of those people who does that sort of thing. Something went wrong, and by the time they saw her at the hospital it was too late. She never mentioned a word to us so we knew nothing about it. Your father and I are heartbroken because we loved her very much. It's hard to understand how a good girl like Jo could have let something like this happen to her, but it doesn't matter now. Dear Jo's gone.

The tone of the letter changed markedly.

How are you, Boy? We've heard that . . . (the next few sentences were blacked out by the censor) . . . *treating you okay? Now you look after yourself, Boy.*

"Jesus Christ," said Frank. "Life's so bloody unfair. You poor bugger. What can I do to help?" Frank did his best to console his friend, but nothing he said really helped.

Bruce had thought he was immune to grief by now, that he had suffered enough heartache, hardship, and misfortune to last a lifetime. But, like his parents, he doted on his sister. He could understand how Jo had felt upon discovering she was pregnant: she would have been worried that her parents would never forgive her for bringing shame upon the family. Like them, he found it hard to imagine how she could have let something like this happen. But the thought of his beloved Jo feeling trapped and desperate enough to seek out a backstreet abortionist made him feel physically ill. He bridled at his mother's phrase "got herself in the family way," as though it were only Jo to blame. He was filled with rage at the cowardly Yank, and at the Americans in general.

The following day, Josefine greeted him with a smile. It faltered when she saw his face.

"What's wrong?" she asked.

"I've had bad news from home," he said, struggling to control his voice. "My sister's dead."

"My God," she said. "How?"

The concern in her face undid him. He sobbed as he told her the circumstances, and by the time he finished he was weeping uncontrollably.

Josefine put her arms around him and held him, thinking of Jelka and the many other girls who had found themselves in the same tragic situation.

"I don't know what to say," she said softly. "I know what it's like to lose a sibling, but at least I have hope that Polde will return . . ."

She held him as he wept. The warmth of her embrace comforted him. After a minute or so, he took a deep, shuddering breath and dashed the back of his hand across his eyes. She released him, but took his hand and held it tight. At that moment he felt closer to Josefine than he had ever felt to anyone before.

"Tell me about her," she said.

"Her name is—was—Jo," he said. "She was beautiful. She was a terrific writer, and could paint. She would have been an artist, I think. She wasn't like anyone else I know. She was a free spirit. I can't believe . . ."

He closed his eyes and his mouth stretched wide with grief.

"This bloody war," said Josefine.

"This bloody war," Bruce echoed.

The second event might have been just as tragic.

As much as she tried to keep her head down, Josefine was still a committed partisan. Her contact had told her many times about the plight of the people in Gornja Radgona—or Oberradkersburg, as the Germans called it—just across the river from Radkersburg. Many of the townsfolk were sympathetic to the partisans and they were being terrorized by a local anti-partisan militia group. Food supplies had been cut off and both citizens and partisans were starving.

Josefine, in one of their increasingly regular tête-à-têtes, mentioned to Bruce that she sometimes took food across the border.

"I want to help," said Bruce at once. "Why don't I get some of my mates to pool some food from our Red Cross parcels? We all get well looked after on the farms around here, so we can spare stuff from our rations. We did it for the Russians at the Maribor camp. We could do the same for the partisans. It mightn't be a lot but it's something."

Josefine looked at him gratefully. "That would be wonderful," she said. "Every little bit helps."

"And I could even deliver the stuff," Bruce continued. "I could do my Houdini act from the camp, deliver the supplies across the border, and be back before roll call."

"No," Josefine said flatly. "It's too dangerous. I can't let you take the risk."

"So who does take the risk? You?"

"Perhaps," she said. "But that's different."

"How is it different? Or," he said, on a sudden impulse, "we could do it together."

Josefine thought for a long time. Eventually, she nodded. She mentioned, as if it were a trifling matter, that she was sometimes asked to deliver documents and small arms to the partisans on the other side of the border and that, if they were crossing into Slovenia, she might be asked to do the same again. She didn't tell him how her last assignment crossing the Mura with her basket of eggs had so nearly cost her everything.

They talked through the details of how they would go about it, and by the time they parted, they had a plan. Bruce would coordinate the collection of Red Cross items—he had no difficulty in persuading his fellow prisoners to contribute to the partisan cause—and Josefine would alert her contacts in Slovenia.

Two weeks later, they went on their first mission together, Bruce wearing a set of Gustl's clothes and Josefine in her usual geriatric outfit. To all appearances, they were an old lady and a farm laborer, and they would scarcely have aroused suspicions had they not been out and about in the middle of the night. Bruce was carrying a German military rucksack stuffed with food, chocolate, and cigarettes, while Josefine carried a bag in which there were several pistols and a grenade. It went without a hitch. So, over the next three months, they did it again, and again, and again, and yet again.

In June 1944, for their sixth excursion, Bruce had the rucksack and an old grain bag tied with string, both filled with Red Cross supplies. Josefine had been given a sheaf of papers and a couple of maps. She didn't know the significance of the maps but presumed they detailed German troop movements.

They took a roundabout route from their rendezvous near the camp to reach the Slovene border. They knew when and where to cross the rail bridge without being challenged. Once across, they were on the outskirts of Gornja Radgona, close to where they were to deliver the food. The journey had taken less than an hour. Josefine went on ahead, and when she was some distance away Bruce followed; Josefine had decided that they would look less suspicious individually than they would if they were together.

Bruce could see her stooped form up ahead as she hobbled along Panonska ulica in the moonlight. Suddenly a flashlight beam splashed her shadow on the wall. Bruce saw two, three men step out of a side street and surround her. He stopped, and sensed the presence of other men in the darkness around him.

One of them addressed him in Slovene. He didn't understand the words, but he recognized the peremptory tone, and there was no mistaking the gleam of moonlight on gunmetal. The man was in uniform, but not a German uniform, so far as Bruce could tell.

"Who are you?" the man repeated, this time in German. "What are you doing out after the curfew?"

Bruce said nothing.

"Hands above your head. Now!" the man barked. "You have no right to be on the streets. Come with us." Bruce was marched at gunpoint toward the doorway of a small hotel, where Josefine had also been taken.

"In here," his escort commanded.

The lobby of the hotel had mud-brick walls and a soaring, vaulted ceiling fit for a cathedral. The walls were decked with Nazi paraphernalia, and the large, intricately inlaid Louis XV desk—probably the reception desk in peacetime—was strewn with papers bearing the German eagle and swastika. It was all Bruce could do to pretend he had no connection with Josefine, who was being restrained by two men in mismatched uniforms. They must, he realized, be the Slovene militia whom Josefine had said were terrorizing the locals.

A boorish-looking man behind the desk studied them.

"Who are these two?" he asked in Slovene.

"They were out in the street after curfew."

"Find out who they are and what they were doing," the man said, nodding at Josefine. "Her first."

As Bruce looked on helplessly, Josefine was frog-marched to a room off the lobby. The door closed behind her. He was terrified, but not for himself.

"What is this curfew? I don't know anything about a curfew," Josefine said in Slovene, taking the initiative.

"Of course, you know about the curfew," one of the men scoffed. "Everyone does. It's been in place for a week."

"I don't live in this town," she said. "I'm on my way home to Podgrad. I've been looking after my sick sister in Norički Vrh all day. That's why I'm out late. She's very ill—I think she's dying—and I couldn't leave her. No one said anything about a curfew."

Norički Vrh was a tiny village on the outskirts of Gornja Radgona. Podgrad was just two miles to the west. Despite her fear, Josefine controlled her tone—a mixture of cantankerous indignation and vulnerability. She averted her eyes whenever they looked at her and bowed her head to avoid any direct contact. She was quivering under her matronly dress, hoping the soldiers wouldn't notice.

"Who's the man out there?" the other asked.

"How should I know?" Josefine replied. "Probably just someone else minding their own business."

"Watch your mouth, old lady," he snapped.

The two men conferred as Josefine watched them from beneath her shawl. She felt nothing but contempt for these traitors, who were worse, as far as she was concerned, than the Nazis themselves.

"Right, you old fool," the first man said. "You know the rule now: in by ten. If we catch you out after curfew again, we'll throw you in the cells."

Josefine made a show of rising stiffly and leaning on her stick.

"Now fuck off," said the man with a dismissive wave of his hand.

"And don't forget who's in charge. If we say there's a curfew, there is one. You'd do well to remember that."

Josefine walked across the lobby without looking at Bruce, who was pushed toward the office. She made her way down the steps and tottered along the dark road. When she felt she was a safe distance away, she turned into a side alley and leaned against the wall.

There was nothing she could do but wait.

———

Bruce jiggled his left leg nervously and clutched his good-luck charm, his grandmother's greenstone pendant. It had served him well so far.

"Why are you here outside after ten o'clock? What were you doing?" the militia man asked in German.

"I . . . I'm from Austria. I came across the border looking for work," stammered Bruce, aware of how unconvincing he sounded.

"Give us your papers," the man ordered, and when Bruce hesitated, "Right now!"

"I've lost them," Bruce replied. "Fell out of my pocket when I was plowing the fields. I haven't had a chance to get them reissued."

"You've lost them?" the man said, his voice heavy with ridicule. He pointed to the bags. "Show us what's in there."

With Bruce watching helplessly, one of the men unbuckled the rucksack and emptied its contents on the desktop. Everyone looked at the tins and packets. The labels in English made it clear that Bruce was no ordinary farmworker passing through. Tinned meat, jam, condensed milk, cheese, and biscuits were unobtainable by all but the most senior German officers. And the Gauleiter himself probably found soap and chocolate hard to come by, yet here was a man claiming to be a farmworker with many bars of both.

"Liar!" the man shouted. "You're no farmworker. You've stolen this stuff. Who did you steal it from? Tell me now—where did you get it?"

"It's not stolen," Bruce protested. "I did some work for a farmer and he gave me these things instead of paying me."

"Bullshit. These are British goods. What farmer gets their hands on British goods? Where did you get them from?"

Bruce felt his face flush and his gut tense; he had endured the horrors of war, been abused, and almost killed, but he had never experienced the terror that comes with the certain knowledge that a lie is about to be exposed. He was on the edge of panic. He felt as though he were about to vomit. He didn't know what to say.

The militia men untied the grain bag and emptied that, too. There was more of the same, along with salmon, sugar, and coffee to boot. It could have been solid gold, the way the men reacted.

"Real coffee! Where would a scumbag like you get real coffee from? That confirms it. You're no worker; you're a bloody thief."

"I'll tell you the truth," said Bruce, hanging his head. "I got it from a German soldier, who gets it from a prisoner-of-war camp. I didn't want to get him into trouble."

"Bullshit. How could someone like you afford all this?"

"I didn't pay. I did him a favor," Bruce replied.

"What kind of favor?" the man asked.

"I gave him eggs and fresh milk," Bruce said.

A mirthless, disbelieving grin crossed the interrogator's face. "Oh, yes? And how much milk does one have to pay a crooked German soldier to get a tin of real coffee?"

Bruce simply shrugged. "It's the truth," he said.

The men conferred.

"We should call the boss," one soldier suggested. "The old fool won't like being woken at this hour, but he should be told we've captured a thief with a stash of English food and stuff."

The others seemed less convinced.

Bruce could do nothing but sit and miserably await his fate. He thought it must have been two or three in the morning. It would take an hour to get back to the *Arbeitskommando* in Radkersburg if all went well. If he wasn't there by five, well, the game was up.

The militia men arrived at a decision. The leader picked up the telephone. Bruce knew that his life was about to become much more difficult—impossibly difficult—if they made that call.

"Hang on a minute," he said. "You can have everything. Just let me go."

The leader paused, the receiver still to his ear.

"I've also got *Zigaretten*," Bruce volunteered. "Plenty of them. You can have the lot if you just let me out of here."

The leader put down the receiver.

"Show me," he said.

Bruce reached into his pockets and pulled out several packets of English cigarettes. The men's eyes goggled. He might as well have produced diamonds. Cigarettes, particularly the prized foreign ones, were universally coveted and these soldiers craved them as much as anyone.

"The boss will be pretty unhappy if we wake him up," the leader mused.

"Especially if it turns out this guy is just a crook," another ventured. "He'll be really pissed off."

"We definitely don't want to piss him off," the leader said. "Best let him sleep."

He seemed to make up his mind.

"Okay, you thieving liar. Leave everything here and get the hell out of this place. And don't ever come back. Next time we'll shoot. Understand?"

Bruce nodded, stood, and walked to the door. The back of his neck prickled as he walked across the lobby to the main door. The night air had never felt so good on his skin or so sweet in his lungs. He strode briskly along the street, resisting the temptation to break into a run. Several hundred yards from the hotel, he sensed movement in an alley to his left.

"Keep walking," said Josefine. "I'll find you outside town."

———

Bruce didn't have long to wait before he heard her shuffling footsteps and the click of her stick on the pavement. When she saw him, she dropped the stick and ran to him. He folded her in his arms and they clung to each other. Josefine sobbed silently, tears of anguish wet on her cheeks.

"Thank God," she said. "Thank God."

They kissed, tenderly at first, then more passionately.

At last, Josefine broke off.

"I love you," she breathed. "I couldn't have lived with myself if . . ."

They kissed again.

Again, it was Josefine who drew away, and this time, she broke his embrace.

"We must get going," she said. "We don't have much time to get you back to the camp."

It was only a few miles back to the *Arbeitskommando*, but they had to travel along disused trails and paths that took them well out of their way. There was light along the horizon when Bruce made it to the camp, so elated that he hardly noticed how fatigued he was. It was only later that it caught up with him, how close he had come to losing Josefine, and she to losing him.

———

Instead, though, and against all odds, they had found each other. In the days that followed their close shave in Gornja Radgona, their love burgeoned. There was no longer any need to hide their feelings; they began to spend every possible minute together.

"You must have a girl at home, Bruce," Josefine said one day, as they lay beside each other in the barn. Their kisses and caresses had become more and more ardent, until both recognized they had reached a kind of impasse: he expectant, she reluctant.

"I'm married," Bruce blurted out. He couldn't deceive her. Not now.

He felt her stiffen. She sat up and hugged her knees.

"I should have told you earlier, but I was too scared of losing you," he said, stroking her back. "But don't be upset. I'm soon to be divorced. My wife and I weren't happy. She's found herself an American soldier."

"Is this true?" Josefine asked. Bruce saw the gleam of her eyes as she studied him in the half-light. There was something of the old frost in her voice.

"It's true," he said. "You know me well enough by now. I wouldn't lie to you."

She was quiet for a long time.

"What's her name?" she asked.

"Doreen," he replied. It seemed strange saying her name there, in the barn.

"Doreen," she echoed. "Do you love her?"

"I used to think so," he admitted. "But we weren't in love when I left New Zealand. And I'm definitely not in love with her now."

She considered him.

"Americans. Both Doreen and your sister," she mused.

"Yes," he said. "Both Yanks."

"It serves you Kiwi men right for coming so far to fight someone else's war."

"You don't sound as though you have much sympathy for us."

"Oh, I'm sorry for you," she said. "I'm sorry for everyone whose lives have been ruined by our European war."

She lay back down and kissed him, softly, her hair falling over his face.

"But the war has brought us one good thing," she murmured.

———

The inevitable happened. It wasn't the most romantic of places—the hayloft over the pens where the cattle were kept, with the sounds and smells of the animals drifting up to them. The late-afternoon sun slanted in through chinks in the boards, lighting motes of dust.

"Are you sure?" he said.

"If you swear you love me," she said.

"I swear," he replied.

"Then I'm sure," she said. "In Slovenia, women will not do this unless they're married. Not respectable women, anyway."

"You're a thoroughly respectable woman," Bruce said.

"Not for much longer, I think," she said, and giggled.

"Are you sure?" he said again.

She left him in no doubt she was sure.

———

Their clandestine meetings became a regular thing. He would slip out of the camp, and they would meet somewhere on the outskirts of Radkersburg. Everything would have been fine had they been a bit more discreet. But love has few boundaries and passion will always conquer caution. They both knew the risks they were taking, but any opportunity to be together was worth the gamble.

One day, just after they had met as usual with a passionate kiss, Josefine gave a start.

"What is it?" Bruce asked.

"Over there," she said.

Bruce followed her gaze, and saw a man turn around and hurry away from them, his shoulders hunched.

"That's Kramer," she said. "The one I told you about—I'm sure it was him who betrayed us at Uncle Josef's."

They saw Kramer mount a bicycle and begin pedaling furiously in the direction of *Arbeitskommando* 296/L.

"You'll never make it in time!" Josefine said, her hands to her mouth. Bruce had already taken to his heels.

"I have to try," he yelled over his shoulder. "If I don't, we'll be separated forever." He knew that if he were discovered his escape route would be closed off and he would be transferred to another work camp—most likely a disciplinary camp. It would definitely mean more time in the cooler. The penalty for Josefine's liaison with the enemy would be harsher.

He ran as fast as he had ever run. As he drew close to the camp, he could hear shouting. "*Raus! Raus! Appell! Appell!* Out! Out! Roll call! Roll call!" He knew he was too late.

When he reached the window with the loose bar, he peered in and saw that against all odds, the room was empty. He wasted no time in removing the bar and wriggling in. When he emerged from the hut, he found a knot of prisoners and guards standing around something. Craning to see what it was, he saw Frank writhing on the floor, his eyes rolled back in his head, his legs jerking wildly and his arms thrashing. He realized at once what had happened. As soon as he had heard the call to muster go up, Frank had realized Bruce was outside the camp. He had created a diversion in the faint hope it would give Bruce time to make it back before the roll was taken. It had. By the time they had dragged Frank off to the sick bay and got the men assembled, they found all present and accounted for. Bruce was the only prisoner fully dressed but the guards didn't seem to notice.

"We owe you, Frankie," Bruce said a day later, after the camp doctor was satisfied that his mysterious seizure was unlikely to recur.

"Bloody right you do," Frank replied, thankful that his friend's absence hadn't been discovered.

Chapter Nineteen

———

Josefine, Ruše and Smolnik, August to September 1944

There was an urgent hammering on the door. Josefine woke with a start: it was after two in the morning, and she had only just drifted off to sleep. The heat of the humid summer night—it was late August, the hottest time in Limbuš—and her own turbulent thoughts had kept her from sleeping. Her first thought was that the SS were about to arrest her. At that hour, whoever was pounding on the door was there for a reason.

The banging came again, frantic this time, hard enough to rattle the hinges. The voice she could hear shouting for attention was unmistakably Slovene, but that didn't mean anything. The visitor might have been from one of the many anti-partisan militia groups.

There was a brief pause, and then a male voice spoke, again in Slovene.

"How long until the Drava freezes?"

It was a code. Josefine knew she could safely open the door. There was a boy, probably only fifteen or sixteen, standing on her doorstep, hands on knees, breathing hard.

"I've just come from Bezena," he panted.

"You ran all that way?" Josefine asked.

"It's urgent," the boy replied. "There's been an escape from the POW camp. Lots of prisoners. You must come quickly."

After the second episode with Kramer, Josefine had decided she had to go back home. Gustl and Mitzl had approved of this move; neither had made any secret of their opposition to her relationship with Bruce. The rest of her family, as it turned out, were similarly united in their opposition, whether out of concern for her—wartime romances ending in death and desertion were a familiar story by now—or out of xenophobic bigotry, it hardly mattered. Nor were the few friends she consulted any more encouraging.

"What happens when the war ends and he goes back to the other side of the world?" they asked.

She wasn't sure she had an answer to that.

She found that when she was with Bruce she had no doubts. But when she was away from him they crowded in like weeds, especially in the lonely, small hours of the morning.

For this reason, action was a welcome diversion. She dressed as quickly as she could, throwing on a simple floral cotton dress and a black embroidered shawl. The courier recited the directions for her and she repeated them. When both were sure she had memorized them, he left at a run, anxious to complete his round before dawn. Josefine fetched her bike from the outside shed and, with only the moonlight to guide her, rode off toward her destination.

On the outskirts of Ruše, three miles from Limbuš, she hid the bike in the undergrowth and struck out into the forest. Her path lay along the banks of the Drava. It had been an easy walk along a wide, smooth track in the prewar days when she, her siblings, and Jelka used to play there as youngsters; now, it was overgrown with weeds and brambles. She dared not use a flashlight, so it was slow going. She proceeded more cautiously as she neared the clearing where the rendezvous was supposed to take place, because she knew that the partisans would have posted sentries. They would be well armed and jumpy. Sure enough, even though she was expecting to encounter someone, and even though he was expecting her, she and the partisan lookout gave each other a fright. Josefine couldn't help but stifle a yell as she all but tripped over the man who was crouching to the side of the path cradling a submachine gun.

There was hardly any need for the passcode and counter-code—not even the Nazis would send a young woman into the forest alone at night to locate a partisan cell—but they performed the ritual anyway.

"How many escapees are there?" she asked.

"There's over a hundred," the partisan replied, a hint of pride in his voice. "We attacked the work site on the railway at Ožbalt. We freed the prisoners and we're getting them out of here."

"All of them?" said Josefine, aghast.

"All of them," chuckled the partisan.

An escape of this magnitude would stretch the escape lines to the limit. One or two escapees—half a dozen, even—were reasonably easy to move without being detected, but with over a hundred the odds of discovery rose a thousandfold. Maribor would be crawling with Nazis by morning and the search would be exhaustive. All routes in and out of town would be blocked and the Germans would scour every suspected escape route within a fifty-mile radius.

———

In all, there were 105 Allied POWs in the clearing, and there was barely enough room to stand. Twenty or so partisans watched over them. Josefine learned that the mass escape had begun as an unplanned thing: on August 30, 1944, seven British POWs had simply walked away from the railway work site at Ožbalt, about sixteen miles from Maribor. They had already communicated with the partisans, and they had been holed up for the night in partisan-controlled Lovrenc—or St Lorenzen, as the Germans had renamed it—with the Ljubo Šercer partisan brigade. Because it was a fairly remote spot, tucked away in the hills and not easily accessible by road or rail, it was relatively safe. The plan was to lie low overnight and then move the men in the morning.

But Slovene hospitality intervened. The partisans took the escapees to the local bar and the slivovitz flowed freely as both the escapees and their liberators celebrated the success of their venture. Every time another of the citizens of Lovrenc dropped by to pay their respects to the foreigners, it was necessary to tell the whole story again. The action grew in scale and valor in every successive version, so by midnight everyone had convinced themselves they were little short of superheroes.

It was sometime in the early hours of the morning—no one could remember exactly when or by whom—that the possibility of liberating the rest of the railway gang was mooted. It was such a self-evidently excellent idea, and it was so liberally toasted with yet more slivovitz, that there was no possibility of a last-minute change of heart when, shortly after dawn, the seven POWs and the hundred-strong Ljubo Šercer brigade moved back toward Ožbalt. The rising sun in their eyes only exacerbated their already blinding hangovers. Their grim faces only enhanced the spectacle they presented as they attacked the Germans at the railway site. The partisans in Lovrenc had more varied uniforms than the German Army had battalions. While they were mostly stolen or battle-plundered from the German and old Yugoslav armies, there were also a few Italian uniforms, some British, a smattering of Greek, and some of indistinguishable origin. Tunics were mismatched with trousers; buttons of various sizes, shapes, and colors were sewn on where the brass or silver ones had been ripped off; original insignia had been torn off or stitched over to remove any suggestion of Nazi allegiance; and patches of whatever material was at hand covered any tears or holes earned in battle. Some still had bloodstains left by their previous, and presumably dead, owners.

They may have appeared to be a motley bunch of misfits, but these men and women were brave, battle-hardened professionals who had sworn to defend their country, whatever the cost. And they were well armed with whatever weapons they had been able to lay their hands on, mostly stolen from dead Nazis.

The only guard on duty at Ožbalt was an old, round-faced Austrian with an ancient rifle, probably not even loaded. He threw it away and shoved his hands in the air as soon as he saw the partisans emerge from the shadows of the rusting railway huts. It was over before he realized he'd pissed his pants.

Another fat and unfit guard came out from one of the huts when he heard the prisoners cheering and, seeing the partisans in force, dropped everything—including his lunchbox—and bolted in the opposite direction. He would likely have been shot, had he not tripped and gone sprawling. The remaining guards, who had been inside enjoying a chat and brewing a pot of *Ersatzkaffee*, gave up without a hint of resistance. Seventy-nine POWs were freed without a shot being fired.

The partisans found themselves with eighty-six prisoners on their hands, not to mention the contingent of cowering guards. Under different circumstances the goons would have been shot then and there, but these were Austrian senior citizens and even the normally ruthless partisans didn't have the heart to execute them.

The action wasn't finished yet. Two of the Kiwi escapees, Phil Tapping and Alf Lloyd—both of whom had served in 25 Battalion with Bruce—knew of a group of French and British farmworkers in the vicinity. Spurred on by the success of the Ožbalt operations, it was decided that these people, too, should be liberated.

Freeing the ten French and nine British farmworkers proved to be even easier. The few guards at the two farms almost died of fright when they saw the mass of men, including the heavily armed partisans, advancing upon them. That brought the total number of prisoners on the run to 105. The easy part was over. Now the much more difficult assignment was to get over a hundred people across the mountains and rivers to Otok, where they would be airlifted to Bari in Allied territory in Italy.

———

Josefine and her fellow National Defence guides were confronted with a challenge the likes of which they had never faced. But there was no time to dwell on the problems; they had to move as quickly as they could. The farther away from Maribor the escapees got, the safer they became.

As they started out, they were at least blessed with good weather. The planned route to the partisan-controlled airfield at Otok was a trip of some two hundred miles over rugged mountains, along treacherous trails crisscrossed by swift rivers. It would normally take well over a week, assuming they encountered no Nazi patrols, no unforeseen obstacles, and experienced a generous dose of good luck. Any delay increased the risk. Summer storms were not uncommon, and both the rivers and the trails could become impassable, and were, in any case, made more dangerous by torrential rain.

The plan was for the guides to move the escapees in groups of five or six, leaving some distance between each party so that, if they were attacked by a Nazi patrol, only one group would be caught. Josefine was assigned one of these small parties, and her task was to guide it from the outskirts of Ruše to the next partisan rendezvous past the tiny village of Smolnik and toward Rogla, from where they would be guided across the slopes of the Pohorje. Although the distance was not great as the crow flies, it would be a full day's strenuous walk, taking a circuitous route with numerous detours in order to evade detection. German spotter planes were buzzing the district, so they had to keep close to cover at all times, and she would have to rely on local farmers, villagers, and partisan lookouts to warn her of the whereabouts of any German patrols or checkpoints.

They made good progress, better than Josefine had dared to hope. But even so, by the time they stopped the escapees were dog-tired. It had been a hot day, and the walk over rough ground and steep terrain meant that they were in desperate need of rest and water. While they sheltered, Josefine and an escort—a partisan fighter who went by the name of Dušan—were sent ahead to make contact with a farmer, a known partisan sympathizer, whom they hoped would house and feed them overnight prior to the handover the following day.

"Are you sure this is the place?" Dušan said, as he and Josefine crouched under cover and studied the farmhouse. It was an old, slightly run-down house with whitewashed walls, green-painted shutters, and a clay-tiled roof. The paint was fading and peeling badly in places. A large, timber-sided barn, big enough to accommodate all the escapees and their escorts, sat about a hundred yards behind the house, nicely concealed by a row of sycamore trees.

"Yes, I'm sure," she said. "The farmer has helped us before."

"Let's move, then." Dušan checked the breech of his rifle and cocked it. When they were certain there was no one approaching from either direction, he and Josefine walked briskly to the door of the house and knocked.

They waited. No one came, so Josefine knocked harder. She heard the sound of movement from within.

She frowned. Something didn't feel quite right.

"Is anybody home?" she called out. "I can hear someone in there. Please come to the door."

Silence.

"Anyone there?" she called out again.

Still silence.

Dušan banged on the door with the butt of his rifle. This time, Josefine heard the occupant approaching the door. A key rattled in the lock. The door opened just wide enough for the watery blue eye of a middle-aged woman to size up Josefine and Dušan. The eye widened when she saw the gun.

"What do you want?" she asked sharply. "What do you mean by banging on my door like that? Tell me what you want or go away."

Josefine was in a quandary. She had been expecting the farmer to answer and was loath to declare herself and her mission to a stranger whose allegiances were unknown, but they had no alternative. She could only hope the woman was the farmer's wife.

"I need your help," she said. "We're partisans. I know you've helped us before and we're grateful. We don't want to put you in any danger, but we have many escaping British soldiers we need to feed and house for the night. Can you help?"

"What?" said the woman. "What is it you want me to do?"

"We need food, water, and beds for the night. The barn would be perfect."

The woman stared at her.

Dušan was losing patience.

"Let us in," he said, and shoved the door open. The woman staggered back, muttering a curse in German. Dušan closed it behind him. In the narrow, dimly lit hallway, there was a sideboard cluttered with religious icons and family photographs—common enough in all Catholic Slovene households. But, among them, discreetly placed so as almost to hide it, Josefine spotted a framed portrait of Adolf Hitler.

The woman's demeanor had suddenly changed.

"You caught me unawares," she said, eyeing Dušan's gun. "I was asleep and when you woke me I had a bit of a fright. Of course, my husband and I will do anything we can to help."

"Where's your husband?" asked Dušan.

"He's out working on the farm," she replied. "I'm expecting him home anytime now."

Josefine caught Dušan's eye and directed his attention to the sideboard.

His face lit with a slow, humorless grin.

"What's this?" he asked, stepping forward and picking up the picture. "I think I recognize this man."

The woman had gone very pale.

"Please don't hurt me," she said.

Dušan whipped a big, ugly-looking knife from his waistband and wound his hand in her hair, forcing her up against the wall with her pale throat exposed.

"So you were going to help us, were you? Or were you going to wait until we were under your roof and then run off to the Švabi? Is that it?"

"Please," she repeated.

"Was that the plan?" Dušan demanded, his voice low and dangerous.

"No, I swear," she whimpered.

Josefine wasn't sure she could watch. Dušan came with a fearsome reputation; he had encountered plenty of collaborators before and few had survived unscathed. He pressed the point of the knife to the woman's cheek, just below her eye. Josefine saw a small, dark bead of blood gather on the blade. The woman began moaning.

"You're a traitor," Dušan growled. "You've probably heard what we do with traitors."

The woman stopped making her terrible noise, and something like defiance stiffened her quivering jowls.

"Yes, I've heard what you do, you dogs," she said. "To people who believe in the true leader, the Führer."

The ball of blood broke and ran like a tear down her cheek.

"What happened to the farmer who lived here before?" Josefine asked.

"I don't know," the woman replied, rolling her eyes toward Josefine. "My husband and I are Volksdeutsche. We moved here from Štós a month ago. The farm was empty. I swear."

Dušan made a noise of disgust. "Where's your Nazi-loving husband?" he said.

"He's away. He'll be back in three days."

Dušan released the woman suddenly, and stepped back. She slid to the floor and crouched there, her back to the wall, and touched her fingers to the small cut on her cheek.

"We can't leave her here," Dušan said to Josefine.

"No," she replied. She knew this was true.

"I'll deal with her."

"I'll help you," the woman groaned. "Please don't harm me. I'll help you."

Josefine and Dušan eyed her.

"You're coming with us," Dušan said at last. "We'll not take the chance that you'll tell your fascist friends. Best we pass you over to *our* friends."

"You partisan scum!" the woman shrieked from the floor. "The glorious German Army will wipe you out, you pig!" Dušan aimed a kick at her that caught her on her shoulder. The fight went out of her. Dušan hauled her to her feet and between him and Josefine, they poked, prodded, and pushed her all the way to Smolnik, where they handed her over to the locals. They had their own methods of dealing with traitors.

They learned from the Smolnik villagers that the previous occupants of the farm, staunch partisan supporters, had "disappeared" (the standard euphemism to describe the fate of the many thousands of Slovenes who, like Polde, had vanished without explanation, to be executed, deported, or sent to concentration camps). The locals believed the family had been taken because of their partisan connections but no one could be sure. Their farm had been leased to the collaborators for a peppercorn rent, a fraction of its true market value.

The escapees were brought to the barn and housed for the night, unaware of what had transpired earlier. The following day, a partisan detachment and a guide from Smolnik arrived to escort them on the next leg of their long, arduous journey.

Josefine seldom heard the outcome of the actions in which she played a small part. But the August mass escape of the workers from Stalag XVIIID was regarded by the partisans as one of the greatest victories of their war. All but one of the little groups made it to Semič on September 10, 1944. The other group of six men was ambushed at night by a Nazi patrol and killed. The remainder—ninety-nine men in all—were airlifted from Otok to Bari in Italy on September 17, 1944.

Had it not been for Josefine's sharp eyes and even sharper instincts, she might not have noticed the small, almost-concealed tribute to Hitler on the cabinet and the outcome for her party might have been very different.

———

Josefine had little time to dwell on the success of her mission. Just days afterward, Dejan summoned her to another briefing. There were men she didn't recognize in the dimly lit little room, hard-eyed, fit-looking men who were introduced as members of the National Liberation Front.

"There is to be an airdrop tonight," Dejan explained. "We will receive medicines that need to find their way to our patriotic doctors. There will be other supplies as well, which will be of more interest to our friends in the Liberation Front. Our resources are stretched, so we want you to accompany them to the drop zone and help load the goods."

Josefine nodded, her heart pounding. Ever since the Allied airdrops had commenced earlier in 1944, the partisan movement had become crucially reliant upon them. Other regions, such as Semič and Otok, where the partisans were more firmly in control, had permanent landing strips, or could at least receive goods by parachute in reasonable security. It was a different story around firmly occupied Maribor, where it was a risky business indeed. Coded messages were passed to and fro for weeks in advance, designating drop zones and times, which more often than not were changed at the last minute to confound anyone who might have intercepted them. Even then, there was a good chance there would be an SS reception committee when they arrived at the appointed place and time. Even if no word of a drop reached the enemy, conditions were ideal, and the cargo was parachuted to exactly the right point, it was difficult to light a drop zone and unload everything without attracting attention from the Nazis or collaborators.

All the same, cancellations were rare and usually only due to the weather, as a cancellation would mean inadequately armed fighting detachments, insufficient medication, and almost certainly more casualties.

Josefine's first airdrop was going exactly according to plan. The weather was clear, there was little wind, and the hum of the aircraft was heard right on cue. Shortly after it had faded, the pale silk of the parachute canopies could be dimly seen in the light of the flares used to mark the remote field. They were bang on target. As soon as they touched down and their chutes collapsed, men and women darted forward to slash the cargo nets and gather the sacks and cases for hauling to the waiting truck. Josefine and her friend Nushka were in charge of accounting for the medical supplies and seeing them safely stowed. They had nearly finished this work when a figure, doubled over the unmistakable shape of a rifle barrel, materialized from the darkness.

"*Boche!*" he called. "Run! We'll hold them off as long as we can."

Other ghostly shadows could be seen bobbing around in the flickering light of the still-flaming flares. The lookout raised his rifle and fired a volley of shots in the direction of the silhouettes. The muzzle flashes and repetitive crackle of gunfire momentarily stunned Josefine into paralysis. But then she grabbed Nushka's arm.

"Run, Nushka! I know where we can hide, but we must hurry. Come on. Faster!"

The rat-a-tat-tat of German machine guns, amplified by the stillness of the night, was answered immediately. The partisans scattered, some harbored by sympathetic farmers and others concealed in the many bolt-holes known only to them. Josefine was running faster than she'd ever run before.

They didn't stop until they reached the farmhouse of family friends Dragan and Branka Tomčič, where they hammered on the door. A bleary-eyed and frightened-looking Dragan opened it.

"Quickly, please," Josefine gabbled. "You must help us. The Švabi are after us. We need to hide before they find us." She had no time to explain what she was doing out so late at night—Dragan had a pretty good idea—and no time for friendly greetings.

"Come," Dragan ordered, as he grabbed a key off a hook by the door and led them to a shed at the back of the property. He padlocked the door once they were inside just to be sure they would be safe. It was a prudent but unnecessary precaution. Having seized the truckload of contraband, the Nazis were satisfied with their night's work. They recognized the futility—not to mention the danger—of pursuing the partisans into territory they knew as well as their own backyards.

When Dragan decided that the coast was clear, he unlocked the shed. Josefine and Nushka emerged tentatively.

"I think it's safe," he said. "Come to the house and have a drink. You look like you need it."

Josefine shook her head. "We don't want to put you in any more danger than we already have," she said. She embraced Dragan.

"Wait," he said. When he returned, he was carrying two baskets of eggs. "I'd be obliged if you would take these into town and sell them for me."

Josefine understood. If they were stopped on the road, they would have an alibi.

It wasn't until she reached the safety of her own house that the night's terror caught up with her. While she'd managed to maintain an icy calm and a clear head throughout, she found herself shaking and sobbing uncontrollably as soon as she was in her own bedroom.

It passed and, when it did, it was replaced by a deep-seated satisfaction. She had once again played her part in resisting the occupation.

Chapter Twenty

—

Bruce & Josefine, Radkersburg, February to April 1945

The rumors flew thick and fast. According to one, the prisoners at *Arbeitskommando* 296/L were to be recalled to Stalag XVIIIA, from where they would be forced to march from Austria into Germany. Bruce was friendly with one of the guards by the name of Helmut Fischer, and he said that he had heard other prisoner-of-war camps had been emptied and their inmates forced to march anywhere up to a thousand miles through the snow. Radkersburg was only 150 miles from the border with metropolitan Germany, but Bruce could only imagine the hardships they would suffer if they were forced to walk there in this bitter season.

According to another rumor, the prisoners were to be used as human shields when the Russians advanced on Germany. To be taken by the Red Army would be the worst fate imaginable for German soldiers. Their barbaric treatment of captured Russians on the Eastern Front meant they could hope for no quarter now that the jackboot was on the other foot. Bruce had seen how badly the Nazis had treated Russian prisoners of war; the Germans knew that the Russians were capable of even more heinous brutality. A human shield of POWs might deter the invaders. Or at least delay them.

According to yet another story, Hitler was preparing plans to liquidate every Allied prisoner of war in German hands. This seemed improbable, but in this war the age of wonders was far from past.

Frank and Bruce spent much of their time discussing which of the rumors to believe.

"I don't fancy sitting around to find out who's right," Bruce said. "I reckon we should shoot through."

Frank heartily agreed. They knew they could escape the camp any time they chose. The question then became: what next?

In mid-February 1945, Helmut whispered to Bruce that the Soviets had taken Budapest. Word around the camp was that the Third Ukrainian Front of the Red Army would be moving on Vienna shortly and advancing into Styria toward its capital, Graz, soon after that. The Russians would have to pass through Radkersburg on the way. Helmut also said that he'd heard the Wolfsberg prisoners of war would be set on their Long March to Germany in April.

"The time's come, Frankie," Bruce said.

"Reckon it has," said Frank. "Not a moment too soon. The novelty of being a kriegie has just about worn off for me."

Josefine had returned to Radkersburg a month after the Ožbalt mission. Now that it was obvious that the German Army was on the verge of defeat, the partisan focus was on preparing for the final onslaught and the liberation of Yugoslavia. Josefine had little to do in this effort, so she and Bruce had plenty of time together. Now, in early March, the sound of artillery, like distant thunder, signaled the onrushing end of the war.

"We'll be separated soon," Bruce said to Josefine. They were lying in the barn.

"I know," she said. "I lie awake at night dreading it."

"Frank and I have decided that the time's probably come to make a run for it."

"Where will you go?"

"We reckon we'll head east and try to hook up with the Russkies. The word at the camp is that there's some sort of directive for POWs to head for Odessa. They'll ship us home from there."

Josefine was silent.

"It won't be forever," Bruce said, stroking her hair. "And I promise you this. As long as there is breath in my body, I'll come back for you."

"I'll wait forever, if I have to."

"You won't have to wait forever. And just imagine it: the two of us, together, after the war."

Josefine was quiet again for a long time.

"It seems too good to be true," she said.

It was a moment before Bruce realized she was weeping.

"Shh," he said. "Shh."

———

"Will these do?" Josefine asked. She had laid out two suits on the straw. Bruce considered them.

"Nice fabric," he said. "Very nice. And they're well made. They look like they're probably custom-made. Where did you get them?"

"Never mind where I got them." Josefine smiled. "Try one on."

In fact, Josefine had stolen them from a senior German officer. She had dressed in smart clothes; tied her hair into a severe, official-looking bun; and knocked on the door of the mansion the general shared with his Austrian mistress.

"*Guten tag.* I have been sent by the general," she told the pretty young thing when she answered the door. "Himmler has made a surprise visit to Radkersburg and a dinner is being held in his honor tonight. I am to collect his dress uniform. He asks me to tell you he will be late."

"The Reichsführer is here? Am I not invited?"

Josefine simply gave a prim smile and shook her head.

The general's mistress registered displeasure, but she showed Josefine to the officer's wardrobe.

"I expect you know what to take," she said. "I'll leave you to it."

When she was gone, Josefine hunted through the clothes and selected two tailor-made suits. She packed these carefully into a green canvas army-issue garment bag, leaving the dress uniform on its hanger. She wondered what the general's mistress would think when she saw it was still hanging there.

———

"It's not the best fit," said Bruce, pulling at the loose fabric on the trouser waist. "The pants are in danger of falling down and the cuffs need shortening. The jacket's not right, either. It doesn't hang well and needs to be taken in a bit."

Josefine set to work making the necessary alterations. It took several fittings before Bruce was satisfied. She had to alter Frank's suit based on some rudimentary measurements Bruce had taken of him.

"It's unbelievable," Josefine said one day in good-humored exasperation, after he had asked for yet another minor adjustment to the sleeves. "After the clothes you've been wearing, I would have thought anything would do."

Bruce gave her a pained look. To him, clothes weren't something to do in half measures.

Eventually, through Josefine's considerable expertise as a seamstress, Bruce's suit fit him as perfectly as a Savile Row bespoke suit.

He couldn't begin to describe how it made him feel, to be wearing decent clothes again. And Josefine seemed to be no less pleased with the fruits of her labors.

"I don't think I knew before how handsome you are," she said admiringly, cocking her head to one side to examine him.

"Oh, I scrub up," he said, in English, but the German translation defeated him. All he could say was "*Danke*."

———

Bruce and Frank settled upon a date for their escape. Sunday was the logical day, as they had no work duties and would both be at the camp. What's more, there were usually fewer guards about, and those who were had become much more relaxed. In fact, they had become almost obsequious, anxious to curry favor with the POWs because they knew the war was lost and wanted to end it on good terms with the victors.

A few nights earlier, Josefine had also "borrowed' a bicycle from another German officer who was settling in at the local *Buschenschank* for a night's drinking and had left it outside. A nod from the proprietor of the wine bar told Josefine all she needed to know, and she wheeled the bike away undetected. That was transport for one. Bruce had suggested they use the large farm wheelbarrow to carry the other.

At the appointed hour of 7 p.m. on Sunday, March 24, Josefine approached the camp. She passed the suits—each wrapped in brown paper and secured with string—through the wire to Bruce, who noticed her hands were shaking violently.

"Are you cold?" he asked.

"No," she replied, although it was only a little above freezing. "I'm afraid."

It was true. Although she had undertaken far more dangerous missions for the partisans, she was as afraid as she had ever been.

She was accustomed to endangering her own life, but she remembered as though it were yesterday the terrible hour she had spent in the alley in Gornja Radgona waiting to find out whether Bruce had been arrested or shot.

"I'll be back in three hours," she promised.

Just before ten, Bruce dislodged the removable bar for the last time. He changed into one of the Berlin-tailored suits, Frank into the other, and they slipped out. Bruce considered replacing the bar to baffle the guards, but decided there was no need.

Once outside, they hid their camp clothes under a heap of fallen leaves. Bruce had with him a small suitcase that he had stolen from a guard. In it were his few personal possessions: a couple of books, some clothes, photos of his parents and siblings, and, of course, the chamois leather he used to spit and polish his boots.

A little down the road, they saw Josefine waiting with a bicycle and a farm wheelbarrow.

"Thank God," she said. "I was worried you might not make it. I thought something had gone wrong."

"We're fine," Bruce replied. "Not a problem. Old Geiringer was fast asleep snoring his head off and that fat, stupid oaf, Heinz, was rotten drunk on schnapps. The other goons were too busy talking to notice anything." He switched to English. "Frank, this is Josefi—"

"I know who you are, love," Frank interrupted in his broad Lincolnshire accent. He had never bothered to learn any German. "Now I see what all the fuss has been about."

He held out his hand and Josefine took it and shook it gravely.

There was no time to waste. Frank climbed into the wheelbarrow and Josefine covered him with a heap of old clothes. Bruce mounted the bike. This was the only part of the plan on which they had disagreed. Bruce thought he should be the one to push the heavy barrow, and that Josefine should ride the bike. But her argument—that her

German and her local knowledge were far better than his, allowing her to pose as a bona fide local—won the day. So off he wobbled; it had been many years since he'd ridden a bike. He immediately enjoyed the feeling of the wind in his hair. It evoked memories of childhood, and the long-lost feeling of true freedom.

Josefine followed behind, pretending she wasn't struggling with Frank's weight. It wasn't far to the farmhouse, but she was exhausted after a couple of hundred yards. So far, they hadn't seen a soul. It was unlikely they would meet any German soldiers, but any who were out and about at this hour would be vigilant. It now occurred to Bruce that he should have replaced the bar in the window. If a guard happened to check the hut and see the hole in the grille, they might come looking.

Bruce looked back over his shoulder, just in time to see Josefine set the barrow down again. She breathed heavily for a few minutes. He was on the point of riding back to her when she hefted the handles again and began trundling it doggedly forward. She lurched as Frank sneezed, the sound muffled by the clothes but audible. She hoped that, if a German patrol were to stop her, Frank wouldn't get a fit of the sneezes.

As soon as she made it through the farm gates, she dropped the wheelbarrow with a thud. She pulled the clothes off Frank, whose wide eyes gleamed in the moonlight, filling with relief when he saw that they had reached their destination and all was well. Bruce had already stowed the bike in the hayloft. Josefine took the clothes to the house, then returned to put the wheelbarrow away in the barn. Bruce and Frank were now safely installed in the loft. They immediately set to work stitching old sacks together to make mattresses, which they stuffed with straw. They then ate the first of the Red Cross rations Josefine had stored there for them.

"Listen to that," Frank said. "Those guns are bloody close."

"Reckon they can't be more than a few days away," Bruce agreed. "We're nearly there, Frank."

"Nearly there," said Frank. "So close, and so bloody far."

———

For two days, their biggest problem was boredom. Then, in the early afternoon of the third day, Bruce and Frank heard someone stumbling about below. Josefine only visited at certain times, so it was unlikely to be her. They heard the sound of feet scraping against the rungs of the ladder to the loft.

Bruce and Frank exchanged glances. Then, as quickly and quietly as possible, they burrowed into the straw.

Heavy boots clumped across the floor. There was a pause, and then a sharp object prodded Bruce's thigh.

I've been bayonetted, he thought, stifling a cry.

Whoever had jabbed him had registered the resistance in the straw. The second thrust was harder, and pierced his thigh. He yelped and burst from his hiding place.

"I surrender!" he said, raising his hands above his head, certain he had been discovered by a German guard. A gangly youth reeled backward and fell over, dropping the pitchfork he was holding. Bruce felt a surge of relief.

"It's you, Grigor," he said.

Grigor, the farmboy, was Russian. He was worked harder than the other POW laborers, often slaving for twelve hours a day, with no break and little food. Mitzl sometimes slipped him a biscuit or a morsel of meat, but any kindness shown to Russians was actively discouraged by the Nazis. The punishment if she'd been caught would have been meted out to Grigor, not to Mitzl.

"Please don't tell the goons where we are," Bruce said in German.

Bruce had always gotten along well with Grigor, or as well as the constraints of the language barrier would allow. But both of them knew that Grigor would earn privileges if he betrayed Bruce and Frank—some extra food, maybe, perhaps even a few hours off. Still, Bruce saw something in Grigor's eyes that suggested he could be trusted.

Josefine came into the barn below them. She had heard Grigor instructed to fetch hay, and had followed him.

"Grigor," she said in Russian. "Please do not betray these men. They're good men. If the Germans find out they're hidden here, they'll be captured and I'll be tortured. Please say nothing."

Grigor shook his head emphatically.

"These German bastards have taken everything from me," he replied. "I'd shoot them if I had a rifle. I'll give them nothing. I'll not say a word. Your secret is safe with me."

He smiled at Bruce, gave him a thumbs-up, moved to the far corner, and pitched the hay over the landing into the barrow below.

As he finished pitching the hay and went to descend the ladder, Bruce stopped him.

"*Spasibo,*" he said, laying his hand on his heart.

The boy just grinned and nodded.

———

With Grigor complicit, Josefine found she had more opportunity to visit Frank and Bruce in the barn. She brought them food and water and, just as important, news from the approaching front. The Soviet advance was accelerating. On April 2, after Bruce and Frank had been hiding for just over a week, word came through that the Russians had taken Nagykanizsa in Hungary, about sixty miles away. The following day, Tuesday, April 3, Murska Sobota, which was much closer to Radkersburg, was also captured, and it was clear the Red Army would soon reach the Mura River bordering Austria and Slovenia.

"You must leave soon," Josefine said. Her voice was brusque and businesslike, but there were tears in her eyes.

"Yes," Bruce said. "But it won't be for long. I promise you."

"Promise me again," she said.

"I promise," he replied, looking deep into her eyes. "The war will be over soon, and then we'll be together. Properly together."

They were alone in the loft. Frank's forays down the ladder to the barn to relieve himself often coincided with Josefine's visits, and Frank noticed they lasted much longer at those times, too.

She stroked the ugly, granulated scar on his forearm.

"Your poor arm," she said.

"You know, I've grown quite fond of that scar," he said. "If I hadn't been injured and the wound hadn't gotten infected, I might have joined the Greeks fighting in the hills. Or I might have gotten away. Or I might have been killed. But I got sent to Corinth, and from Corinth to Maribor, and from Maribor to Wolfsberg, and from Wolfsberg to Radkersburg, and from Radkersburg to here. To you."

She kissed the scar gently and looked up at him. She was weeping properly now, big tears rolling down her cheeks.

"If Polde hadn't been taken, I would never have carried the note to the prison camp. And, if Jelka had not betrayed me, I wouldn't have come to live with my cousins. So many terrible things made this wonderful thing happen."

"If the war hadn't happened, I would still be in New Zealand and you would be making a Slovene boy very happy. So many terrible things."

"No more," said Josefine. "Let there be no more terrible things."

"Amen to that," said Bruce.

———

Random shelling of Radkersburg started the next day, April 4. A Russian invasion of the town seemed imminent. For now, the main action was twelve miles to the north, between Radkersburg and Sankt Anna. Josefine cautiously ventured toward the river, careful to steer clear of German troops, to check out the respective positions of the Germans and the Soviets. She could see that the Nazis were well dug in along the Mura. They plainly meant to mount a fierce defense. She reported what she had seen to her Austrian partisan contacts, and to Bruce.

Sure enough, the Russian advance seemed to stall as it ran up against the German rear guard. As more information filtered through, it seemed that Bruce and Frank might have to wait a little longer for their freedom. They resigned themselves to being holed up for a few more days.

Nor was there any immediate pressure to move on. Josefine had overheard the old Austrian guard telling Gustl that Frank and Bruce had escaped from the *Arbeitskommando* and wouldn't be coming to work. She held her breath, praying that Gustl wouldn't give the game away; she knew how heartily he disapproved of her relationship with Bruce. But she needn't have worried. He'd asked whether they were likely to be caught, but the guard shook his head.

"No, no one even bothered to raise the alarm. If they want to go and take their chances with those Communist barbarians, then good luck to them."

He had also said that the camp was being emptied. The POWs were being marched to Markt Pongau, 150 miles away beyond the border with Germany. Frank and Bruce had made their move just in time.

———

Midmorning on Thursday, April 5, a line of German staff cars rolled up to the Rossnegger farm. There were no courtesies extended; an SS officer just bashed on the door and made the announcement.

"You are to vacate the farmhouse by three o'clock this afternoon. No later. Our men will be occupying a number of buildings in this area and yours is one of them. We'll also be requisitioning your barn. Our mechanics will be moving in."

Gustl knew better than to argue. Josefine, who had been standing in the hallway behind him, was stricken. She saw two trucks already parked at the barn, with soldiers unloading tools and machinery. She'd had no chance to warn Bruce and Frank, who were still in the loft and who would surely be discovered if the Germans decided to go exploring.

"What can we do?" she said to Mitzl. "What if the Švabi find them? What will happen to them then? How can we help them?"

"Pepi, you know there's nothing we can do. We just have to sit tight and hope no one discovers them. The Nazis will probably be gone in a couple of days."

Josefine was not reassured. She helped her family shift as many of their possessions as they could to a disused farmhands' quarters at the back of the property. She flinched when she heard a volley of gunfire, but when she investigated it turned out to be a pair of soldiers using a milk churn for target practice. Other shots and noises like shots rang out over the farm throughout the course of the day, and there were periodic bursts of shouting. Every time, she imagined that it was the end of Bruce and Frank.

That night, when all was quiet, she crept to the barn, only to find it securely padlocked. She didn't dare call out to the two men, in case there were Germans sleeping inside. She listened for a long time, but heard no sign of life. For all she knew, Frank and Bruce might be dead. If they weren't, she feared they would soon run out of food and water, and she had no idea when, or how, she might replenish their supplies.

The following day, she visited the barn again, hoping it might be unattended or that there might be some sign that the Germans were about to abandon it. But it was a hive of activity—men and machinery everywhere, amid the hiss and crackle of welders, the clanging of hammers and wrenches—and it looked as though they had settled in for the long haul. She went again in the afternoon, but nothing had changed, and that night she found it locked up tight again.

It was the same the next day, and the day after that, and the day after that. Josefine felt a rising sense of panic. If the men had not been discovered and shot, then they would surely be forced to break cover before they starved or died of thirst.

"Please, God," she prayed nightly. "Please keep Bruce and Frank safe. Please make the Germans go. Dear Lord, I beg you to protect them."

On the fourth day, she considered telling the Germans that the men were there and asking for mercy. But she dismissed this option. Although everyone knew the war was a lost cause, the Nazis were as brutal and vindictive as ever—perhaps even more so, out of wounded national pride. She had heard that only a week earlier, on March 31, eight prisoners were gunned down in nearby Murska Sobota. She had little doubt that if she led the Germans to Frank and Bruce, or if they were found, they would be shot. And if she revealed she had knowingly harbored them, it was virtually certain that not only she, but also her family, would face a firing squad.

She even considered offering herself to the mechanics in the hope that she could hide food somewhere in the barn during the transaction. But she knew Bruce well enough to know that he would not lie quietly and listen to her being violated below. There really did not seem to be anything she could do but pray.

On the fifth day, her persistent vigil paid off. She crept up to the barn at night and found that the padlock had not been secured. She could hear men talking on the other side. It sounded as though two, perhaps three, of the mechanics had stayed behind after the rest had left. She realized they would probably check the door when they, too, retired for the night. She rushed back to the laborers' hut and grabbed a large pot of cold semolina that was sitting on the stove, ready to be reheated the following morning. She filled a bucket with water and hurried back to the barn, straining under the weight. She was relieved to find the door unlocked and the mechanics still deep in conversation. She opened the door carefully and quickly climbed the ladder, carrying the water. Her heart was pounding. She wasn't afraid of being discovered by the Germans; she was afraid of what she might find.

She gently set the bucket on the boards of the loft and paused. After a silence that seemed to last an eternity, there was movement in the straw. She could have shouted for joy. They were still there, and they were alive.

None of the three could speak, for fear of being heard. Josefine crept softly back down the ladder and returned with the pot of semolina. Bruce's hand found hers in the dark and squeezed. It told her all she needed to know. She wanted nothing more than to stay with them, but she knew she had to leave the barn before it was locked. So she gave Bruce's hand an answering squeeze, then climbed down the ladder. She hadn't exchanged a single word with her beloved, but she paused in her walk back to the laborers' hut and gazed heavenward with tears of pure gratitude stinging her eyes.

"Thank you, Lord," she said. "Thank you."

———

Josefine slept that night for the first time in five nights. She woke on the morning of April 10 and knew at once that everything was different. The bass rumble of the big guns had become overlaid with the rattle and crack of small-arms fire. It was clear the battle was closing in on Radkersburg.

To her joy, she saw that the Germans were preparing to leave. Trucks were being loaded, men hurried this way and that, and, amid much shouting and the roar of diesel engines, the entire contingent departed just after midday. Josefine hurried at once to the barn, which was unlocked and empty apart from an abandoned motorcycle and sidecar in an advanced state of disrepair. She climbed the ladder and found Bruce and Frank lying pale and gaunt on their mattresses.

"Josefine. My darling. You saved our lives," said Bruce.

After they had eaten the food she brought, they told her about their ordeal. They had been caught completely by surprise by the arrival of the Germans, and had been forced to hide in the hay. None of the Germans had bothered to climb the ladder, but nor had there been any opportunity, day or night, to escape the barn. Their food had run out on the first day but they managed to conserve water, stretching it out to last three. At night, when the place was locked up and empty, they scavenged for any food or water. All they found in five days was a couple of half-eaten chunks of black bread and a few apple cores.

The deprivation was worse than anything Bruce had experienced at Salonika or on the nightmare train journey to Maribor—at least then they had something to eat even if it wasn't enough. Their thoughts became totally fixated on food. They craved even a tiny morsel of cheese or a sliver of dried meat or a few crumbs of stale bread—anything edible would do. They knew they could survive for some time without nourishment—it would be a lack of water that killed them first—but that didn't quell their insatiable obsession with food.

Bruce had even started hallucinating.

"He kept going on about dogs flying through the loft, would you believe?" Frank said, and Bruce reluctantly translated. He didn't remember any of this with clarity. "Then he reckoned he could see a banquet laid out with roast this and poached that and fried this, that, and the other. That was all I bloody needed: him going on about food. And then he said there was an angel telling him to climb the walls, and he claimed he could see fireworks and all. I thought he'd gone stark raving mad."

"Poor Bruce," said Josefine, horrified.

Frank had managed to calm him down. On the fifth day, he was completely lucid again. They decided they would have to surrender, but had agreed they could hold on for one more day. The sound of the guns encouraged them to believe that deliverance was at hand—even if they wondered whether they might be targeted if the Russians spotted the military activity at the farm.

"And then you appeared," said Bruce in German. "You, my guardian angel. You saved us."

"Tell you what. Semolina never tasted so bloody good," said Frank, as though he had understood.

———

Now the Germans were gone. Josefine learned that the unit occupying the farm had been ordered to withdraw to the defense of the Mura.

The following day, they heard that Gederovci, less than three miles away, had been taken by the Russians.

"This is it," said Bruce. "We'd better go to Radkersburg tomorrow. Uncle Joe should be there to meet us."

"I'll come with you," Josefine said when he told her the plan.

"Never," he replied. "I won't let you."

"You must take me," she argued. "I know the area better than you or Frank, and I speak Russian. You have to take me."

It made sense. Bruce relented.

On the morning of April 12, they set off for Radkersburg, Bruce riding ahead on the bike and Josefine pushing Frank in the wheelbarrow covered in old clothes. Since Frank spoke no German, they had all agreed he was best kept out of sight. Josefine had instructed Bruce to save himself if they encountered a German patrol. She trusted herself to talk her way out of trouble. Bruce had nodded, but he'd already decided he would stay with her no matter what.

They saw no soldiers, so abandoned both bike and barrow soon after leaving and struck out across the fields toward Radkersburg, traveling parallel to the main road to avoid the German forces. They reached Radkersburg safely, and resolved to make for the center of town. Josefine had a piece of white cloth ripped from an old sheet, but none of them imagined the truce symbol would protect them in the heat of battle. Her fluency in Russian was more likely to pacify any Soviet aggression.

They were moving quickly across the intersection of Hauptplatz and Langgasse when the first shot whined past them, embedding itself with a dull thwack in the gray stone wall of a turn-of-the-century building. A shower of masonry shards pattered on the road, and the report of the gun that fired the round reached them a split second later, sounding from behind. Other shots immediately rang out from in front of them. They were caught in cross fire.

"Down," Bruce shrieked, grabbing Josefine by the arm and pulling her toward him. "We'll have to crawl from here. Look, there's some shelter by that old house."

They slithered across the rough cobblestones using their elbows. There was an explosion a few yards away on their left that set their ears singing and showered them with stones. There was another ahead of them and to the right, and, as the smoke and dust from the detonation hung in the air, they used the cover to clamber frantically to the other side of the road. There they huddled together, trying to press themselves into the old stone walls. To have come so far only to be injured or killed by a stray bullet was not how they wanted it to end.

The fighting continued unabated for at least half an hour. Stray rounds and ricochets sent debris cascading over them, and the sweetish, acrid smell of cordite was overwhelming. Bruce marveled at how calm Josefine was. It was years since he and Frank had been under fire, and it was terrifying.

Finally, there was a lull in the fighting. They made a run toward the Russian lines. Men were lying behind low walls and piles of rubble with their rifles leveled down the street. They glanced at the three civilians incuriously. Bruce saw the red star on their helmets.

Fifty yards farther on, Russian soldiers were walking upright, talking cockily, carrying ammunition cases, unreeling spools of communications wire. Josefine spotted someone who, to judge by the peaked cap and the lapel insignia on his field uniform, was a senior officer.

"I'm a Slovene partisan," she announced in Russian. "I have two British prisoners of war with me who have escaped from the Germans. They're trying to get to Odessa. Will you help them get away?"

"We still have a war to fight here," he replied. "I've got to focus on my immediate task: finishing off these stinking Nazis. My men have enough on their hands without babysitting a couple of runaways."

"These men have risked their lives to escape and have found their way to the Allied lines. They're on the same side as you. Surely there's something you can do to help?"

The officer considered her request.

"If they want to be treated like our Allies, they'll have to prove they're our allies," he said. "They'll have to do their bit and help my men get the situation here under control. That means fighting for us. They'll be expected to do their duty like all my soldiers, and that includes serving on the front line if necessary."

Josefine explained the terms to Bruce.

"Please don't do it," she pleaded. "Come back to the farm and wait until the fighting's finished. It'll be over soon enough and, when they've taken Radkersburg, the Russians will probably escort you somewhere safe—well away from the firing line."

"There's no guarantee of that," Bruce said. "The Russians may not want to help us at all. They may force us to fight somewhere else. We're here now and at least we've got a chance to get away. We might as well stay and help them."

They argued for a minute or two, as Frank looked on, uncomprehending. "Blimey, what a place to choose for a bleeding lovers' tiff," he muttered.

Then he saw them come to some sort of agreement, and clasp each other, a short, fierce embrace. Bruce bent his neck and took off the greenstone pendant he always wore. It was the one that had belonged to his grandmother; the one Bruce took everywhere as a good-luck charm.

He gave it to Josefine. They kissed briefly. Josefine ducked down the street back the way they had come. Bruce didn't even watch her go. He stalked toward Frank, his face set in an expression of agonized grief.

"Here I thought you wore that necklace for luck," Frank said.

"I did," he replied. "She needs it more than me now."

"Not so sure about that," muttered Frank.

There was a sudden burst of firing from the German lines, the direction in which Josefine had gone.

"Come on," said Bruce. "Let's help Uncle Joe win this fucking war."

Chapter Twenty-One

—

Bruce, Radkersburg to Sopron, April 1945

Don't know about you, Brucie, but I thought we might have been past all this," Frank said. For the third time in the war, Bruce was in action. He was just as apprehensive as he had been the first time—perhaps more so, because he felt he had so much more to live for—but he was prepared to do whatever he had to. He and Frank cut incongruous figures, dressed in their dusty tailored suits with frayed knees and elbows and clutching SVT-40 rifles. They were posted behind the front in a backup unit, ready to move forward should they be ordered to. They were positioned opposite the same intersection they had crossed earlier. Watching it over the sights of his rifle, Bruce realized how fortunate they were to be alive. All it would have taken was one trigger-happy Russian and they would have been lying out there on the cobbles, dead.

He ducked as a burst of machine-gun fire dislodged splinters from the eaves of the building alongside him.

"Got to hand it to those Krauts," he said to Frank. "They aren't giving in easily."

"You're bloody right there," Frank agreed.

———

"*Komm*," said a Soviet soldier, clapping Bruce on the shoulder. He and Frank followed, running in a half crouch to a barricade comprising blocks of masonry and lengths of timber. Bruce understood that they were being pushed up to the front line, whether because the Germans were mounting an attack or the Russians were themselves making an assault he couldn't tell.

Bullets whined and cracked overhead. Bruce found a gap in the rubble pile that would serve as a loophole and pushed his rifle through it. Every now and then, he saw German soldiers running from the cover of one building corner or doorway to another. He loosed a few rounds, but wasn't sure whether he hit anyone. The fire from the Soviet side had become intense, and it was clear the Nazis were falling back in the face of it.

Soon, the shooting tapered off, as the battle shifted to another street. And soon after that all fell relatively quiet. Radkersburg had been taken by the Red Army. Bruce hadn't felt in as much danger as he had in Greece—there wasn't the intensity of Thermopylae or Molos—but it was a different feeling emerging victorious from a battle. At least Bruce could claim to have played a part in one triumph after the military disasters of Greece.

———

The Russians were now pressing forward and didn't want two Allied soldiers tagging along. Bruce and Frank were relieved of their rifles. No thanks were given nor any acknowledgment of their help tendered. A dirty, crumpled map was roughly shoved into Bruce's hands and they were given vague directions in almost unintelligible German.

"Go this way," the Russian said, waving his hand toward a decrepit farmhouse that didn't appear to have a road anywhere near it. "Carry on along there and you'll get to Sank Tenner and Feastenfilled," he continued, clearly unable to pronounce Sankt Anna and Fürstenfeld. "There should be more of us there. They might be able to help."

An ancient Mosin-Nagant rifle was handed to Bruce, a Nagant pistol to Frank and they were sent on their way with a letter to be given to a senior Russian officer explaining that they were Allied soldiers and were to be treated accordingly. The map was next to useless—it was all in Russian, so Bruce didn't understand a word—and there were no landmarks that either he or Frank could make out.

As they moved out of the village, heading in what they thought was the right direction, the roads were packed with frightened refugees. There were German soldiers everywhere—some clearly trying to fall in with the main defensive effort, which had withdrawn south across the river to Gornja Radgona; some heading in the opposite direction. No one seemed to care about a couple of civilians who were far too smartly dressed for a war zone. Frank and Bruce traversed the first couple of miles completely unmolested.

Three miles east of Radkersburg, Frank nudged Bruce.

"Hello, what have we here?" he queried. There was a group of five German soldiers in the roadway.

"What do we do?" Bruce asked.

"Brazen it out," Frank said. "They've got too much on their plate to bother with the likes of us."

As they got closer, they saw that the soldiers' hair under their forage caps was silver. They were likely prison guards brought to the front line as Hitler became more desperate in the dying days of the war. Indeed, as he studied them, Bruce recognized one of them from his early days at Maribor.

"That's bloody Klaus Weiner," he said to Frank. "The bastard deserves to be shot for what he did to us."

"So it is. So he does," Frank replied.

The old men saw them approaching.

"Halt," one of them called half-heartedly. "Who are you? What's your business here?"

"Fuck off," Frank replied in English. "Get out of our way before we shoot."

Bruce worked the bolt on his rifle and aimed it directly at Weiner.

"Drop your weapons," he ordered in German.

The soldiers smartly complied and raised their hands.

"*Bitte*," Weiner whimpered, hands high in the air. "Don't shoot. Don't harm us. Let us go. *Bitte*."

Bruce eyed him with distaste. He had been a first-rate bully in Stalag XVIIID. Now he cut a wretched figure.

"What do we do now?" Frank muttered.

"Buggered if I know," Bruce replied. "Don't know about you, Frank, but I can't in all conscience allow these blokes to be slaughtered. I reckon that's what'll happen if the Russians get hold of them. They're just harmless old fools, now. We have to let them go."

"Agreed, but what's to stop them shooting us as soon as our backs are turned? Do we tie them up or what?"

"Tying them up means the Russkies will get them. Let's just take their guns and let them go."

Bruce collected their guns, watched tensely by the Germans, whose hands were still high in the air. One of them was praying quietly. Bruce stood back and uncocked his rifle.

"*Viel glück*," he said. "Good luck."

The five looked momentarily baffled, then delighted as it became clear that they weren't to be summarily executed or frog-marched to the Russian lines. Frank handed them five cigarettes each—almost half his supply—and waved his hand.

"What's Kraut for 'fuck off'?" he asked Bruce. But no translation was necessary. The soldiers were only too happy to oblige. They ran toward the Mura as fast as their old legs would carry them.

———

A short distance farther on, Bruce spotted an abandoned Zündapp military motorbike on its side, its sidecar cocked in the air. A heap of blood-soaked cloth in the field a little off the road was presumably the rider.

"He won't be needing this anymore," he said to Frank, nodding in the direction of the corpse. "It'll make life a hell of a lot easier for us."

"I dunno," Frank said, but he helped Bruce heave the machine upright again. Gasoline had soaked into the ground beneath the fuel tank, but Bruce figured there was enough left to take them some considerable distance. He straddled the machine and kicked it into life.

Frank muttered to himself, but climbed into the sidecar.

They were feeling confident—cocky even—when, according to the speedometer, they had ridden fifteen miles without seeing so much as a Nazi helmet or a Russian forage cap. But then they saw soldiers in the roadway ahead. It only now dawned on Bruce what a risk they had taken. If these were Soviet soldiers, they would shoot the riders of a German motorcycle on sight. If they were Germans, Bruce and Frank's civilian clothes would be a dead giveaway and they would surely be halted and recaptured.

Sure enough, even as Bruce slowed and looked around for an escape route, the soldiers were unslinging their weapons.

"Halt," one of the soldiers yelled in German. "Stop now. Get off the bike and raise your hands. If you don't, we'll shoot."

For a moment, Bruce considered complying. But a giddy impulse swept over him. They had come too far to be denied their freedom by an almost-defeated German Army. He hooked his toe under the gear lever, gave it two sharp jerks, opened the throttle, and let out the clutch. The machine roared and the Germans dived to either side as it raged toward them. The sidecar struck one a glancing blow and Bruce saw him tumble in the dust. He swerved just as he heard the first shot fired behind him. He swerved again as there was a ragged fusillade. Frank was yelling incoherently from the sidecar, which was in danger of shearing clean off. They hurtled into a bend, and Bruce took it without slowing, the wheel of the sidecar lifting from the ground. For a moment, Bruce thought they were going to leave the road, but the rear wheel slithered, the sidecar landed with a crash, and they were away.

"Fuck me!" Frank yelled.

Bruce drove them as far as he dared, and far enough, he hoped, to evade any pursuit from the patrol. Then he eased the machine to a halt and killed the engine.

Frank had slipped his suit jacket off his shoulder and was studying a red welt on his upper arm where he'd been creased by a German round. "That wasn't your brightest idea, Brucie boy."

They dumped the Zündapp and proceeded on foot, careful to ensure they skirted around any danger areas. For the rest of the ten-mile journey, they were not once challenged. They reached Fürstenfeld, near the Austrian border with Hungary, in the late afternoon. The Russians were clearly still struggling to gain control; a pall of smoke hung over the town and there was the crackle of small-arms fire. Bruce and Frank kept to the fields and skirted the town until they were fairly certain they were behind the Russian lines. Then, after a short debate about the best way to proceed, they stood, raised their hands, and began walking down the middle of the road. Bruce held the precious letter aloft in his right, and the two of them shouted, "*Angliyskiy, Angliyskiy!*"

A soldier stepped out of a doorway with his rifle leveled at them. Another followed, then another, and they were surrounded by men aiming guns at them. Bruce offered the letter, but it was ignored. The soldiers motioned them to walk ahead of them, and they were shepherded to a building walled in with sandbags. A man wearing an officer's uniform glanced at them indifferently. Bruce offered him the letter, too, but he waved it away. After a short conversation in Russian with the soldiers, Bruce and Frank were escorted to another officer. He sent them on to a third, and he to yet another. Soviet bureaucracy clearly functioned as inefficiently on the battlefield as it had in the prewar civil service.

Finally, they found a senior apparatchik who was interested enough to read the letter. He directed a barrage of questions at them in Russian. Bruce asked him if he spoke German, but he didn't; he quickly became exasperated and made a dismissive gesture. The soldiers took them away to a tiny log cabin and motioned them inside. The door was closed behind them, and they heard a bolt shot home. They were locked in.

There were two wooden-framed folding camp stretchers with partially ripped green canvas covers and a couple of moldy army blankets lay on top, but it was still bitterly cold, even in spring. The split-log construction of the cabin left wide gaps in the walls that did nothing to keep out the breeze. Bruce and Frank were terrified; they were still tormented by the memories of the last time they had been locked away without food or water.

They hammered on the door and shouted, *"Angliyskiy, Angliyskiy!"* but it seemed that no one spoke English, and no one seemed interested in finding anyone who did.

"Spricht man Deutsch?" Bruce yelled in frustration.

"What's that you're saying?" Frank asked.

"I'm asking if anyone speaks German."

"Is that wise?" Frank said nervously.

Bruce was wondering the same thing.

———

After he had been calling for ten minutes, the bolt rattled and the door opened, framing a diminutive man wearing a Soviet sergeant's uniform. His appearance set him apart from the other Red Army soldiers Bruce had seen. He wore old-fashioned horn-rimmed spectacles, crudely mended with sticky black insulation tape. His dark hair was cropped short and his hooked nose looked slightly too large for the face it graced—especially since he didn't wear the extravagant Stalin moustache fashionable among Russian soldiers. Most strikingly, he was as well dressed and groomed as it was possible to be, considering the drastic shortage of new uniforms, the nonexistent laundry facilities and the hardships of war.

Bruce and the soldier connected instantly.

"I'm told you have been asking if anyone speaks German," he said in a quiet voice. "I speak it well. My wife is German. Born in Russia but of German descent."

"My name is Bruce Murray. This is Frank Butler. We were English prisoners of war. We've escaped and we're trying to make our way to Odessa."

"I'm delighted to meet you," the man said, offering his soft hand. "My name is Arkady. Somehow I find myself a sergeant in the Soviet Army. I will do what I can to help you."

———

The following day, after a breakfast of lukewarm *kasha*—boiled buckwheat porridge—Bruce and Frank were interrogated again. This time, there was an officer present who could speak a little English, but he chose to communicate in Russian with Arkady, who translated. All the preliminaries went without a hitch: name, rank, serial number, battalion details. It was only when they were questioned about their war service that the mood changed.

"We were both captured in Greece," Bruce explained, "and we've been in POW camps in Slovenia and Austria for the last four years."

When Arkady translated, the portly officer went red in the face and launched into a furious rant, directed at Arkady but clearly intended for Bruce and Frank. Arkady replied, but that only seemed to incense the officer further. He spat a few more words, and glared first at Bruce, then at Frank.

Arkady tried again, and Bruce heard the word Radkersburg. He assumed Arkady was repeating what he had told them: that they had assisted the Russians in that action.

The officer waved his hand as though shooing a fly. Something resembling an argument ensued, with Frank and Bruce watching on helplessly, unable to understand anything beyond the fact that it didn't seem to be going well.

When finally the officer pushed his chair back with a savage scraping noise and stormed out of the room, he didn't so much as address Bruce and Frank. They were bundled off back to the shed. Arkady accompanied them.

"I'm sorry, Bruce. I did my best, but the Captain is a good Army man, and if the Army says jump, he jumps. With respect to prisoners of war, the official Red Army position is clear. Order Number 270 states, and I quote, 'There are no Soviet prisoners of war, only traitors.'"

"What will happen to us?" Bruce asked.

Arkady hesitated before replying.

"Just last week the Captain had five deserters executed. These were men from his own ranks, not foreigners. He said in there that he thinks you deserve to be shot. His mind's made up and I have come to understand that it is best to take him literally. I'll do my best to protect you but I can't promise anything."

———

"Well, looks like we're in the shit good and proper, Brucie," Frank said when Arkady had gone.

"Again," said Bruce.

"Again," agreed Frank. "So what do we do this time?"

Bruce thought about it.

"The only thing we can do is try to show them we're not cowards," he said. "We'll have to volunteer to fight for Uncle Joe, just like we did in Radkersburg. It's worth a try, don't you think?"

Frank groaned. "Anything's worth a go," he said. "Who knows?"

Bruce summoned Arkady and explained their proposition. Arkady was skeptical but marched off to put it to the POW-hating captain. After an anxious wait, he was back.

"Well, wonders will never cease," Arkady said. "The Captain was in favor . . . No, he was positively enthusiastic about your plan. He gratefully accepts your offer of help, and welcomes you into the ranks of the Red Army. You are to report for duty in the morning."

"You beauty," said Bruce, feeling weak with relief. Frank, who had been watching his face anxiously to see what news Arkady had brought, punched the air in delight.

"How many frying pans and fires is that now, do you think?" he crowed.

———

As the battle for Fürstenfeld wore on, Bruce and Frank were assigned to Arkady's unit, which was involved in logistical support

behind the front lines. They unloaded munitions from trucks, helped
bear stretchers with the wounded, and delivered supplies to forward
positions. It wasn't difficult or particularly dangerous work and the
Soviets treated them well enough. Bruce even found himself enjoying it, perhaps because it seemed like an atonement for being captured, or vengeance for the deaths of Blackie and Logie, or perhaps
because he just wanted to do his bit to end the war. Fürstenfeld was
taken the following day: April 15.

What followed shocked Bruce to the core. Helmut and several of
the other guards at Wolfsberg had regaled the prisoners with lurid
stories of Soviet excesses—rape and pillage, torture and murder—but
Bruce had been inclined to dismiss these as the kind of demonizaton
of the enemy that armies go in for. But shortly after Fürstenfeld had
fallen, as they were returning from a stint unloading ammunition,
Bruce, Frank, and Arkady came upon the hellish reality. Among the
ruins of the town, they saw a knot of men, all in the uniforms of privates in the Soviet Army. The sound of women screaming came from
within the circle. There could be no doubt about what was happening.
Four men were raping the women as the others, trousers around their
ankles, called encouragement and waited their turn.

"Fucking animals!" Bruce shouted, but even those who heard him
took no visible notice.

"Leave it, Bruce," Arkady said. "They'll kill you if you try to stop
them." Arkady grabbed Bruce to prevent him from charging at the
rapists.

Bruce might have allowed himself to be pulled away. But one soldier, reeling drunk and with a bottle in his hand, had become frustrated when arousal eluded him. When frantic hand stimulation failed
to make a difference, he finally gave up. As his comrades taunted him,
he hauled his trousers up, stepped forward, and delivered a swift kick
between the legs of the already bleeding woman, shouting abuse as
he did so.

As she writhed on the ground, he took out a pistol and shot her in the head. Bruce could take no more. Impulsively, without considering the consequences, he twisted free of Arkady's grip and charged at the men. He swung his boot into the groin of the nearest rapist.

"*Svoloch!*" the doubled-up soldier shouted. "Bastard!"

Bruce was set upon. He was bludgeoned with anything that came to hand—fists, boots, broomsticks, metal spikes, rifle butts—before Arkady was able to assert his authority by firing a shot from his pistol into the air.

"Disperse!" he yelled. "Get out of here, or I'll see to it that the last thing you ever see will be a firing squad."

For a tense moment, the men faced Arkady. Then one of them turned and began walking away, buttoning his trousers as he went. The others followed one by one, leaving the five bodies—one dead, and Bruce and the women severely injured—lying on the bloodied ground. Frank and Arkady dragged Bruce away, leaving the sobbing women to scramble off as best they could.

———

As consciousness returned, Bruce realized he was lucky to be alive. He was confined for a day to his quarters, a single room he shared with Frank and two others in a small farmhouse commandeered by the Russians. Frank stood guard in case of retaliation by the rapists. There was none. On the second day following the beating and still heavily bandaged, he was well enough to eat and joined Arkady and Frank for a lunch of watery borscht and stale blini.

"We can't stay here, Arkady," he said. "We've done our bit. Now we need to get on to Odessa. Can you help us?"

Arkady agreed he would do what he could. That afternoon, he took them before a man he introduced as the divisional commanding officer. The man heard their case, raising his eyebrows when Arkady told him that they had volunteered to serve alongside their Russian allies. It may have been Bruce's injuries, no doubt interpreted as hard-earned battle scars, that swayed his decision but, after a few minutes' deliberation, he told Arkady that he would agree to their request.

Early the same evening, Arkady appeared, his excitement obvious. "I have two bits of news, both good," he said. "The first is that you're leaving tomorrow morning."

"What's the second?" asked Bruce.

"The second piece of good news, especially for me, is that I've been ordered to escort you. A truck will take us to Szombathely in Hungary, and from there we'll be transported to Veszprém, where we'll join other Allied servicemen who are being taken to Odessa."

They gathered together the few belongings they had, packed them in their rucksacks, and readied to leave. The following morning, they boarded a decrepit old GAZ truck with canvas sides and packing cases serving as seats. They had only been on the road an hour—crashing and heaving over the pitted and potholed surface—before Bruce's arse went numb, and there were red stripes on the backs of his legs that matched the gaps between the parallel boxwood panels. Here and there, the truck stopped so that other Allied soldiers, mostly those freed from POW camps, could also be loaded into the truck. Bruce and Frank would have preferred walking. The trucks moved at about the same pace.

The journey to Szombathely took them through scenes straight from a nightmare. The living conditions of the peasants on the farms and in the villages were the most primitive Bruce had ever seen, and the extent of the poverty was distressing. But it was the carnage that affected him the most. The roadside was littered with dead bodies, some squashed after being run over by tanks; others with mangled faces; and many grotesquely disfigured by bombs, land mines, and grenades. The dead—and probably a few still dying—lay heaped on top of one another, bulldozed out of the road to make way for military traffic and tanks. No one seemed to care and no attempt had been made to bury them. They were left where they had been shoved to the verge. From a distance, these mounds of human flesh might have been mistaken for a gently undulating landscape, were it not for the protruding arms and legs.

Where bodies lay singly, they were stepped over by soldiers or run over by tanks as if they were inconvenient obstacles standing in the way of military progress. Anything of value—boots, watches, wallets, tunics, cigarettes—was plundered. The Russians could see no point in leaving boots on a dead man; he had no use for them. Photos of loved ones were either ripped to pieces or discarded; there was no black market for personal mementos.

The butchered children moved Bruce more than anything else; lifeless then and, he suspected, with little to live for before.

Most incredibly, life was going on among it all. Here and there, smoke rose from the chimney of a building that was more or less un-scathed. Women hoed the fields beyond the windrows of corpses as the stream of military traffic passed them by.

The worst treatment was reserved for the Germans. The fortunate were those who were shot; the less fortunate were tortured, abused, and left to die an agonizing death. Bruce and Frank saw a row of four German soldiers tied to railway tracks, unable to move, knowing they would be dissected by the next train. A short distance along the same line, they saw the remains of others who had been dismembered by the last train through.

Life seemed to be of little value to the Soviets. Perhaps they had seen so many of their comrades killed on the battlefield, or executed by their own for cowardice, treachery, or desertion, that it mattered little to them that a few more innocents might perish. Even Arkady seemed unaffected by what he saw. Bruce asked him about this.

"I cannot ask you to pardon the unpardonable," Arkady said. "But perhaps you can understand. Most of the Red Army comprises young men who knew nothing but potato fields until they were conscripted. Since then, they have known nothing but death and destruction. They have seen the Germans butcher their comrades and their country-men, and now they find they have the chance to mete out the same punishment. It is too much to ask them to show mercy. And they are not sufficiently wise about the world to know that not everyone who speaks in a different accent is a German. So—this." He waved at the world outside the truck.

"You don't seem like most of the other soldiers," Bruce said.

"I am—I was—a schoolteacher, so I have the privilege of educa-tion," Arkady said. "For all the good it has done me."

"Your wife is waiting for you?"

Arkady was silent for a moment.

"My wife, Olga, is probably dead," he said at last. "She was arrested and transported east in 1941. To where I don't know. I've heard nothing from her. She was one of hundreds of thousands of Russian-born Germans deported. Russia has been our only home, and we are loyal citizens, but that made no difference. I have some hope, but not much. Not many people return from the east."

———

Toward the end of that first harrowing day on the road, they passed through one village—Bruce couldn't remember its name—that had been completely destroyed and then pillaged, either by the retreat-ing Germans or the advancing Russians. Wrecked tanks, still burning days after the battle, were scattered across the landscape, and Bruce could see the charcoal-black bodies of the crew who were too slow to scramble out slumping from the top hatches and, on the ground beside them, the bullet-riddled bodies of those who had been quick enough. One of the charred bodies still sported a shock of blond hair even though his face had been burned beyond recognition.

Just before they reached the Hungarian border, they were ordered off the truck and told to march. They weren't far from Szombathely—about fifteen miles away—and were to be picked up by another truck a few miles down the road. The last few miles continued in the relative comfort of an open-decked cattle truck. Fresh cow dung covered the floor, but a sudden cloudburst washed most of the muck away.

The men were housed overnight at a campsite on a farm on the outskirts of Szombathely where soldiers of all nationalities were gathered, also awaiting transport to Odessa. It felt like a prisoner-of-war camp, not least because it was guarded by armed Soviet soldiers. Subsistence rations were dished out but most, like Bruce, Frank, and Arkady, preferred to forage for their own food, which the guards permitted them to do. Spit-roast rabbits were cooked alongside potatoes and pumpkins scavenged from the fields. In the evening, the camp was filled with the savory aroma of roasting meat—horse, cat, and dog steaks sizzling on makeshift grills over open fires. A French soldier even showed Bruce and Frank how to roast a hedgehog. He smothered it in clay and set it to bake among the coals. When the clay was blackened and hard, he broke it open. A cloud of savory steam rose, and the smooth, pink flesh was revealed, the prickles remaining embedded in the clay. Bruce and Frank devoured it without a qualm. Meat was meat and they'd had very little of it over the past four years.

A convoy of trucks took them from Szombathely. Soon after leaving, it swung to the northeast, away from Veszprém and toward Sopron, which was on the way to Vienna. Arkady had no idea why. The detour would add almost seventy miles to their journey, but the Russians made it clear that Sopron was the next stop and that was that.

Bruce was shocked by what he saw as they traveled through war-torn towns and villages. The Red Army had left a trail of destruction, taking whatever they wanted from the impoverished locals—food, drink, livestock, valuables of any sort, and, whenever and however it suited them, their women, often forcing husbands or lovers to look on at gunpoint. From the back of the truck passing through a village, Bruce and Frank saw another pack rape being committed, but they were powerless to intervene. Bruce knew the same thing was happening wherever the Soviets went. Women were discarded or shot after the soldiers had satisfied themselves and were seeking solace again in the vodka bottle. Inevitably, Bruce's thoughts fled to occupied Austria. He knew that, as Arkady had said, it was too much to ask for an unsophisticated Russian soldier to differentiate between an Austrian and a German; the language was the same after all. And, quite apart from the thirst for vengeance, a conquering army always takes what it wants from the conquered. Young men seemed to want one thing above anything else. Bruce was haunted by visions of the kind of scene he had witnessed twice, only instead of the face of just another anonymous victim glimpsed between the shoulders of gloating soldiers, it was the face of his beloved Josefine.

Bruce tried to write to her.

I will try and tell you about something of what has happened since I last saw your dear self, he wrote. *The first few days I cannot write about because I was in the very depths of hell.*

Chapter Twenty-Two

Bruce & Josefine, Radkersburg and Europe, April to June 1945

Josefine had made it back to the Rossnegger farm without incident after she had left Bruce with the Russians. There, she spent what she described to Bruce as the worst night of her life, apart from the five terrible nights when he and Frank had been trapped in the barn. With the sound of the fierce fighting sometimes closer, sometimes farther away, she clutched Bruce's greenstone pendant and wondered if he had survived, and whether she would ever see him again.

The day after they had parted tearfully on April 12, the fighting engulfed the farm. Around the middle of the morning, there was a whoosh from the sky and a crash from another part of the house. When Josefine went to investigate, she found the entire front of the house ablaze. *We did everything we possibly could,* she wrote to Bruce, *and carried buckets and buckets of water to douse the flames . . . I was no longer afraid of the shooting when the house went up in flames.*

Together with neighbors who saw the smoke, they did their utmost to get the fire under control while one of the fiercest battles in Austria raged around them. As Josefine was hurrying from the well with a bucket of water, she saw an object fall close by. It was a grenade. She didn't even break stride—and luckily the grenade failed to explode.

Theirs was a losing battle. They managed to salvage a few personal belongings once the flames died down, but the house was destroyed along with virtually everything in it.

The Rossneggers and Josefine shifted into the small laborers' cottage that they had occupied when the Germans commandeered the farm buildings. It shook and rattled violently as the battle raged. Plates and cups crashed to the floor and smashed, cutlery was strewn everywhere, and furniture toppled to the ground, but, remarkably, a dozen Rogaška Slatina crystal glasses they had rescued from the fire remained intact. They shook and wobbled on the shelf, but didn't tumble; the tinkling of rims knocking against one another sounded like an orchestra of xylophones with the rhythmic boom of bomb blasts providing the bass. The dust and debris were suffocating, and shrapnel and rock splinters almost as deadly as the gunfire itself came at them from all directions.

For three days, our place was on the front line, Josefine wrote. *But thank God we were lucky [and survived] . . . even you, who mean everything to me, could not comprehend what we suffered in those terrible days.*

The inevitable happened. The Red Army triumphed and the Germans withdrew, but not before the Rossnegger farmhands' quarters—their last refuge—was also destroyed, rendering them completely homeless.

Whatever dangers she had courted and dodged in her life, Josefine reckoned the peril she and her family found themselves in now was the greatest they had ever faced. *The Russians are brutes*, she wrote to Bruce. *In my whole life, I have never prayed for my safety as much as I did then.* She traveled to her uncle's house in occupied Rikte Stoor to escape the depredations of the marauding Red Army. Even so, she wrote, there were many times when she was sure she would be shot. And, once the immediate danger was past, she and her family had to face the reality. *We have now become genuine beggars,* she wrote. *Our house is gone and we have to look for somewhere to live.*

————

At Sopron, Frank and Bruce were ordered onto another truck, bound for the railway station at Veszprém, where they would meet up with other Allied servicemen and Soviet soldiers who would accompany them through to Odessa. But Bruce had gone cold on the idea of Odessa. It felt too much like running in the opposite direction from the one his heart told him he should be taking. He was determined to return to Austria. He needed to be sure Josefine was safe.

Somewhere along the way, someone had told him that there was a British and American diplomatic mission based in Budapest. Asking around, he learned that it would be possible, in theory, to catch a train there. At the first rest stop, he asked Arkady to take him to his superior officer. Frank went along for the ride.

With Arkady as an interpreter, Bruce requested permission to go to the Hungarian capital.

"I need to get in touch with some British officials based in Budapest," he said. "It's very important I talk to them. As a liberated New Zealand POW, I'm entitled to make my own way through Hungary. I'm no longer a prisoner and I wish to leave tomorrow."

The officer stared at Arkady incredulously as he translated.

"*Nyet!*" he shouted. "*Nyet! Nyet! Nyet!* You must go to Veszprém. That's an order—you're under our command now."

Bruce went to protest, but Arkady shook his head. There was nothing to do but to resume the journey to Veszprém.

They were on the outskirts of the town, just about to turn toward the railway station, when Arkady asked the driver to stop. The remains of a large aircraft were scattered all over a field, and men were rummaging in the wreckage and loading pieces of it into a pair of trucks. Arkady wandered over to see what was happening.

"What's going on?" Bruce asked.

"This was a Tupolev bomber," Arkady replied. "They're taking anything that still has value to the airbase near Budapest."

Frank saw the look on Bruce's face.

"You daft bugger. You wouldn't, would you?"

But, of course, Frank knew he would. Bruce had seen his opportunity. The two trucks had been loaded and the drivers were ready to go. Bruce walked toward them, with Frank following reluctantly behind. As the second truck passed, they simply leaped aboard.

That was the last we saw of our good friend, the Russian soldier, poor fellow, Bruce wrote to Josefine. *I hope he didn't get into trouble.*

Bruce felt guilty about leaving without saying goodbye, but he knew Arkady would have been duty bound to prevent him going. His need to see Josefine was greater than any debt of loyalty.

———

The airfield was around thirty miles from Budapest. After leaving the truck, Bruce and Frank tried to hitch a ride the rest of the way, but no one seemed interested in stopping to help a couple of itinerant Allied soldiers. But, just as they were beginning to wonder how they would manage to cover the remaining distance, an open-decked ZIS-5 appeared, grinding slowly along the road. Bruce and Frank jogged alongside it and, as it passed, they hopped aboard. They were in Budapest by evening.

It took most of the following day to get an appointment with a senior British officer at the diplomatic post. Arkady had all their identity documents which, as Bruce wrote to Josefine, took quite a lot of explaining.

And even once they were granted an audience with a British functionary, if Bruce had been expecting to be greeted with thanks for their service in Greece or sympathy for the four years they had endured as prisoners of war, he was to be disappointed. It was his first brush with British bureaucracy, and he was not impressed. Even after he was admitted to the office and instructed to sit down, the man at the desk carried on writing, ignoring Bruce. The desk was enormous. "Snotty," as Bruce dubbed the man, sat on an old, creaking banker's chair. Oak filing cabinets lined the wall, with dog-eared folders sticking out of half-opened drawers.

Finally, Snotty put his pen down. "Why are you here? What do you want?"

"Sir, I'd like permission to make my way back to Austria. The Russians or British must have control of the situation there by now, so it should be safe for me to return. I need to go back for personal reasons. It's very important, sir, and I'm prepared to serve with the British or Russians in the region if necessary. Whatever I need to do to get back, I will do. I'm desperate to—"

Bruce was only partway through his explanation when Snotty picked his pen up again.

"Out of the question, I'm afraid," he said, busying himself with his papers. "You must return to the care of the Russians. You're under their control until you get to Odessa. Understand? Request denied."

"But, sir, I don't think you—"

"Perhaps you didn't hear me, Private," Snotty interrupted. "I said no. What you ask is impossible. Now clear out. I have much more important things to do than listen to some antipodean POW making a stupid request to return to a war zone. Go down the corridor to my junior assistant and get him to sort you out some temporary papers. Interview over."

Everything inside of me just went dead, Bruce wrote to Josefine. *I knew that it would be impossible for me to come to you once I reached Odessa.*

After being cleared by the authorities and given their temporary identity papers, Bruce and Frank were handed over to a Russian named Igor, who spoke passable English. He was to accompany them for the rest of the journey and had strict instructions to guard them diligently, given that they had escaped from their escort at Veszprém. Igor seemed a nice enough bloke, not unlike Arkady, although he was much more conventionally Russian to look at—a squat fellow with a crop of black, curly hair atop a round, fleshy face with a dark five-o'clock shadow. Igor informed them that they were to be put on a train in two days' time, bound for Bucharest.

"Nothing can do but enjoy Budapest," he said with obvious satisfaction. "And now, we go to bar."

———

After two days in the Pearl of the Danube, during which Bruce and Frank saw as much as they could of the fabled city—they even went to the cinema where, to their surprise, a movie featuring Spencer Tracy and Clark Gable was playing—it was time to move on. They were loaded aboard cattle trucks with other Allied servicemen and Russians returning from the front line. It wasn't unlike the accommodation on the journey from Salonika to Wolfsberg, although it was far less crowded, slightly more sanitary, and the food and water were adequate. But they had been aboard for four hours before the train finally lurched and pulled out of Budapest's Keleti train terminal. The bridge between Buda and Pest had been destroyed by the retreating Germans and there was now only one way through: a newly constructed Soviet bridge. Since crossings were restricted, long delays were standard.

That set the tone. The trip to Bucharest was painfully slow, and punctuated by frequent stops, mainly to allow Russian troop and munitions trains to travel unimpeded. Most of those on the troop trains appeared to be rotten drunk, judging by the whooping and hollering and the lively Russian folk songs sung horribly out of tune. Instead of taking the direct line via Szeged, they were told their train was being diverted to Szolnok. Rumors started circulating among the Allied servicemen that they were being redirected and would be sent to Soviet concentration camps.

Bruce asked Igor if these rumors could be true.

"Bruce, you not serious?" Igor laughed. "That never happen. You ally—we fighting same enemy. We Russians look after friends. Only enemies and traitors sent to salt mines. Relax. Everything be okay."

Bruce wasn't altogether reassured, but there was nothing he could do. His disquiet grew—and the conspiracy theorists' murmurings became louder—when the train actually reversed direction. Frank and Bruce had all but come to expect the worst when they pulled into the station and discovered that they were in Subotica in Yugoslavia. There was another train disgorging a large concentration of Soviet soldiers onto the platform.

"I don't like the look of this, Frankie," Bruce said.

"Me neither," Frank replied.

But, instead of being manacled and shipped off to a forced-labor camp, they were treated by the Serbian Red Cross to small food parcels, and the Russians on the platform put on a spontaneous display of Cossack dancing to the accompaniment of an accordion.

———

From Subotica, the train headed to Timişoara in Romania, where they were told they were to remain for the night before proceeding to Bucharest. Bruce arrived in the Romanian capital on April 25 and his first port of call was once again to the British authorities, whom he hoped to convince to allow him to return to Josefine in Austria. He was again refused. *They were very sorry*, he wrote to Josefine, *but they could not help us to return to Austria if the Russians did not wish us to do so. There was nothing for it but to return to the Russians and go with them to Odessa.*

After that, Bruce was downhearted.

I lost faith in everything except you, my darling, he wrote.

His options now exhausted, he and Frank found themselves temporarily at a loose end in yet another great European capital. The war seemed to have bypassed Bucharest. Most of the magnificent buildings were intact and some of the luxurious hotels would have footed it with the best on the Champs-Élysées. The Romanians were friendly and welcoming. Some were too friendly. Bruce was sitting in a café with a group of Russians and other Allied soldiers when a middle-aged woman came in, accompanied by a group of young women who fanned out among the tables.

"My girls beautiful, yes?" the older woman asked their table.

"Yes, very beautiful," one of the soldiers answered.

"We sit, yes?" the madam inquired.

"Of course," the soldier replied.

"What you want?" the woman asked. "Girls do everything. Like e-ver-y-thing." She pronounced every syllable. "How you say, blew job? Or tie up? What you want? One girl? Two girls? Three? You have as many girls you want. All cheap but give good time. Romanian girls best of all."

Igor was an eager customer. He went off with one girl and didn't return until an hour later. Bruce declined all offers, but they kept on coming.

"Romanians be like this with Nazis before," Igor explained, holding up crossed fingers and still wearing a satisfied grin. "They join our side in 1944 but to we Russians they still be enemies. They frightened that Russians send them to gulag. New British document best chance for new start. Romanians want to put past behind them. They sell anything, e-ver-y-thing like she say, for identity papers. Or cash. Or good meal."

"What do they think I can do for them?" Bruce asked. "I can't arrange passports."

"Is desperate," Igor shrugged. "Try anything for new papers."

———

The two-day journey from Bucharest was uneventful. The train traveled to Ploești, where important Romanian oil fields had supplied the Germans, followed by Galați, close to the Ukrainian border. At Galați, where the narrow European railway lines made way for the wider-gauge Soviet tracks, they boarded an ancient, soot-covered Russian train that looked as if it hadn't been cleaned for a century. But it got them to Odessa without breaking down. Two and a half weeks and 1,300 miles from Radkersburg, they chugged into the ornate railway station at Odessa. Bruce and Frank were relieved to have finally arrived, but Bruce's relief was tempered with despair. He was far away and moving farther from where he wanted to be.

As soon as they arrived, they were taken to a temporary transit camp for Allied servicemen. This, they were told, would be their home for a few nights. It was worse than any of the stalags, worse even than Corinth and Salonika. Excrement spewed out from the overflowing latrines, there was no running water of any sort, and there were more rats than there were humans. The bunks, if you were lucky enough to score one—and Bruce wasn't—were planks of knotty timber laid in rows with mattresses that were supposed to be straw but felt more like hardened sacks of concrete. It was still bitterly cold at night, yet there was no heating. Those fortunate enough to have greatcoats—which Bruce was—could have sold them for a black-market fortune.

One night there was enough. In the morning, a British POW went about inciting the men to riot in protest at the conditions.

"We're supposed to be their bloody allies," he said, "not common criminals. We were better off under the Jerries. This shithole isn't fit for animals."

He was unanimously supported, even though most, like Bruce and Frank, were doubtful that the Soviets would be moved. But, to everyone's surprise, the delegation of POWs was received sympathetically, and before the day was out, they were shifted to a facility which a large sign proclaimed to be Camp 138, a former sanatorium. Here, they enjoyed real beds in shared villas, although the camp was surrounded by an imposing wall, with armed Russian guards posted at regular junctions. But they were still prisoners; the Allied soldiers weren't allowed out unless they had a Soviet escort.

In this respect, Bruce and Frank were luckier than most, because one of the guards was none other than Igor, whom they hadn't seen since they were whisked away at the station. Igor was more than happy to take them wherever they wanted to go. Since they were to be stuck in Odessa for a few days, they decided once again to make the most of their predicament.

By 1945, the Pearl of the Black Sea had lost much of its luster, partly through neglect and partly because of the damage inflicted during the Axis occupation and its recapture by the Soviets in 1944. Formerly grand and extravagant buildings—those still standing—looked shabby; the peeling paint and crumbling facades were a faded reminder of a more glorious past. At best, the sightseeing provided a diversion from the boredom of the camp. At worst, the depressing surroundings, the Red Army–themed street names, the destroyed buildings, and the run-down monuments served as stark reminders of the Stalinization of the Soviet Union. Then, on May 2, quite out of the blue, they were told to get ready to depart the following day.

"We've got our sailing orders, Igor," Bruce told his friend. "We leave tomorrow."

"Too bad," said Igor, but then his face lit up. "We go one last night on town. There's a good-known bar here in Odessa and we make plenty merry."

"We're out of here first thing tomorrow," Bruce protested, although he knew they were trapped. "We'll never make it if we're on the grog all night."

"Bullshit, Bruce. Get off arses and let's hit bars." Resistance was futile.

Bruce lost count after twelve. He had no idea how many times *"Na Zdorovne"*—the Russian version of "Cheers"—was shouted, muttered, and then slurred, but he vaguely remembered someone saying twenty. They skipped as many rounds as they could, and consequently, at three in the morning, Bruce and Frank were still standing—just—but Igor was slumped in a corner of the bar unable to get to his feet. It was the first time they had ever seen him drunk. They made an unsteady trio as they weaved their way back to the camp, Bruce and Frank doing their best to keep Igor upright without toppling over themselves. Igor never did say farewell. They laid him on his bunk, unconscious and unresponsive, to sleep it off.

"Goodbye, Igor," Bruce slurred. "You've been a good friend."

Igor was still out when Bruce and Frank, groggy and still half sloshed, gathered their meager belongings and marched out of camp. They made their way along Primorskiy Boulevard and down the famous Potemkin Steps to the port of Odessa, where their ship, the Norwegian liner SS *Bergensfjord*, was ready for embarkation. They were about to become truly free men at last.

Early that morning, May 3, 1945, as the ship was maneuvered away from dock and nosed into the Black Sea, Bruce uttered a silent prayer and bade *"proshchay"* to the Soviet Union. He couldn't say he was sad to leave.

The sea voyage was surreal. After the horrors they had so recently witnessed, they found themselves acting more like passengers on a cruise liner, eating well, admiring the scenery, and considering their sightseeing options in the next port. The ship stopped at Istanbul for a short time, then sailed through the Dardanelles and through the Greek Islands. The seas were a lot kinder than they had been on that turbulent trip from Cairo to Greece in 1941, and the beauty of the islands surpassed anything Bruce had seen on that first roller-coaster journey to Athens. They sailed close to the coastline and passed by many famous sites. From this distance, they all seemed untouched by the ravages of war. Bruce wondered how the Greeks he had met had fared, particularly his friend Costas, who had harbored him in Kala-vryta. He hoped they had survived unscathed, too.

Meanwhile, of course, he had to deal with a rising sense of help-lessness. On the trip from Odessa to Naples, *every day was a lifetime to me*, he wrote to Josefine. *Nothing to do but think and dream of you, Josefine, the ship couldn't go fast enough for me. I listened to the radio whenever it was possible but of course never anything was said about Radkersburg.*

Bruce was informed that he was to disembark in Naples to await another ship, which would take him to the Middle East and then on to New Zealand. The *Bergensfjord* was carrying on for Marseille, and from there on to Gibraltar and the Firth of Clyde in Scotland. Frank was to go with it.

As had become his habit, as soon as they docked in Naples, Bruce intended to petition the authorities to allow him to travel to Austria. This time, he had what he thought would be a surefire plan. In Istan-bul, he had learned that the 2nd New Zealand Division had fought its way from El Alamein all the way up to Trieste on the border with Yugoslavia, where it remained. He would simply ask to rejoin his unit, as his orders indicated was his duty.

He duly presented himself to the British command post as soon as he could take leave of the ship.

"Sir, I'm a soldier from 25 Battalion of the 2nd New Zealand Expeditionary Force," he explained to the man with a red band around his hat. "I've had word that 25 Battalion is now based in Trieste. I'm asking for permission to rejoin my battalion. Under our military rules, I'm required to make every effort to get back to my unit and, sir, I'm formally requesting permission to leave for Trieste as soon as possible."

The man considered him, not unkindly.

"'Fraid not, soldier," he said at length. "Not possible. Our rules are clear. You're under our jurisdiction and our orders are to ship you back to New Zealand. And that's what we're going to do. The war's all but over, man, and I doubt the New Zealand military will want you back in Europe. Request formally denied."

Bruce couldn't believe it. He decided he would try again the following day, in case he struck a different officer with a different take on the rules.

In the meantime, there were a variety of ways he could spend the time. Tours were being offered. With Frank, he chose to go to Pompeii and Herculaneum. Others opted for the Isle of Capri. Some just headed for the nearest bar, of which there were many.

The following day, May 8, 1945, all thought of returning to British high command was forgotten because, as he wrote to Josefine, *The day after I arrived in Naples, peace was declared in Europe.* Scenes of jubilation erupted everywhere. Like the rest of the soldiery and the civilian population in Naples, Italy, and, for all anyone knew, the rest of Europe, Frank and Bruce hit the bars. There had never been a party like it, not even with Igor. Bruce had double the reason to be elated, because he imagined that, now that Germany had surrendered, there would be no resistance to his request to travel north to Trieste.

He presented himself to the British authorities the following day. This time, he was more candid about the reasons for his desire to rejoin the battalion. It made no difference. Once again, the answer was an emphatic no. The officer was good enough to explain.

"There are two reasons, Private. First, it's impossible for a POW to rejoin their unit just like that. The Army doesn't work that fast. And second, it would be a fool's errand anyway. There's been a spot of bother between you chaps and the Yugoslavs and the border is practically closed. Even if we could let you go to Trieste, you'll never get any farther."

Then it was time to say goodbye to Frank. Bruce tried to find the words to tell Frank what their friendship meant to him. Frank had helped him through some of the very darkest times; he had literally saved Bruce's life and risked his own. He couldn't think of a more loyal friend.

"Shot of you at last, ya useless bum," was all he could find to say, tears rolling down his cheeks.

"Get on with you, ya silly sod," Frank replied gruffly. "It's not as though we've been through a lot together, or anything like that."

———

Bruce climbed aboard the truck that was to take him to Taranto to meet his ship home. He was miserable, of course: Taranto was in the opposite direction to Trieste. When he petitioned the authorities there to let him travel north, he got the usual reply.

Since he was desperate, his last attempt to get to Austria was his boldest. He traveled to Bari, around fifty miles from Taranto, where there was a large airfield. *I became friendly with some airmen*, he wrote to Josefine. *One of them, after hearing my story, broke the rules and flew me up to Trieste, where once again I was with the New Zealand Division.*

In Trieste, Bruce was less than six hours by train from Radkersburg. But the situation was complex. The partisan hero and now leader of Yugoslavia, Josip Broz Tito, was locked in a bitter dispute with the

New Zealand forces occupying Trieste. Bruce might as well have been 12,000 miles away in Wellington. *There was likely to be trouble there at any time between the various parties concerned*, he wrote. *Everyone would have been very pleased to help me, but for a New Zealander to cross the border into Yugoslavia I soon discovered was quite impossible.*

He returned to Bari. He had missed the ship that was to take him home. Instead, he received orders to return to Naples. There, he was to wait for yet another ship. He'd been in Italy almost a month when he embarked, and it was sixty-six days after he'd left Josefine that he disembarked in Liverpool, almost seven thousand miles from Radkersburg.

He was exhausted, disappointed, and disillusioned.

Chapter Twenty-Three

—

Bruce & Josefine, Wellington and Radkersburg, April to September 1945

And so the paper war began.

Bruce's first few weeks in England proved that bureaucracy had not only survived the war unscathed, but had positively flourished. After years of playing second fiddle to the army types—and stung by the insinuation that they had shirked their duty while others risked their lives—civil servants were once again able to assert their authority. They demanded forms for this, signatures for that, documents for something else, and proof of identity for everything. It didn't matter to them that POWs had endured four years behind wire; these inflexible pen pushers insisted everything be done by the very large book. The rules were the rules and, where a rule didn't exist, they would create one. Swathes of red tape were suffocating postwar progress.

The military wasn't much better. When Bruce had filled out all the paperwork, there was a raft of inspections to deal with. As he wrote to Josefine, for the first two weeks in England he was obliged to submit to all manner of examinations—medicals, X-rays, inoculations, vaccinations, dental treatments. He was even measured and fitted with a new uniform.

Bruce hadn't expected a hero's welcome when he arrived in the UK—he wasn't sure what he expected—but he did anticipate some acknowledgment of his service to the Commonwealth. But the Brits seemed indifferent; they were more interested in the weather, the price of bread, the upcoming general election, and the gossip at the local pub than the plight of those who had spent some of the best years of their lives in the service of their country. The highly anticipated, four-years-in-the-making dream of a return to freedom was a depressing anticlimax.

It was fortunate Bruce had one place left to turn.

"Well, if it isn't the bloody bad penny that always turns up," Frank said when he greeted Bruce at the station. "I thought I'd seen the last of you."

Frank was as much of a rock for Bruce as he struggled to find his feet in peace as he had been throughout most of the war. The monotonous predictability of the past four years had been traded for the uncomfortable uncertainty of the future. But at least Frank was in familiar surroundings. He listened to Bruce's doubts and fears and did his best to buck him up. He offered expert advice on how to handle English bureaucrats. And, most important of all, he was simply there, always willing to take Bruce to a pub and lift his spirits.

Meanwhile, Bruce tried everything in his power to get back to Austria. His prospects seemed even more remote in peacetime Britain than they had in war-torn Europe. He contacted the Red Cross; they apologized that they were unable to help then, but said they might be able to later when things had settled down. He tried to arrange independent travel, but he was denied a passport to travel in Europe, let alone in Austria or Yugoslavia, which were all but cut off. As a last, desperate resort, he even applied to transfer from the New Zealand to the British Army, in the hope that he might be posted to a location from which it would be possible to make his way to Austria. His request was denied. As the date of his repatriation loomed, he wrote and wrote and wrote to Josefine of his despair and his determination. *I have been almost around the world since I last saw you, my Josefine,* he wrote, *and every yard has been hell to me . . . Have faith in me, I will come to you. With you I have everything, without you nothing.*

Finally, the time came. On August 8, 1945, he again bade farewell to Frank and boarded the transport ship for the long trip home. He was looking forward to seeing his family, but he wondered what home held for him now. Would he get his old job back at Prestige? Would he be able to cope with daily life? Would soldiers who had seen out the war on active duty be as condescending toward ex-POWs such as himself as he had found them to be in Britain? What about his remaining friends? How had they fared in the war? Would he still have anything in common with them? He had found true friendship behind the barbed wire. Those who had suffered with him had forged a unique bond that could never be created outside the camp compounds, and it wasn't just confined to fellow kriegies. There was Ulrich Hutmacher, the Heidelberg rugby fanatic; Matte Baumgartner, the Anita lingerie production manager; Helmut, who had alerted Bruce to the Long March; and, of course, Arkady and Igor. From this distance, his other, prewar friendships—with the exception of those with his dead mates Blackie and Logie—seemed shallow by comparison.

And into all of these doubts and uncertainties, another blow fell. The first round of mail he received aboard ship included a card. He recognized it at once, because he had sent it to Josefine at what he had thought to be her address; he had lost the paper on which he'd written it the night he escaped. The card was marked "return to sender." Just as he was desperate for news of her, he now realized she might not even know he had survived.

———

Bruce arrived back in Wellington on September 5, 1945. He was met by his parents, who were older and sadder than they had been when he left. Their first embrace contained less joy than grief for all the tragedy that had beset them since he departed. His sister Jo's absence had created a deep void he knew could never be filled.

He dropped in on Doreen.

"Oh," she said when she opened the door. "I wondered when you'd be back."

They faced each other awkwardly.

"Well, I suppose you'd better come in."

Bruce walked into the house they had shared. It was a strange sensation. Many of his things were still where they had been when he'd left, but it had none of the feel of home.

"Is he here?" he asked.

"No." Doreen grimaced. "He's buggered off back to America. I haven't heard a dicky bird from him."

"Sorry to hear that." Bruce meant it, although he wasn't surprised by the news. "I'll get those papers filled out as soon as I can. No sense in waiting."

"Oh," she said. She looked out the window, chewing her lip. "I don't suppose there's any chance we might—"

"No chance at all," Bruce interrupted.

Her face hardened. "Right. Well, you'll still have to sign to say you're at fault. Otherwise I won't agree to it."

"Fine," he said, smiling a little at the irony of the situation. He stood up. "Dad and I will be back with a truck to pick up my stuff. Thanks for the tea."

And that was that.

———

He had told Josefine to write to him care of his sister Betty. He was elated to find several letters waiting for him. He had never really doubted that she would survive—it seemed they had come through far too much for fate to thwart them now—but the relief he felt as he held the envelopes with her handwriting made him dizzy. They were concrete proof that she was still alive.

Every day, on his way home to his rented digs, Bruce stopped at Betty's to check for more mail. Among the bills, letters from Doreen's lawyers, correspondence from the Army, and the odd few lines from Frank, there was often a letter from her—but not nearly often enough for Bruce. He would read and reread every letter until he almost knew it word for word.

———

Months passed, and Bruce couldn't seem to settle down. After years of doing what he was told every waking hour, the sudden restoration of his freedom to go anywhere and do anything was disorienting and strangely terrifying. The only decision that posed no problem was when and where he might eat: as often as possible at the best places he could afford. Having been denied decent food for years, Bruce made sure he ate well.

He did get his old job back at Prestige, but somehow it wasn't the same. War, captivity, and the atrocities he had witnessed had changed Bruce. His outlook on life was now tinged with a darkness that cast a shadow on everything. He could remember the good times before the war, but they seemed impossibly remote, more like the recollections of childhood, of a time that had gone and could not come again.

He couldn't bear to set foot in the Midland Hotel. The loss of Blackie and Logie hit him harder than he could ever have imagined. He had grieved for them in captivity, but it was here, back in Wellington, that their absence assumed its full significance. Bumping into their old mates brought back memories too painful to confront; Friday nights were melancholy without his two bosom buddies, and even Sunday-morning hangovers weren't the same. Bruce made a point of visiting Blackie's and Logie's parents every couple of weeks. They were grateful, but the visits were desperately awkward. Apart from a few reminiscences, there wasn't a lot to talk about, and Bruce found himself crippled with guilt that he had survived the war while his mates had died. After a while, he decided he was making things worse for everyone, so he stopped going.

Guilt was everywhere, straining every relationship. His friends who hadn't served seemed embarrassed by their relatively cushy life on Civvy Street and tended to avoid Bruce, even though many had tried to enlist and been rejected. And a few of those who had seen the war out on active duty displayed a certain superciliousness toward those who had been captured. Nothing Bruce could ever put his finger on but a sort of battle-proven smugness that, in their eyes, elevated their military status above that of a POW. At least that's the way Bruce saw it. Even a good number of the girls looked ill at ease. The Americans had swept through Wellington like a plague, and many young women who had been left behind couldn't welcome their men back with a completely clean conscience.

In short, it seemed that nobody in peacetime Wellington could look anyone else in the eye anymore.

———

Bruce felt as though his life were on hold. He was merely biding his time before he could return to Austria to be reunited with Josefine. The authorities continued to put obstacles in his path. And, meanwhile, the news from that part of the world was disturbing.

In the period immediately after hostilities ceased in Austria and before peace was declared in Europe on May 8, Austria was terrorized by the conquering Russians. The Austrians were treated as badly as the Germans; after all, they spoke the same language. Yugoslavia and Austria had supposedly been "liberated," but the Russian view of liberation was tainted by a sordid sense of entitlement. Whatever they wanted they assumed was theirs as of right.

In Radkersburg, houses and buildings had been reduced to rubble and life was anything but back to normal. Many, like Josefine, were homeless and surviving on whatever scraps of food they could scavenge or steal. Soon after she had returned to Radkersburg and was living temporarily with her aunt and uncle, the Russians looted the Hamlers' house. The very little in the way of possessions Josefine had managed to retain was stolen, but she was luckier than most, in that she was neither raped nor shot. Many women dressed as dowdily as possible, wearing ankle-length dresses, matronly clothes, and no makeup to deter the Russian rapists. They needn't have bothered. The Russians didn't much care what the women looked like; as long as they had two legs that could be forced apart, their basest needs were satisfied. Children were not exempt. Infants were tossed to the ground or bashed against walls to shut them up while their mothers were violated. Some had their skulls crushed because they dared to cry.

It wasn't just rape and murder. There were random beatings for no reason at all. A drunken soldier might take offense at a friendly greeting and retaliate with a timber plank, or a broad-shouldered muscleman might pick a fight with a skinny runt just for the fun of it. If the victims were pummeled to death, it was of no concern to the

Russians, who would move on to the next bar to demand their free booze. There were honorable Russian soldiers, but, sadly, the vicious behavior of the many eclipsed the common decency of the few.

Josefine quickly learned to keep her mouth shut and look the other way. She walked long distances along little-known streets and alleys just to avoid the Red Army soldiers.

And persistent rumors of horrors occurring across the border in Yugoslavia were circulating. The Yugoslavian political matrix had always been complicated; now, with the war against the Germans won, the partisans turned on the so-called "national traitors"—the Chetniks, Domobranci, Ustaše, and other Nazi collaborators. Many fled to Austria. Josefine saw thousands passing through Radkersburg, most on their way to meet up with the British troops around Bleiburg, who they hoped might offer them some protection. She could no longer feel the same depth of hatred toward them that she had felt during the dark days of the war. She preferred the thought of reconciliation and national unity, but she was among the minority.

Rumors also reached Josefine that thousands of collaborators, soldiers, anti-communists, and civilians had been slaughtered by partisans in the Tezno forest near her hometown of Maribor, executed and dumped in mass graves. For a week, reports reached her daily of further massacres. She wept, fearful for the future of her country.

Josefine learned that Jelena Kunstek was a victim of the postwar retaliation. Her son had been born with spina bifida, and the locals, particularly the devoutly religious and the irrationally superstitious, had deemed this to be God's judgment for her cavorting with Nazis. After the Germans had been driven out, Jelka was tarred and feathered, completely shorn of her beautiful black hair, and marched through Maribor to the taunts and abuse of the local Slovenes. As the procession crossed the bridge over the Drava, Jelka somehow ended up in the water. Josefine heard she jumped; she also heard Jelka was pushed. Either way, she drowned, and no one seemed to know what had become of the infant, who was supposed to be in an orphanage somewhere.

Peace has come, Josefine wrote to Bruce, *the peace for which we waited such a long time, but it is not the peace we wished for.*

Worse still, she had no news of her family, spread so far and wide by the war. *I have been inquiring for over three weeks,* she wrote, *but always nothing. Neither father nor sister have given any sign of life. I don't know what to make of it; is the post so bad or is nobody still alive? But, my beloved, surely fate cannot be so merciless.*

Most shocking of all to Bruce was the complaint at the foot of one of her letters. *I am already in despair,* she wrote, *not having had news from you for so long.*

He had written screeds and screeds. He had sent news, and thoughts, and commiserations, and encouragements. He had renewed the pledge of his love and his vow to marry her over and over again.

In her next letter, she wrote, *I'm very sad because I have still not received any mail from you,* and finished by writing, *Everything would be easier to bear if I could only get more mail, but nothing comes from you at all.*

What was going on? Some disruption to mail services was inevitable, but surely something would get through? Bruce had finally gotten Josefine's lost address details—they were on the letters she sent—and sent mail to both her Slovene address, Limbuš 12A in Maribor, and the Rossnegger farm at Altneudörfl 65 in Radkersburg to make sure he covered both options. Surely one of those letters would have gotten through?

As he listened to her fretting on the page, the doubts rising like weeds to choke her faith in him, he felt as though he were being buried alive.

———

As it happened, Josefine's family did survive, but hardly unscathed. Despite the dangers of Anica's work as a senior officer in the partisan movement, Josefine learned that her sister had come through. She also learned that her brother Roman had returned to Limbuš after being hospitalized in Belgrade, so seriously wounded fighting against the Germans in the final battles to liberate their country that he had nearly lost his right foot.

The most dramatic news of all was that a few weeks after the end of hostilities, Josefine's prayers were answered. There was a knock at the door of the makeshift building in which they were living at the Rossnegger farm, and she opened it to a man whom she initially thought was one of the many beggars drifting across the face of Europe. He was skinny to the point of being skeletal, and his filthy clothes hung off him in tatters.

But there was something about him, and suddenly, she knew who he was.

"Polde," she gasped.

After his arrest, Leopold Lobnik was first sent to a forced-labor camp in Croatia. Then, in August 1943, prisoner number 1790 was transferred to the Flossenbürg concentration camp in northeast Bavaria, close to where the Lobnik family had once spent happy holidays. He was officially classified as being *Schutzhäftling politisch* ("Protective Custodian Political"), a designation reserved for prisoners deemed to be opponents of the Third Reich or racially inferior beings. They could be held indefinitely without trial. After Flossenbürg, where he endured the same barbaric conditions that characterized all Nazi concentration camps, he was transferred to one of the most brutal camps in Nazi Germany: Dachau.

There were close to three thousand Yugoslavs among the 12,000-strong complement of Dachau at the time. At first, it served as a forced-labor camp for the local munitions factory. But as the war drew on and Nazi policy shifted, it became one of the installations charged with administering the so-called "Final Solution to the Jewish Problem." Polde lived day and night under the plume of smoke from the crematoria, a constant reminder of the fragility of life in Dachau. The acrid smell of burning flesh and the sickly odor of death had left its mark—quite apart from the physical abuse and the privation that he had suffered.

He had been liberated by the Americans in the closing days of the war, on April 29, 1945, and they had trucked him to Vienna. No one was going to Slovenia. From Vienna, the British stepped in and took him all the way to Radkersburg.

Josefine gave him some of the clothes Bruce had left with her, and which had ironically remained safely hidden while her own effects were looted. She wrote to Bruce, *Do not be angry if I have given Polde some of the clothes you left with me. He had nothing when he returned, just the clothes he had on his back.* When he was freed, Polde weighed just seven stone, and was riddled with disease and suffering from malnutrition. He could barely walk and his body was covered in festering sores.

The Almighty God in Heaven has heard my prayer, Josefine wrote. Polde was alive. But, like the peace she had longed for, the return of her brother was not the wholly joyous event she had imagined it would be. All the laughter had gone from Polde's eyes and, even before she learned what he had endured, she somehow knew it would never be back.

—

Chapter Twenty-Four

Bruce & Josefine, Wellington, Radkersburg, and London, October 1945 to December 1947

Beloved Bruce, Josefine wrote. *I could go home now to Maribor, through the Commission. You'll probably understand how I would love to leave the Rossneggers. But I believe that when I'm in Yugoslavia, it will be impossible for us to be together. So, darling, write to me very soon if you are still coming, then I will still stay here and gladly continue to wait and work . . . Because you know, my darling . . . I have not seen my siblings and my father for such a long time, and I will endure that for an even longer time if I know you are coming.*

Every week she wrote. And every day, she told him, she asked Mitzl if there was any mail from her dear Bruce. Every day she was disappointed, but still she wrote, sometimes twice a week. She even had some of her letters translated into English so that Bruce would be able to read them in his own language.

The Rossneggers picked up their mail from the post office at least three times a week, Josefine wrote, and she couldn't understand why there was never anything from Bruce. All she had received from him was a single letter that she found among a pile of mail left on the table. She declared it her most treasured possession. *I read that letter very often. I've read it more than fifty times,* she wrote. But her doubts and confusion were clear. She knew Bruce had survived. Why was he not writing to her?

———

The tone of her letters grew ever more miserable. She couldn't settle down. She told Bruce that the Rossneggers said it was because she needed a husband, and they offered no shortage of candidates. Everyone, even her friends, told her to forget this Kiwi soldier and marry a good local lad who would look after her in the customary Slovene way. She had to endure constant jibes about the soldier who everyone was convinced had forsaken her. Even her best friends mocked her:

> [Marija] *often says: "He will not come back." She wants to laugh at me, but she shouldn't. Please remember me and come here soon. I'm waiting, and as I have said to myself, I will keep on waiting for as long as I live.*

In another letter, she wrote:

> *My love, people always say . . . I am stupid to believe that you will come back. But, my dearly beloved, I am proud to say that I don't listen to other people who know nothing.*

Bruce replied, irate at the malicious attempts to destroy their love for each other:

*I wonder if they will admit that when I arrive, you can tell them to have a
care, all of them. I'll return but not as a prisoner of war . . . Tell them all my
memory is good, so that one day in the near future they will be able to say all the
things they are saying to you to me. Remind them of the fact that I'll return not
as a prisoner of war but as an ex-soldier of the famous New Zealand divisions.
Where there is a debt owing it shall be paid. My love for you is only equalled
by my hatred for those who willingly make you, my beloved girl, suffer.*

He wrote again, imploring Josefine to trust him:

*I beg of you to have faith in me. Even when I was a prisoner of war, the
German guards couldn't stop me from coming to you, not one single time did
they stop me from coming to you, and nothing will stop me now . . . As soon
as it is possible, I will come to you again and leave Europe with you.*

When her next letter arrived, it was plain that she hadn't received
his latest one, either. It was like talking to the empty air, and it was
driving Bruce slowly mad.

———

Then, one day, a letter arrived from Josefine that was, to judge by
the thickness of the envelope, many times longer than any she had
written so far. Bruce tore it open and read it with a mixture of fear
and longing.

He had only read two pages when he had to set it down to wipe the
tears from his eyes.

Josefine had been looking for a bracelet that she had lost, she wrote,
and she couldn't explain why, but she had decided it might have found
its way into the oak wardrobe in her cousins' room. She eased the
wardrobe open, and normally she would never have been so nosy as to
open the painted wooden box covered with a square crocheted napkin

that she found tucked in the corner. But perhaps she suspected what she would find all along. When she lifted the lid, she found letters—dozens of them—all unopened and all addressed to her. She knew immediately they were from Bruce. Her emotions ranged from relief that Bruce had not deserted her to outrage that the Rossneggers had deliberately conspired to hide the mail from her. She had known all along that her family, and especially the Rossneggers, were opposed to what they regarded as her infatuation with a foreign scoundrel, but she had not really imagined they would go to the lengths of intercepting Bruce's mail.

She told Bruce she spent all that day and night reading and rereading the letters, and then the following day she had composed this very long letter, explaining what had happened to his correspondence and how she felt.

To you, my sweetheart, she wrote in closing, *I give you my life, my love—everything. Your Josefine.*

Dearest girl, Bruce replied. *I could cry when I think how unkind fate has been to you, keeping from you those letters assuring you of my love . . .*

For Josefine, the world was almost back on an even keel. Her family was safe—scarred, but safe—and her faith in Bruce, like her faith in the return of Polde, had been vindicated. She could begin to look to the future again.

———

As soon as he was formally discharged from the Army, on March 6, 1946, Bruce started making arrangements to get on a ship to Europe. He didn't much care where it was headed, as long as it took him closer to his one true love. He thought it would be easy: just pick a date and pay for the passage. Unfortunately, it wasn't. As he explained to Josefine, *One simply cannot walk down to a ship and get a ticket to any port in the world. One must first have a permit to leave New Zealand . . .* Even with the necessary documents, which sometimes took months to process, berths were scarce—VIPs, government officials, and wealthy dignitaries took priority—but Bruce was hopeful, declaring, *It is possible to get a ticket now and then.* He promised Josefine, *I will do all in my power to hasten our reunion.* Since September 1945, he had written a blizzard of letters to all the relevant agencies and consulates and ministries seeking permission to join her.

He received no replies.

Finally, he was granted permission to travel to England. All the same, it was several months before he could get a berth on a liner to Southampton; it was only through a late cancellation that a space in a cabin came free and, with just a single suitcase and the few bob he had left after paying the fare, Bruce made the trip back to Europe as he had promised. He arrived in the UK in August 1946.

He immediately set about applying for the necessary visas and approvals to allow him and Josefine to be reunited. Naïvely, he assumed that, now that he was in England, a couple of calls to the authorities and filling out a few forms would be all it would take to get the necessary consents. How wrong he was. His attempts to get permission to travel to Slovenia failed. The Yugoslav Consulate wrote, *With reference to your application for a visa to Yugoslavia, I regret to inform you that it has not been found possible for the authority to grant your request.*

Bruce tried another approach. *I went to London, darling, to the British Foreign Office.* This experience proved to be one of the most frustrating in the whole long campaign. After waiting for forty-five minutes, he was peremptorily informed that the official was "too busy to be bothered with trivial matters like some antipodean nobody chasing a foreign peasant."

His second attempt resulted in a face-to-face meeting, but the outcome was the same. The pompous desk wallah—who sported a perfectly groomed moustache, waxed and twirled at the ends, and who wore a three-piece pinstripe and a blue-and-yellow polka-dot bow tie complete with a matching pocket handkerchief—eyed him contemptuously as he entered.

"Captain Beresford-Chudleigh," he announced, without extending his hand or making any attempt at a polite greeting. "Captain in the Great War, you know. The real war, lad, charging the Hun from the trenches with rifles and bayonets. Nothing like the life of Riley you lot enjoyed. You can address me as Captain or Sir."

"Sir," Bruce responded, opting to use the more deferential term in the hope that he might ingratiate himself with the self-obsessed administrator. "I need your help to get my fiancée from Austria to England. I've come here all the way from New Zealand—"

"Get on with it, man. I have appointments to keep. I don't have all day."

Bruce explained his situation as succinctly as he could: how he had met Josefine, her role in the resistance movement, how she helped him escape, why he had traveled back to Europe, and why he needed the Foreign Office's assistance to get her to the UK.

"I'm not sure why you've come to me." Beresford-Chudleigh sighed. "It's the Austrian or Yugoslav authorities you should be talking to, not me. Damn it, man, you're wasting my time. Nothing I can do."

His word was final.

If Josefine couldn't come to Bruce, he would have to go to her. He made another attempt to get approval to go to Austria. *I applied to the Military Permit Office in London again for permission to travel to Austria but once again I was refused. I then wrote another letter to the visa branch in Vienna to find out why you had not received the permit to come to England.*

Austria had very strict exit and entry controls and Yugoslavia had closed its frontiers to all foreigners. Josefine couldn't leave Austria because she had no identity documents—and it was almost impossible to get any because she wasn't Austrian—and returning to Slovenia had been out of the question since Tito shut its borders.

Has everything we have done, the sacrifices we have made, all been in vain? Are the authorities [ever] going to issue you with an exit permit? Bruce lamented. It now seemed that, having smashed down all the barriers created by Hitler, Stalin, treacherous collaborators, and an over-protective family, their love would be smothered in red tape and battered down by rubber stamps.

He wrote regularly to every individual, government department, and embassy that might be able to get Josefine to England or him to Austria: the Home Office, the War Office, the Foreign Office, the Cabinet Office, even the Prime Minister's Office. He contacted MPs, opposition leaders, the Yugoslav, Austrian, and New Zealand author-ities—anyone he could think of. Where he could get appointments with senior civil servants, he made them; where he couldn't, he just turned up unannounced and waited. He was in some of the offices so often that many of the receptionists knew Bruce by name and chatted about the weather, politics, and life in general. Some even promised to put in a good word for him.

Still, he was frustrated at every turn. *Every government office in any way connected with this matter has been visited by me, all to no avail.* But the more rejections he got, the more determined he became. *I have spared nothing—expense or effort—I have never given up trying to get you here.*

He refused to give up. *I have written three times to the authorities in Vienna . . . I wrote [another] long letter eight pages, to be exact . . . [in which] I explained our case fully . . . I then wrote another letter . . .* Exasperated, he told Josefine, *I have done so much letter writing and so much filling in of forms in this last nine months that I am heartily tired of pen and ink.*

———

On December 3, 1946, he received a reply from the visa branch in Vienna. He opened the envelope without hope, and could barely believe his eyes when he read: *With reference to your letter, I can inform you that your fiancée has been notified that she will be granted a visa for the UK.*

No "pleased to advise you," no "congratulations," no explanation of what would happen next—just a dampening final sentence that somewhat took the gloss off Bruce's excitement: *I wish to stress however that this office has no control over the issue of passports by the local authorities and it is therefore not possible to say how long this will take.*

These proved to be prophetic words. A month passed, then another. Three. Nothing. Six months later, still nothing. On August 18, 1947—almost nine months after the authorization was granted—Bruce suffered another setback, this time from the Friends Committee for Refugees and Aliens: *We have just received a list of names from the Exit and Entry branch of fiancées who are not yet (approved) to travel and I'm sorry to say that Miss Lobnik's name is among them. We very much regret not being able to complete the arrangements.*

———

Love, as they say, conquers all. This is not necessarily or universally true, but persistence and determination help to make it so. More than fifteen months after arriving in the UK and battling against the combined bureaucratic inertia of three war-ravaged nations, word reached Bruce that his Josefine was on her way to him at last. She had received all the necessary documents and permissions; she had tickets for a flight to London.

Bruce hardly dared believe it. He only dared believe it was true as he watched the plane land one gray English winter's morning. And he only truly believed it when he saw, among the men and women and children wandering into the arrivals hall, the slight frame of his beloved Josefine, her black hair bouncing off her shoulders. She looked around uncertainly, then caught sight of him. She didn't smile, as he had imagined she would, and nor did he. They faced each other for a moment or two, mesmerized, and when finally they hurried into each other's arms they were both weeping. They clung to each other as though they needed reassurance that this was not just another dream from which they would soon awake.

"*Hier bist du*," he said. Here you are.

"*Hier bin ich*," she replied. Here I am.

Author's Note

The main characters in this story all existed but, because some of the facts cannot be verified, some of their names have been changed. Of course, Bruce and Josefine were real people. Bruce's military record and the parallel narratives of others enable his war to be reconstructed in some detail. Some of Josefine's partisan activities were recorded in the citations for bravery she received, but, largely due to the resistance movement's obsession with secrecy, others were never recorded. Some dramatic license has been the inevitable consequence of this absence of documentary evidence.

Bruce Murray and Josefine Lobnik were married on December 27, 1947, at Cleethorpes, where they lived for two years before returning to New Zealand in 1949. They had three children: Anemarie, Gregory (honoring a promise Bruce made to himself to name their son after Grigor, the Russian farmboy who saved Bruce and Frank from discovery and recapture), and Tanja. After their heroics during the war, Bruce and Josefine lived a peaceful, unremarkable Kiwi life, making a home for themselves in Johnsonville, Wellington.

Blackie, Logie, and Frank Butler were real people and their names have been altered only slightly. Frank was a saddler and harnessmaker from Swallow in Lincolnshire and did serve with the RAVC. Blackie and Logie were Bruce's best friends and served with him in 25 Battalion. Both died on the same day, November 23, 1941, at Sidi Rezegh. Blackie was killed when he recklessly charged into an artillery barrage, knowing that death was certain, and it was believed by those close to him that he did so out of shame over a sexually transmitted disease contracted from a Cairene prostitute.

Bruce's sister's real name was Elsie Dell Murray; Jo was a nickname. She did become pregnant to an American GI and died on March 5, 1944, after a botched abortion. She was just nineteen.

Josefine's father, Jožef Lobnik, was persecuted by the Nazis because of his family's partisan connections. Anica and Roman were Josefine's siblings and their service in the partisan movement is a matter of record. Anica was in the armed divisions and later a liaison officer for the Maribor partisans. She was imprisoned and tortured by the Švabi. Roman was twice seriously injured in desperate partisan battles. Exactly when they joined the partisans—and the specific reasons that prompted them to do so—are not known, but Josefine wrote that Anica was with the freedom fighters for a very long time, so she would have been one of the early recruits. Bruce refers to the arrest of both Anica and Roman in 1941 and confirms that the teenage Roman withstood the Gestapo interrogation and torture: *the Germans learned nothing at all from him and so they were released, he and his sister* . . . Polde, Josefine's other sibling, was captured and languished in the Flossenbürg and Dachau concentration camps. His concentration camp records show that he was first registered at Flossenbürg on August 9, 1943. After the war, Polde—by then an irreparably damaged man—disappeared again. There were rumors that he had been shot while crossing the Drava, but no one knew for sure. His family never saw him again.

Bruce summed up the whole Lobnik family succinctly when he wrote, *All in all, this was quite a family of partisans.* He added, *they fought as surely as my brother, my father and myself on the side of democracy.* Josefine later gained two half brothers, Silvo and Branko, who were born after the war.

The Ožbalt escape was one of the largest mass escapes of World War II and has been well documented in books and television documentaries. Ninety-nine of the original 105 POWs made it safely to Italy.

Josefine was a decorated war heroine: she received two awards for bravery. One has long since been lost but the other, awarded by the wartime Supreme Commander of the Mediterranean Theater, Field Marshal Sir Harold Alexander, was prominently displayed at her local RSA club. It read:

> *This certificate is awarded to Josefine Lobnik as a token of gratitude for, and appreciation of, the help given to the sailors, soldiers and airmen of the British Commonwealth of Nations which enabled them to escape from, or evade capture by, the enemy.*

Gustl and Mitzl Rossnegger, Kramer, and others from Radkersburg were also real people who are identified by name in the letters written by Bruce and Josefine, as were Josef and Agatha Hamler.

Josefine's best friend, whose real name is unknown, did become pregnant to a German officer.

Ulrich Hutmacher and Matte Baumgartner are based on real guards Bruce regarded as friends, although their actual names have long been forgotten. Psycho, Weasel, and The Skunk are fictitious names but their characters are modeled on various vindictive guards Bruce encountered. Red Cross officials reported on the abusive treatment of prisoners at the Radkersburg work camp, noting that "serious complaints were brought to the inspectors' knowledge" and confirming in one instance that "the NCO in question will be discharged of his command."

Bruce had great admiration for all the Greeks who helped him while he was on the run, and Costas Papadopoulos personifies the spirit of these valiant individuals. On December 13, 1943, in retribution for a partisan attack, the Nazis massacred the entire male civilian population of Kalavryta—almost 700 victims—and razed all its houses and churches. It became known as the Holocaust of Kalavryta.

Two trucks carrying 25 Battalion soldiers to Monemvasia did take a wrong turn and one ended up at Kalamata Bay. The visit by Himmler to Corinth, the German brass band playing "Roll Out the Barrel," the POWs trading watches for bread, and the conditions on the torturous rail journey from Salonika to Maribor and Wolfsberg are all actual events and have been described by a number of ex-POWs.

The Loburgs were close family friends of the Lobniks, and Srečko Loburg did write to Josefine expressing his relief on hearing of Anica's release from a Nazi prison. Jože Fluks and Albin and Marjan Milavec were real people who were executed by the Nazis. Their final letters have been recorded as they were written. Albin and Marjan were executed on December 27, 1941. Ivan Milavec died fighting for the partisans on November 28, 1941.

Bruce did serve with the Red Army. His military record confirms this, stating that he "served with the Russians on the Hungarian, Austrian and Yugoslav borders." He also recorded that he "was with the Russian Army that [had taken] Budapest and Platten See when they crossed the Hungarian–Austrian borders." Bruce had mixed feelings about the Russians. He had encountered both the best and the worst of Russian behavior. He concluded that there were the good and the bad, with few in between. Some, like the escorts who accompanied him to Odessa, were educated, intelligent, upright human beings—decent, hardworking, law-abiding blokes who were in the Army to fight for their country. Regrettably, they were in the minority. Others may have started out with noble intentions but surrendered to their basest instincts when they realized that war provided them with the opportunity to rape, loot, murder, and exact revenge with impunity. Bruce always talked fondly of his Russian companions. Arkady and Igor weren't their real names but they did treat Bruce kindly and certainly did have a gargantuan thirst for vodka. Josefine had nothing good to say about the Soviets who raped, pillaged, and plundered their way through Austria.

Doreen was not the name of Bruce's first wife and, as depicted, she is a fictitious character. The circumstances of their marriage and subsequent divorce are not known.

In 1955, Bruce applied to the Immigration Division of the Department of Labour and Employment to secure entry permits to bring Jožef, Anica, and Roman to New Zealand. He and Josefine were concerned about the political situation in Communist Yugoslavia. The application was rejected.

———

This is not an authoritative record of the events of World War II. To have compiled such a dossier would have required much more research than was justified in the context of a love story. The timing of events, as they are narrated, may not always be consistent with the actual time lines recorded in history and the locations not necessarily geographically precise.

And as for Bruce and Josefine's story, there is a blend of fact and fiction in these pages. Remarkably, Bruce and Josefine kept a cache of letters, carefully packed into a cardboard box, doubtless as a lasting reminder of their wartime hardships and the obstacles they had to overcome to be together. The letters, unopened since the end of the war, provided a wealth of information on the events that shaped their lives and gave an invaluable insight into their wartime experiences. Excerpts from correspondence between Bruce and Josefine have been accurately reproduced, as have the letters that Polde, Roman, and Srečko Loburg wrote to Josefine; in some cases they have been translated from Slovene and German into English.

Some of the incidents recounted are based on known but sometimes sketchy facts, handed-down memoirs, occasionally incomplete records, recollections, and supposition. Like many World War II veterans, Bruce and Josefine were loath to talk about their wartime exploits. Modesty and painful memories of suffering prevented them from revealing all they had experienced. But there is enough verifiable material to enable the story to be pieced together from mostly credible sources: enduring memories of dinner-table discussions when alcohol had worked its magic and loosened reluctant tongues; media coverage of the rare interviews they granted; official military records; government-commissioned New Zealand and Yugoslav war histories; unbiased reports from neutral observers like the Red Cross; oft-repeated anecdotes at POW and 25 Battalion reunions; eyewitness accounts of others whose experiences were similar; extensive independent research; and, most illuminatingly, the box of personal letters written during and immediately after the war that record a good deal of their anguish and the adversity they were forced to confront to realize their dream of a life together. Relevant excerpts from newspaper stories recording their wartime exploits have been summarized in the Appendix. Where the fundamental facts are known but the corroborating details uncertain, I have at times created circumstances to fit those facts and, where necessary, I have created events as I imagined them to be.

My regret is that neither Bruce nor Josefine lived to see their remarkable story of courage, conviction, and love finally recorded.

I hope they would have approved.

Acknowledgments

I intended to write this book twenty years ago. Bruce and Josefine had always been reluctant to talk about their wartime feats but in 1998, several years after Bruce's death, I finally persuaded Josefine to tell their remarkable story. Our family had just shifted to France, and Josefine had agreed to share her account of the events that had brought her and Bruce together. Tragically, she was killed in a car accident in Slovenia just three days before she was due to visit us in Aix-en-Provence and her memoir was never recorded.

I have therefore had to construct the story from a profusion of diverse sources. In this respect, thanks go to my wife, Anemarie, and her sister Tanja, whose recollections of the exploits their parents recounted have been invaluable—as was their help in recovering the box of letters written by Bruce and Josefine, which documented their struggle to overcome adversity and find fulfillment. Particular thanks to Anemarie; her support and inspiration made the task of researching and piecing together her parents' story more rewarding, and her insightful comments on the early drafts of the manuscript helped to make it a better book.

A story can be interesting, but the way in which it is told determines whether it enthralls the reader and does justice to the subject.

In this respect, there are two people who have had a major influence on the development of this book; it is immeasurably better for their input. Initially, Jennifer Barclay's advice and honest appraisal took an unstructured and sometimes disjointed manuscript and gave it both form and shape. Without her guidance and encouragement, the manuscript would have sat, forgotten and curling at the edges, in some bottom drawer. More recently, John McCrystal's professionalism and storytelling artistry added the magic that transformed it into what I hope is an enjoyable read. If it's not, that's my fault not theirs.

I have never tackled a writing project as ambitious as this one, and my sincerest thanks go to Jenny Hellen, Leanne McGregor, Abba Renshaw, Becky Innes, and the Allen & Unwin team for, first, recognizing that the story of Bruce and Josefine might have some merit and, subsequently, for all the support they have given to a novice writer.

Appendix

Many of the events and incidents recorded in this book were covered in newspaper reports, military records, official war histories, eyewitness accounts, and letters written by Bruce, Josefine, Polde, Roman, and Srečko Loburg.

Press coverage

The circumstances of Bruce's capture were explained in one press story: "Exhausted, wounded and alone in Corinth, he threw his rifle in a well and waited for the medical treatment which would accompany capture. After hospitalisation in Kalamata he ended up as a prisoner of war in Maribor . . ."

While the circumstances of Polde's capture weren't reported, the details of Josefine's expedition to the POW camp with her scrawled note were covered in Wellington's *Evening Post*: ". . . it began across barbed wire . . . at a German prisoner-of-war camp near Limbuš in Yugoslavia's Maribor district . . . Biding time in the prison camp close to the Austrian border was 23-year-old Bruce Murray who had been captured in Greece while serving with the 25th Battalion. When Murray was by the camp's perimeter fence, Josefine Lobnik, then 18, slipped a note through the wire seeking news of her brother Polde, who had also been captured by the Germans. The note was in German. Murray had it translated but was unable to help." The story incorrectly reported Bruce's age as twenty-three. He was twenty-five.

Bruce's encounter with The Skunk and the events that led to him calling his girlfriend a German whore were reported in a feature article in *The Dominion* newspaper: "Bruce was charged with agitating, refusing to work and hitting a guard. He had hit a German officer who suggested he might like to share some of his Red Cross chocolate with a woman Bruce had unfortunately described as a German whore. He was shifted to labour camps in Siebing and Radkersburg in Austria."

His refusal to work, subsequent disciplinary transfer to Radkersburg, and second meeting with Josefine were also covered in a story in the *Evening Post*: "Murray, [as punishment for] striking a German guard and refusing to work, was transferred to Radkersburg over the border in Austria. Miraculously . . . he again met the young partisan Lobnik while he was labouring on a farm."

Of Bruce's two unsuccessful escape attempts, the New Zealand Press Association reported the facts without elaborating on the details: "He tried to escape twice and was forced to give himself up on his second attempt after his legs became covered in leeches from having spent five days in a swamp."

Bruce's visits to the Hamlers to listen to the BBC and the removable bar that enabled him to escape from the work camp were covered in a feature story headed "The Brave Yugoslav Partisan and Her Kiwi POW": "Bruce had gouged a bar from a window with a view to another escape. The Hamlers tuned in to the BBC news bulletins regularly . . . and there were many nights when they were joined by Bruce, courtesy of the removable bar, who made the one kilometre journey to catch up on the news . . ."

A newspaper article headed "Love Blossomed Behind Barbed Wire" recounted how Bruce and Josefine ventured from Radkersburg into Slovenia to distribute Red Cross parcels: "Together, they smuggled Red Cross parcels back into Yugoslavia during sorties in which he left the lockup at night, and during this period they were falling in love."

Two separate press reports covered Bruce's escape from the work camp with Josefine's help. One stated: "Russian forces were breaking through from the east and the Germans were keen to get their prisoners back into Germany. The break came for Murray and his English mate, Frank, when Josefine masterminded their escape, disguising one as a civilian and the other as a bundle of clothes. She smuggled in clothes for Murray who rode out of the farm on a bicycle. She concealed [Frank] under food and clothes in her wooden barrow and wheeled him out, a safe distance behind Murray, so as not to create suspicion."

The second report had this to say: "When arrangements were made for Bruce and his fellow prisoners to be moved to Germany in January 1945 the New Zealander and an English mate, Frank, decided the time had come to use the removable bar one last time. Josefine helped the escape by providing a bicycle and a suit borrowed from a German officer." The relocation of POWs to Germany referred to in both articles was known as the Long March or the Death March.

Two separate newspaper stories described the five life-threatening days that Bruce and Frank were hidden in the hayloft, without food and water, while the German mechanics occupied the barn below. One stated: "For about a week she risked her life feeding and chaperoning the two men around Radkersburg as they awaited the Russian occupation of the town. For five of those days, Bruce and Frank lay beneath a pile of straw in a barn which mechanics in the retreating German army commandeered for use after the two escapees had also staked their claim. Josefine recalls this as the most difficult time because she was unable to provide them with food." The second referred to the risk Josefine took in getting food to the men: "The two escapers were hidden under straw in a barn while battles between partisans and Germans raged around them. Josefine and her friends were unable to help them for fear of alerting the German mechanics who had commandeered the farm. Despite the danger, Josefine, fearing they were starving to death, slipped the escapers a tin of semolina after one five-day stretch without food." The latter article was incorrect in one respect: it was the Russians who were fighting the Germans, not the partisans.

The near-disastrous discovery of Bruce and Frank by the Russian farmhand, Grigor, was featured in a press article on Bruce and Josefine's wartime experiences: "Her heart was in her mouth when she learned how a Russian farmboy called Grigor had discovered the two men while he was pitchforking hay during a feedout operation. Because Grigor did not turn Bruce and Frank in to the nearby Germans, Bruce and Josefine were later to name their eldest son Gregory."

Bruce's meeting with the Russians at Radkersburg and their acceptance that he was an Allied POW was briefly reported by the NZPA: "It was a great relief for the New Zealander when the Russians accepted he was not a German deserter—meaning he escaped the fate of being strung up at the nearest lamp-post or bridge."

In a newspaper article recounting his wartime exploits, Bruce recalled that he and Frank "were propositioned in Bucharest by women seeking new national identity papers and were intoxicated over breakfast on many a morning with the Russian guides."

Bruce's problems traveling without identity documents and a subsequent encounter with Lady Churchill were also covered in a New Zealand Press Association report: "Without any identification papers, it was an eventful journey through war-torn Europe, which included a meeting with Lady Churchill in Odessa as he waited for a Norwegian ship to Naples."

Bruce's endeavors immediately after the war to get to Trieste and then make his way to Josefine in Maribor were outlined in a newspaper story: "He decided to make his way to Trieste where he would be able to catch up with his old 25th Battalion mates and make his way from there to Josefine's family in Maribor, but he found neither was possible." This report was inaccurate in one respect: Bruce did make it to Trieste.

Excerpts from various letters written by Bruce and Josefine

Bruce on learning German at Stalag XVIIID:

I got stuck into learning the language, this, I reckoned, was a must for making outside contacts and an escape. Several [escape] attempts of mine were quite unsuccessful. [Only] the last one was a success.

Bruce on serving with the Russians:

I served with them, not by choice, but because we had a common enemy [and because] the only way I could get out of middle Europe was via Russia.

Josefine on the Soviet Army raping and pillaging its way through Austria:

A much bigger anxiety arrived—the Russians. That's why I went for two days to my uncle in the occupied Rikte Stoor so that nothing would happen to me.

I once again had to think of our dreadful time with the Russians . . . there were many times I feared that I would be shot . . .

Had not the Russians come, but rather the British, everything would be different.

The Russians have stolen a lot. They didn't find your suitcases; if I had known that, I would have hidden my things with yours.

Josefine on Nazi atrocities and Polde's release from Dachau:

You know exactly what my brother and siblings have suffered in the Nazi time, for you were the only person I entrusted this with, when I came home to Maribor, what the Nazis did and how you comforted me.

Roman, who has already been through so much in spite of his youth . . . was so badly wounded he almost lost his right foot.
Roman has been in Belgrade's military hospital until now, but he is now well again.

. . . the Almighty God in Heaven has heard my prayer. Leopold has endured this slavery and now he's free . . . [he] languished for two years in Dachau concentration camp . . . [but] finally got his day of liberation.

Bruce on Polde's incarceration at Flossenbürg:

You have no doubt heard of Belsen, Buchenwald and Dachau, they were bad no denying, but Flossenbürg was especially bad, where the agitators, the proven anti-Nazi, pro-British persons were dumped. The guards were picked SS, picked because of their love for their boss and their hatred of the British. That is where this boy was put away, Flossenbürg.

Bruce on Roman's arrest and interrogation:

Roman was 14 years of age in 1941 when the Gestapo picked him up and tossed him into solitary confinement for 14 days, to soften him up, before they really went to work on him in an effort to make him give the names of the sister's accomplices in anti-Nazi, pro-British activities. One of the methods used was to take him down to the square . . . to witness the executions by firing squad of girls like his sister and boys like himself, for anti-Nazi utterances. This was quite an ordeal for a lad, his sister was in the same prison as he. He had seen her in the courtyard. Each morning he expected he would be joining the partisans at the wall, or that he would see his sister there.

Bruce on Anica and Roman joining the partisans:

At 19 years of age [Anica] was liaison officer in Maribor, Slovenia, for the Yugoslav partisans with a price on her head. At 16 years of age, [Roman] joined the partisans, was wounded twice and remained with them up until the end of the war.

Bruce on jumping the truck from Veszprém to Budapest:

Frank and I walked a short way down the road, leaving the Russian soldier talking to the airmen, and when the lorries came down the road, Frank and I jumped on the second one as it passed us.

Bruce on leaving their passports with the Russian escort:

There was quite a lot of explaining to do as we had no papers, nothing at all to prove we were even British.

Bruce on attempting to rejoin the 2nd New Zealand Division in Trieste:

I was in Istanbul [in] Turkey when I first heard that the famous New Zealand Division had fought its way from El Alamein to Trieste. To me that was really wonderful. I felt certain that once I reached Italy and got to Trieste my people would help me come to you.

I was told that I must go to Taranto and wait for a ship for the Middle East. I asked to be sent to the Division in Trieste but they would not listen to me. I was told that it was impossible for anyone who had been a prisoner of war to return immediately to the Division.

I did all that was possible while I was in Taranto to get to Trieste, nothing I did or said was of any use. To make matters worse, Tito was not very pleased because of the fact that the New Zealanders were in charge and would not allow him any rights. This piece of trouble only made it harder for me to travel.

Bruce on his attempts to communicate and reunite with Josefine:

At the end of one week we received a reply [from the Red Cross] informing us that they couldn't do anything for us immediately but perhaps later when things were better organised.

. . . to reach Yugoslavia or Austria without a permit was hopeless.

The next thing I did was to apply for a transfer from the New Zealand Army to the English Army in Europe, once again the same answer: impossible.

I lost your address the night I escaped.

. . . the day I came aboard the ship, I received the cruellest blow to date. The card which I had sent to you, darling, was returned to me with these words: Return to Sender.

Further Reading

Bardsley, E., 2010, *Barbed Wire and Balkans*, Chesterfield, UK: Bannister Publications Ltd

Batinić, J., 2015, *Women and Yugoslav Partisans*, New York, US: Cambridge University Press

Beevor, A., 1991, *Crete*, London, UK: John Murray Publishers

Carruthers, B., 2012, *German Anti-Partisan Combat*, Warwickshire, UK: Coda Books Ltd

Cawthorne, N., 1993, *The Iron Cage*, London, UK: Fourth Estate Ltd

Churches, R., 1996, *As the Crow Flies*, Adelaide, Australia: R. F. Churches

Cooke, P. & Shepherd, H., 2013, *European Resistance in the Second World War*, Barnsley, UK: Pen & Sword Books Ltd

The Dominion, "The Brave Yugoslav Partisan and her Kiwi POW," Wellington, New Zealand, 7 May 1990, p. 6

Elenio, P., 2014, *The Dominion Post: 150 Years of News*, Wellington, New Zealand: Fairfax Media

Evening Post, "Love Blossomed Behind Barbed Wire," Wellington, New Zealand, 8 October 1998, p. 5

Ewer, P., 2008, *Forgotten Anzacs*, Brunswick, Australia: Scribe Publications

Gilbert, A., 2014, *POW*, London, UK: Thistle Publishing

Gillies, M., 2011, *The Barbed Wire University*, London, UK: Aurum Press Ltd

Goodrich, T., 2010, *Hellstorm*, Colorado, US: Aberdeen Books

Granquist, C., 2015, *A Long Way Home*, Newport, Australia: Big Sky Publishing

Hedley, A., 2009, *Fernleaf Cairo*, Auckland, New Zealand: HarperCollins

Hutching, M., 2002, *Inside Stories*, Auckland, New Zealand: HarperCollins

Kranjc, G., 2013, *To Walk With The Devil: Slovene collaboration and Axis occupation, 1941–1945*, Toronto, Canada: University of Toronto Press

McCallum, J., 2005, *The Long Way Home*, Edinburgh, UK: Birlinn Ltd

Mikulan, K. & Thomas, N., 1995, *Axis Forces in Yugoslavia 1941–45*, Oxford, UK: Osprey Publishing

Milač, M., 2002, *Resistance, Imprisonment and Forced Labor*, New York, US: Peter Lang Publishing

Mountfield, D., 1979, *The Partisans*, London, UK: The Hamlyn Publishing Group

Puttick, E., 1960, *25 Battalion*, Dunedin, UK: Coulls Somerville Wilkie Ltd

Research Institute, Ljubljana, 1946, *Allied Airmen and Prisoners of War Rescued by the Slovene Partisans*, London, UK: Imperial War Museum

Šelhaus, E., 1993, *Evasion & Repatriation: Slovene Partisans and Rescued American Airmen in World War II*, Kansas, US: Sunflower University Press

Šorn, M., "Life in Occupied Slovenia During World War II" in J. Perovšek and B. Godeša (eds.), 2016, *Between the House of Habsburg and Tito: A Look at the Slovenian Past 1861–1980*, Ljubljana, Slovenia: Institute of Contemporary History, available online at <www.sistory.si/cdn/publikacije/36001-37000/36073/ch09.html>.

Stanovnik, J., Pleterski, J., Pirjevec, J., Repe, B., Guštin, D., Bajc, G., Kostnapfel, J., Kmecl, M., Paternu, B., Fabec, F. & Kerec, D., 2008, *Resistance, Suffering, Hope: The Slovene Partisan Movement 1941–1945*, Ljubljana, Slovenia: National Committee of Union of Societies of Combatants of the Slovene National Liberation Struggle

Stout, T. & Duncan, M., 1958, *Medical Services in New Zealand and The Pacific*, Wellington, New Zealand: War History Branch, Department of Internal Affairs

Sweitzer, D., 2014, *My Childhood in WWII Yugoslavia*, Nevada, US: Self-published

Vuksic, V., 2003, *Tito's Partisans 1941–45*, Oxford, UK: Osprey Publishing

Wynne Mason, W., 1954, *Prisoners of War*, Wellington, New Zealand: War History Branch, Department of Internal Affairs

About the Author

Doug Gold has had a long and successful media career. With a business partner, he set up the More FM radio network and, later, was a founding partner of NRS Media, an international media company with offices in London, Atlanta, Toronto, and Sydney. He has won numerous broadcasting awards and consulted for major media networks globally.

Doug lives in Wellington with his wife, Anemarie. He is the son-in-law of Bruce and Josefine.